AMERICAN BLOOD

Also by John Nichols

FICTION

The Sterile Cuckoo
The Wizard of Loneliness
The Milagro Beanfield War
The Magic Journey
A Ghost in the Music
The Nirvana Blues

NONFICTION

If Mountains Die (with William Davis)
The Last Beautiful Days of Autumn
On the Mesa

AMERICAN BLOOD

BLOOD

JOHN NICHOLS

HENRY HOLT AND COMPANY
NEW YORK

Copyright © 1987 by John Treadwell Nichols
All rights reserved, including the right to reproduce this
book or portions thereof in any form.
Published by Henry Holt and Company, Inc.,
521 Fifth Avenue, New York, New York 10175.
Distributed in Canada by Fitzhenry & Whiteside Limited,
195 Allstate Parkway, Markham, Ontario L3R 4T8.

Library of Congress Cataloging-in-Publication Data
Nichols, John Treadwell, 1940–
American blood.
I. Title.
PS3564.I274A8   1987   813'.54   86-25616
ISBN 0-8050-0374-6

First Edition

Designed by Lucy Albanese
Printed in the United States of America
10 9 8 7 6 5 4 3 2 1

This novel is a work of fiction. No character in it
is intended to represent a real person.

ISBN 0-8050-0374-6

I'm sure to go to heaven, boys,
Because I've done my time in hell.

1

NAM

No doubt, some men and women truly believe in the "beautiful madness of war." Deep down they have a lust for all that melodramatic insanity. Richard Nixon, William Westmoreland, Curtis LeMay, Ronald Reagan, Douglas Mac-Arthur—don't you ever believe their pious homilies about waging war so the world can live in peace, be safe for democracy. It all has to be the biggest crock ever invented. Gerald Ford once said, "All wars are the glory and the agony of the young."

Well, I'm young, or I was once when I went to war, but I sure never tipped to the glory of my temporary occupation as foot soldier, on the line, killing all those commies for Mommy, for Christ, for the good old USA. No, from my humble perspective it always seemed like an old man's game, and I can actually picture them now, centuries, millenniums of paunchy old geezers, bespangled in gold epaulets and campaign ribbons and medallions, down on their callused knees, and, with unspeakable urgency, performing fellatio on the great god of carnage, Mars, until finally their idol comes, filling their mouths with a mixture of

blood, maggots, and decaying brains—war jism is what I call it.
War jism.

Love it or leave it, Gerald Ford.

We were just humping along (singing a song) when I saw it. Talk about pretty—la-di-da. I thought it was a cluster of bright blue wildflowers. In fact, right about then that's what I needed it to be. So I veered to pluck a blossom; me, the incurable romantic of our platoon. I planned to stick a flower in the webbing of my headgear, show those hotshot COs leading us into stupid battle a bit of the old Peace, Love, Groovy.

The blue colors reflecting hot sunlight shivered, an iridescent sheen that seemed almost to hum. In fact, the entire bouquet quivered as my exhausted shadow touched it. And that's when the bunch exploded. I didn't even have time to react. "Booby trap!" flared in my brain as big flakes of blueness sailed past me like fragments of shrapnel. Fucking VC, dirty little buggers, never missed a trick. And up went my hands as I toppled backward, squealing like a stuck dink.

No, actually, they don't squeal much, stoic little bastards, by and large. It's us who squeal; us with our big, pink bellies when the metal does its dirty business, and the lights start going out.

There must have been a hundred fancy Asian butterflies feeding on the bloated corpse of that child. Eyes puffed shut, tongue tip pink between swollen lips, huge belly, tiny penis stiff and scratched raw by the feet of flies, fat fetid legs akimbo, rotten crotched in surrender.

By the time I raised back up on one knee, all the lovely bugs had relanded, resumed their feasting. And I? I followed a road less traveled by, and that has made all the difference.

So begins our story about the glory and the agony of the young.

Over there, in country, I often mistook objects like that dead child for something else. Never could understand exactly what was

4

real, what imagined. A common enough plight for everybody: for your basic grunt, your basic captain, your basic general, your basic President of the United States. Everybody, including yours truly, Michael Smith, Michael *P*. Smith—*P*. for prurient, *P*. for paralyzed, *P*. for Paul, if you must know the truth—invented the people, the landscapes, the logic of our pillaging. After all, everyone needs a reason to perish. Can't just say, "Oops, I fell into hell—lawdy, lawdy." No, there has to be high purpose, moral goals for creating a landscape infinitely littered by offal. God forbid any American should expire "in vain." I used to concentrate on that, marching through the dust, humping the rice paddies, over and over again the refrain: "In vain, in vain, in vain." Not me, no sirree bob, huh-uh. I was terrified of dying "in vain."

Actually, I was simply terrified of dying.

So I drifted through it; we all did, all tried to stay alive, and killed anything that interfered, and I never much felt like I was *awake* over there. I was just a groggy member of a somnambulist army, spreading dire consequences wherever it tramped. "Ram, bam, thank you, Nam"—belly open, entrails bulging. Our motto: *When we grease 'em, they stay greased.*

And then I came back to the world, and the "danger" was "all over." And I woke up. And all of a sudden the war was totally real. Things focused, they took on purpose, they had moral consequences. My conscience said, "Howdy, Michael, whatcha been doin' all this time, bro'?"

And then the proverbial excrement hit the proverbial fan.

I remember this. We were in a hamlet; it started to rain. Barrels of rain, dump trucks of rain, reservoirs of hot rain. "Shucks, now we can't torch the hooches!" Like almost you feel underwater; you expect bubbles coming out their noses, rising up from people, chickens, dogs, cattle trying to breathe. "Stow them Zippos, boys. They're gonna drown of their own accords!" We all sought shelter. But this one Vietnamese kid wouldn't get out of the downpour. Maybe because there was a Yankee grunt in the doorway of almost every hooch. Maybe he was retarded. Maybe he was confused. Maybe he was part duck. He was five or six years old, scrawny like they all were, and he just stood in the middle of the muddy plaza. Wearing some Uncle Ho sandals, tattered beige shorts, that's all. Arms and legs knobby and delicate, covered with sores. Not very many fat people over there in Nam, were there? Only in Saigon. They ate garbage like we eat caviar, and thanked their lucky stars profusely for any leavings in a sordid time.

This guy next to me, name of Carp, Thomas Carp—he started hollering: "Hey, get out of the rain, you stupid dink! You'll catch pneumonia!" Mr. Compassionate. Oh, maybe he *was* concerned, who knows how God programs the human brain? Not me. Not Private (not even Private First Class) Michael P. Smith. "Get out of the rain, you stupid little gook!" Carp hollered, but the kid didn't move. After all, there was a gringo man—a nigger, a honkie, a spic—in every doorway. Or maybe—surprise! surprise!—the kid didn't understand English.

"What are you, an idiot?" Carp shook his gun at the kid, then turned to me. "These people got shit for brains, they're fuckin' morons!"

And what did we do to morons, over in the Nam? Simple: waste the retards. So Carp swung around, aimed his 16, and shot the kid, just once—*pop!*—smack-dab in the old breadbasket. No great histrionics followed. Maybe the bullet zipped right through; it didn't knock him over. Little Huan or Duc or Chang just plopped down into a sitting position, and sat there, holding his belly, staring at us. The rain pounded, splashing in puddles, blasting up gooey droplets of mud all over the square. Looked like the earth, in filthy squirts, was jumping up all over the place. Made a reedy battering sound against the thatch of all the hooches. Clattered like marbles in a quaking jar off the tin roof of their cinderblock community center. And there were gooks—'scuse me, Vietnamese human beings—huddled around, too, sheltering under whatever. Wrinkled papasans and mamasans, their arms folded, glaring out at the rain with those eyes they assumed whenever we showed up. Holy Moses, you were never dry over in the Nam.

Surprised me sometimes those Asiatics didn't have moss and big green dripping bunches of weedy slop dangling off them, like creatures from a black lagoon. *We* certainly always carried a rot on us, in all the crevices, between our toes, under our balls. Endless itching in Nam—Jesus. I had sores all over my body, big red welts from the bugs, and a bunghole that throbbed all day, every day. The country inspired endless diarrhea; my pants were always caked from dribbling shit. But at least some of the bugs stopped for a minute during the daily monsoons. Blessed relief.

Kids, too, in apprehensive bunches, lounged around the square gawking into the rain at the shot boy contemplating his navel. But nobody made a move. Any slant stirred now, they knew they might get wasted. No bonfires today, and our outfit was feeling a trifle petulant. So the dinks hung fire and peered at the gut-shot victim, who barely even whimpered. Nearby lay a crumpled bicycle, gleaming.

The guy who popped him, Carp, commenced bitching: "Look at that asshole! Look at that stupid asshole! He can't even die!" Then he addressed the kid personally: "Die, you stupid schmuck! Go ahead, *die!*" And to us: "See? These people are crazy, they don't even know how to die!"

No, that little gook wouldn't croak. "Shoot him again," somebody grumbled. But Carp would have none of that. Mad he might be, but not a madman. "I can't. What do you think I am, an animal? He's only a kid."

"Wait a minute, he'll drown," another guy joked. We laughed. Lot of humor over there in country. Regular barrel of monkeys providing the fun that levered our days.

Rain, rain, rain . . . and nothing happened. Until a monster pig rounded a corner and minced into the plaza, snuffling at the muck, moving forward, swinging its head from side to side, emitting funny salacious grunting noises. It walked right up to Ho Duc Dodo and stopped. Confronted the gut-shot little bugger, fat snout twitching, sniffing curiously. Then poked its head forward, bumped into flesh, started slurping at the belly wound. The kid's hands fluttered against the big snout. The pig snorted, irritated, tossed its head a little, shaking off the hands. Weakening, the hands flapped against the dirt-blotched ears—no silk purses in the offing here. Then we could see the belly, where a glistening bubble of intestine had broken through the skin. The pig weighed maybe two hundred pounds. And in an almost delicate, prissy manner, it began eating the gut bubble. Nibbled tentatively at first, the boy's hands lying loosely against the big head, sort of laxly holding it like you would a basketball, maybe, calculating a free throw. All relaxed and very passive.

Pretty soon the porker got into it, gave a yank, essayed a couple of eager munches. Good stuff, warm guts. Yanked again, chewing. The kid's eyes stayed trained directly at Carp.

"For Pete's sake, shoot 'em both," a queasy grunt grumbled. But no way, José—not now. All of us, dinks and soldiers alike, were fascinated. I mean, it's not every day you see a big fat animal devour a human being alive. And the hog got into it, now, very deliberate, jerking its head from time to time, releasing another few inches of intestinal goodies.

Finally the beast lurched backward, and, attempting to liberate a particularly choice morsel, it jerked little Ho Chi Minh over into a puddle. Then straddled the boy like it was maybe gonna fuck him, and kept eagerly noshing up the guts with a flurry of rips and snuffles. Still alive, our comic commie relief, gazing at the sky now, child eyes drowning in water. Arms danced up a final time and flopped against the tough hide, the right leg jerked a bit; the left foot scooted out. Pig lifted one hoof and pawed at the abdominal cavity, pinning down the body while it tugged for the rest of the glop: entrails, spleen, liver, kidneys, stomach, lungs—yum yum, pig candy.

"Shoot the pig," a dismayed American growled. But nobody could. As I said, not every day do you get front-row tickets for a spectacle like this. We were mesmerized. Rain splashed off the pig like gallons of liquid bullets; rain jumped in all the puddles; a lake spread across the plaza.

That pig kept on for a while, methodical, chewing carefully, making sure it devoured everything. Finally nosed in and chomped the heart, savored the delicacy, then shook its gruff head in satisfaction, glanced once around, and gulped it down. Still beating, that heart? Who knows? Sometimes, I swear, given the dumb courage of those feisty relics from the Stone Age up against our fully automated slaughtering machine—sometimes I swear their hearts just never stopped beating. Took such a licking, but kept on ticking. Like the country, you couldn't really snuff the people. Reminded me of Edgar Allan Poe, "The Tell-Tale Heart." You walked around, you could hear the hearts of all the dead gooks we iced and buried beating on underneath your boots. Occasionally, their hearts were like land mines, they exploded, took off your legs at the knees—stump city. You just couldn't kill them dead enough. Straggling through the jungles you could hear the hearts of their dead beating all over the place, beneath the vines, hidden in elephant grass. A thousand years of their history lay underfoot. You'd walk through the paddies, see bubbles rising where their dead had fallen, their hearts breathing underwater. Like vampires, the gooks—even a silver stake through their chests didn't quiet them. Their earth was composed of all their dead, their massacred communities, their chopped and buggered martyrs, always beating, pumping blood through veins of agony throughout their festering earth. How you gonna defeat a people fighting to defend a land that contains centuries of their own hallowed dead? Maybe if we'd buried *our* corpses in their earth, we would have kicked more ass. Oh yeah, it gave me the royal creeps.

I think, despite the noisy battering-ram deluge, I heard the kid give a mournful squeak when the pig tore out his heart. Then the body lay still. The pig nosed around in the cavity, tonguing up assorted odds and ends. Then stopped at last, glanced up licking its chops, and slowly turned a circle, squinting disinterestedly at all us captivated onlookers. Maybe it got a whiff of danger then, I don't know. Do pigs differentiate between their normal slops and a human being? I figure no: shit is just shit to a shiteater. And hey, who among us really cared? Pigs, buzzards, dogs, Cholon chinks—everybody grew plump on carrion in Nam. So without further ado, this hog gave a twitch, a perky flick of its heels, and trotted off, daintily splashing through puddles, leaving that empty body behind.

The rain pelted and nobody moved, nobody spoke. I was thinking: another VC for the body count. Any dead gook was a VC we could count. Any dead water buffalo was a VC we could count. Any dead dog, pig, chicken, or snake was a VC we could count. You died in Nam, if you were slant eyed you automatically became a VC we could count. By conservative estimates we counted a million and a half VC over there. And it cost us ten million bucks for every number.

And if you could personally prove you had killed enough VC, you earned some in-country R and R. A day off at the beaches, and all the infected zip quiff you could stomach. I recall two grunts fighting over an arm: who had the right to turn it in? "I saw it first!" shouted the big guy. "Fuck you, I saw it first," said the little guy. They had a tug-of-war with that arm, both of them noodled out, gone bonkers, absolutely crazy. They wanted that three-day leave. Finally, the big lummox took out a .45 and greased the little rooster—*K-wham!*—in the middle of his chest. Popped his heart like a balloon. And got his R and R.

Naturally, Carp got to claim this one—the Pig Boy. Always afterward we'd say, "Remember the Pig Boy?" Har de har har. Later, after the rain let up, Carp actually cut off an ear, just to prove it—a democracy needs living proof, you know. In God we trust, all others pay cash. And the Army stores all those ears in a big vault (in the middle of Beverly Hills). Collateral, they say; drawing interest from the big bank in hell.

The ear got Carp three days in Da Nang's Dogpatch, world's most festering brothel, Cunt County, Indochina. Carp came out of it high on smack, and without a case of clap—miracle of miracles! "Oh that Pig Boy," he crowed to us. "That's one dink to whom I owe a lot."

"To whom." Most educated country in the world, our USA. Shoved grammar down their heathen throats in Nam, you bet we did—shoved it down in royal spades.

The glory and the agony of the young.

10

It never stopped, of course. In later years the pundits all bewailed the fact that in Nam Death Had Become an End in Itself.

For those of us poor devils on the ground, genocide sure had an intimate face. "Save their ass—?" My ass. By the time I arrived in country, our single and singular mission in life was to dismember an entire race of people, turning their pathetic country into a bloody soup of human bone, gristle, tissue, feces. In the end we came out Number 2, but nobody can chide us for not trying harder.

Boys became men over there, men became dead, zipped up in green vinyl Glad bags, flown home first class, buried with a twenty-one-gun salute. Pious homilies; patriotic claptrap; saccharine bullshit. Died in the service of murder and mayhem is all it ever amounted to, far as I could see. Honor guard folded up the flag, worms went to work—"Birdy num-num."

We stumbled through it in a kind of killing trance. No rhyme, no reason, no front. Went somewhere, got killed, and killed a lot of the diminutive beaners in exchange. Took a hill, suffered great casualties, gave great casualties, and departed next day, never to return. The slicks came and wafted us home to steak and ice cream hours after major battles. The dust-offs arrived and whisked away those of us missing certain pieces of ourselves. We lined up the enemy bodies and snapped pictures with our Instamatics. Weren't supposed to, but we did it anyway. Then we cut off ears, made necklaces, hung them from the aerials of Amtracs. Pissed on the bodies, defecated in their mouths, stuck sticks up their rectums, cut off testicles, cut off heads, stuffed severed privates into the mouths of dead women. Seemed our basic purpose was to mutilate people and landscape as thoroughly and as horribly as possible, using the most advanced technology ever available to any civilization. "Civilization"—that word has a tart flavor on my tongue. "Civilization," indeed. Jews—excuse me, kikes, Hebes, mockies, yids—in the German holocaust suffered no worse than did the Vietnamese.

11

Agent Orange, white phosphorus, napalm, B-52s, M-60s, Chinooks, Hueys, FACs, Puff the Magic Dragons, F-104s, F-111s, M-79 grenade launchers, radios, concertina wire, Claymore mines, Starlight Scopes, People Sniffers, Bouncing Bettys, butterfly bombs, miniguns, C-4 explosives, M-16s, trip flares, 155 howitzers, Spookys, Gatling guns, K-bar knives, fixed bayonets, .45 automatics, captured AK-47s, water tortures, "Bell Telephone Hour" electrocutions, assassinations, ambushes, hosings, killings, mutilating masturbating death. We treated the entire country like a Free-Fire Zone. A sniper took a single potshot at us, we retaliated with the wrath of God. Saturated their land with unspeakable suffering; committed terracide against their country; committed terracide against their souls. Tried to rub 'em out, kill 'em all. "Waste every last dink and begin again with Americans." "Put all the good gooks in boats, take 'em out to sea, then annihilate everybody left in the country . . . then sink the boats." Never failed to get a laugh, that one.

When I first arrived in country I remember thinking, "This ain't half bad. This is a beautiful place." Then I noticed something wrong. Couldn't land a finger on it at first. Began like one of those cartoon games in the newspapers—"What's wrong with this picture? Find the 15 hidden mistakes." Well, I found them all right. There existed so many cripples in Nam. All these chipper zits prancing around missing limbs, or parts of limbs, or an ear, or maybe a couple fingers, a toe, a foot . . . and it wasn't just ex-soldiers, or farmers—people you might expect. It was lovely young girls, also, and kids of all ages, on crutches, waddling about on stumps, begging with open hands that contained no fingers.

Droves of exquisite deformed human beings.

So many of them that at first they simply blended in, seemed a natural part of the landscape, hard to notice.

But once you snapped on it, gee willikers; the country was a friggin' freak show.

They all should have walked around displaying red, white, and blue stamps on their stumps: MADE IN AMERICA.

Ringling Brothers, Barnum and Bailey: a nation modeled after The Elephant Man.

The VC were like hummingbirds, small and swift and often invisible. By contrast we were huge and clumsy, noisy and awkward, fat and big, always overexposed. Our firepower killed them. Torched the very atmosphere so they couldn't breathe. Poured gases, flames, liquid explosives into their tunnels underground. Burned the earth, leveled the towns, herbicided the forests, poisoned the rice paddies, and bulldozed anything that remained. We laid down so much withering heat that finally the hummingbirds couldn't dart through it. Opened up with M-16s and M-60s and M-79s and 155s and B-52s dropping 750-pounders, and kicked ass on those hummingbirds, you bet. And when it was all over, when the villes were burned and all the animals lay dead and all the leaves had curled up and all the splintered greasy forests smoked fretfully . . . when it was all over and we were stupidly mingling around, gawking at the carnage . . . there it would be again, the fluttery distant buzz of another hummingbird, tiny energetic ghosts flitting through the jungle, setting their teeny-weeny traps to blow off our arms and jaws, our testicles and kneecaps, digging their punji pits so we could be impaled on razor-sharp slivers of bamboo smeared in human excrement.

"What you have to be over here," said a buddy of mine named Rothstein, "is you have to be like a fucking golem. No, not *like*, you have to *be* a fucking golem."

"What's a golem?" asked Michael P. Smith, all-American WASP, Happy Honkie, and otherwise culturally deprived human being.

"It's a Yiddish monster that eats human turds for breakfast, and butt-fucks dinks until they're dead," he replied.

"Is it covered by hair?"

"Hard to tell because it's always so drenched in blood."

Well, who knows why?—time, place, verbal inflection—but that captured my imagination. And ever afterward I saw myself as Rothstein's version of a golem: hairy, bloody, butt-fucking dinks, mouth full of shit, thirty feet tall, and never leaving the home base without my American Express card—an M-16 shaped like Karl Malden's nose.

You'd think after awhile the deaths would merge into each other: the edges of all the bloody details would get blurry . . . but they didn't. I guard a hundred individual memories of atrocity, all bright and polished like photographs in a truly professional scrapbook. And every one seems indignantly unique.

For example, one time we captured four of them, up near Nha Trang, on the beach. A few large metal Conex boxes lay around outside our camp, and somebody had the brilliant idea to jail the prisoners inside. So we locked them in the boxes without food and water for two days. By noon of the second day the temperature at sand-dune level was a hundred and twenty degrees. When finally we opened the Conexes to peep inside, the corpses were already bloated up to twice their natural size. The stench almost knocked us out. We splashed three bags of lime over them, and shut the lids again.

During that same operation we came across dink prisoners who had been handled by other troops working in our area of operations—a man and a woman, hanging in a tree. The woman hung by her long hair from a branch, hands tied behind her back, burned all over by cigarette butts. They must have jammed some C-4 plastic into her vagina and detonated it, no doubt while she still breathed. The legs were erased at the hip; her innards had dropped into a pile on the ground. As an afterthought, a sharpened bamboo stick had been implanted through her midriff and a paper South Vietnamese flag tied to one end.

The man had a crowbar punched through his head, in one ear, out the other, a Chieu Hoi pass was shish-kebabbed onto one end. Rope on either side of the crowbar extended up to a tree branch. No ears, no privates. The privates were located in his mouth. The penis head poked out between clenched teeth like a purple tongue. One hand was chopped off.

Tom Carp took a picture, clicked his Instamatic. He had a penchant for that sort of scene. Some other guys took photos also. I just left it alone—it was boring, I thought. You got burned out after awhile on that sort of candid pic.

We left them dangling in the trees. Unburied Vietnamese are called "wandering souls," they never get any rest. Apparently, it's a terrible thing for a gook to be buried when their body is not whole. That's why, much of the time, we cut off a hand, a foot, a head—and hid them. Just another way to show we meant business, to demoralize them, to capture their hearts and minds, keep 'em honest.

So often death took them by surprise. We rarely mingled around asking questions and assessing the situation before we cut loose. By the time I arrived in country everybody was much too paranoid for that. Law of the land said: shoot first, ask questions afterward. Only good Indian (substitute "gook") was a dead Indian (substitute "gook" again).

One day on patrol we turned a corner and surprised an old man squatting in midtrail, taking a shit. It disgusted us the way gooks defecated outdoors, in public, beside roads, in the fields, any old place. Blasé as you please. So here was a wrinkled old prune sporting a few tattered wisps of hair on his chin, taking a dump in the middle of our trail. He looked up, startled. Then smiled. They always smiled at us, even if they wanted to off us. *Hi, guys, my name is Wang, and I'm your host for the evening.* He had a silly, toothless grin; wasn't even embarrassed. But the smile never really charged up, because our lead man—your friend and mine, Thomas Carp—instinctively shot him.

Just turned the corner, met the unexpected geezer taking a crap, and greased him.

Our reaction? We all laughed. It was the funniest thing. That papasan had looked so foolish squatting there, a turd half out of his ass, when suddenly a great big American with a great big gun just blew him away—*bang! splat! payday!* The whole patrol cracked up. Days later, even, guys would break into the giggles. Stop in their tracks, slap their thighs, point a finger at each other, and say, "Bang, you're dead! Right in the middle of a shit!"

Oh, we hooted and guffawed. "Did you catch the look on the face of that old dink just before he bought the farm?"

Belly laughter, yes indeed. Fellows like us would latch on to anything for a chortle over in Nam. I certainly do wish Bob McNamara and Bob Hope could have been there at such times, to share the jokes, enlarge their repertoires, take it back home to the US public.

Every now and then something so weird happened that it fairly sucked my breath away. Take this little burg near Phu Bai. We had just been flown into the area and were pretty nervous, because in the past couple weeks there'd been several pitched battles between us and the NVA, North Vietnamese regulars. A bunch of them had been killed, but so had a lot of us. Hence we had moved into the ville and very cautiously felt it out. The peasants seemed cooperative, but they were known to support the enemy. So we ignited it. Herded everybody away to the outskirts, and methodically burned down every hooch in town.

Smack-dab in the middle of the operation we heard an incredible noise overhead. Turned out to be a giant Tarhe Sky Crane chopper, looks like a praying mantis or a humongous dragonfly. It rattled directly above the burning village. Underneath it bulged a huge cargo net, plumb full of goodies. Hard to decipher from the ground what they were: looked like big globs of bubble gum, or large chunks of pink cottage cheese.

Then they punched a release button and the net unfurled, dumping the load straight at us. At first, the ordnance just hung together; then it began to separate, becoming distinctly shaped, like individual naked human beings. And that's what it was: a ton of naked bodies falling at us. Only how could that be? I mean Christ on a crutch, I'd witnessed some bizarre antics in Nam, but nothing like this. All of us reacted similarly: stood transfixed, gawking, as dead men tumbled toward us. I thought, Holy cow, some joke. Perhaps a kind of propaganda operation. Store mannequins, maybe with rubber knives stuck in their bellies, the latest scare tactic from PSYOP.

But when they thudded to earth, we understood they were honest to God Vietnamese bodies. They crashed through burning rooftops, splintered a cart, clapped against the 50-mm machine gun on our APC, slammed to earth with crunching blunt thumps, plummeted through treetops tearing out leaves and branches, splashed into puddles left over from yesterday's downpour.

Soon as the first one hit, we started dancing. Bodies landed all over the place—*thump! thump! thump!* I was astonished, and could barely move. If luck had been against me I would have been annihilated by a deceased dink dropped from heaven. And in fact one grunt was actually clobbered—a fellow named Charles Detwiler took a body directly on the noggin, snapped his neck, dead instantly.

Turns out they were NVA soldiers killed in an operation nine clicks away in a hamlet called Do Jan. They took too many of our side with them, so somebody concocted this scheme, called for the Sky Crane, carried it out. I doubt a sense of humor spirited the play; more like a muddled rage. Idea was, of course, to teach the gooks in *this* ville a lesson.

So we were bombarded by enemy bodies. Fortunately, nobody else was beaned. Mistakes like that happened all the time.

I was packed in a chopper with three other dudes, Tom Carp again, a black grunt called Watkins, and a bespectacled jerk, Roger Thorpe, who, because he spoke some Vietnamese, was ordered to interrogate our four prisoners. My inopportune presence was due to a mild shoulder wound, but I wasn't complaining: a hit like that could buy maybe a full two weeks off the line.

The prisoners understood what was up: after the painful formalities, they'd eat the ether. Two of the men wore loincloths; the woman had on black pajamas, and, strange to say, a couple of gold (probably brass or tin) earrings. Half her teeth were missing and she also wore glasses—pretty intelligent mien, to tell the truth. They all squatted, eyes taped over, hands tied behind their backs. Why nobody had chucked the female's glasses, given the blindfold, I don't know. Funny touch. In Nam we were constantly regaled by funny touches.

Carp grabbed the woman's hair and yanked her forward: Thorpe yelled at her in Vietnamese. She didn't speak. Though blindfolded, she nevertheless stared at Carp, her exposed features lidded in that composed defiant way they had when death was a foregone conclusion. Carp finally plucked off the glassses, flung them out the doorway, and they perished toward the jungle. Thorpe yelled at her some more—gobbledy gobbledygook—but she didn't even flinch.

Well, I knew the upcoming charade. Knew Carp, by now, but didn't interfere. I was numb from the battle, still scared from being wounded, and I had an especially virulent dislike of gooks right then. Fuck 'em all, big and small, right up their corrugated tushies. So I merely spectated without comment on the ritual.

Carp rudely pushed the woman over, twisted her around onto her knees, and bent her down, chest and shoulders pressed against the floor matting. Watkins touched the muzzle of his 16 against her temple. Her wrists had puffed where the truss line cut into them. She wore an ID tag, scrawled words in English and in Vietnamese. Carp tugged down her britches: she wore no underclothes. No BVDs, no lingerie from Moscow, nothing. The chopper vibrated and jumped around on the thermals, so he had trouble with his zipper, but then it popped out all right—Mr. America, he called it. From other escapades, I knew already that Carp wasn't circumcised. And for a big man he had a big dick, confounding the prurient clichés then in style.

Her butt was covered with bug bites, angry red welts. I felt a trifle faint from loss of blood. Carp, wailing away at her crouched form, was silhouetted in the doorway against the bright sunglaring jungle. Never did understand how men like him could get it up in a situation like that. But he did. And nobody spoke while he had at her, except Watkins, who kept shouting above the roar of the chopper: *"Don't you move, or I'll blow your fuckin' head off!"* Alan Ladd, John Wayne, Super Fly.

The woman just accepted it, I reckon, knowing that her ghost would flap off and enter the bodies of a hundred other women creeping toward other battles under that green canopy below. Who knows what a female dink thought at a time like this: *I wonder if the Rams will beat the Giants next Friday? Is my hair a little sloppy? Is this shade of polish on my fingernails really me?*

Her buddies didn't speak. Their faces were glazed, immobile, and they seemed to avert their heads slightly, as if respecting her privacy as much as possible, given the difficult circumstances.

Carp finished pretty quick, then Watkins took his turn at that small hump of communist pussy. He was laughing as he came, and whacked her hard for good measure. Thorpe was a fastidious ape, and you're not going to believe this, but the sychophantic dork pulled out a wallet, and from it extricated a blue condom, which he unrolled onto his erection, because damned if he was gonna let some kind of Asian crud compromise his penis. Six pumps later he was happy as a cricket in a hot horse turd. *Playboy* magazine never offered anything to compare with hog-tied Asian nooky.

They offered me a boff, but I declined. Things got a tad loaded for a minute, because if everyone's a participant, there can't be any trouble later on. But I begged off. "I'm wounded, for crissakes. I feel faint. I'm *sick*." And they bought the story, left me alone, accepted my willing complicity.

Carp maneuvered the bitch around still on her knees, aiming out the doorway. Then grabbed her hair again, lifted back her head, and with a clean swipe of his K-bar slit her throat. All of a sudden we were splashed in blood sprayed back by the wind. About the same time Watkins placed his gun muzzle against her welted buttocks, and busted a cap up her rectum. Gore splattered out the front of her and whipped off in the airstream; plus somehow shit from her body backfired and bits of that rotten gunk spattered against us.

Then Carp heaved as Watkins kicked, and she toppled, tailing down behind us, hands forever bound, black pants flapping around her ankles.

The other prisoners they didn't bother to interrogate. Just dragged them over to the doorway, slit their throats, shot them in the noodle for emphasis—you could never kill a slant too thoroughly—and pitched them jungleward.

So I was laid up for a spell, out of action, on the ward at the surgical hospital, recuperating, mending, getting better so I could go back to work: Uncle Sam takes pretty good care of his conscripted gunslingers.

I met a nurse first day there, and liked her immediately. Name of Barbara Cicarelli, a quaint no-nonsense bitch who exuded an odd sort of tough sex appeal that kind of tickled my fancy. Wiry, almost scrawny—as a kid she must have been a tomboy. Checked in at five-three, five-four, and had nondescript brown hair that always looked askew on her bony head. Cheeks pitted, badly scarred from acne that must have hounded her adolescence—she was twenty-four by the time we met. Folks considered her ugly, but she had fierce, intelligent eyes underneath bushy, joined-together eyebrows. Gave her a startling expression, like a hawk, maybe, or a raven. And she had a wonderful voice that didn't jibe at all with her angular, titless body. Kind of low, half-husky, half-gravelly—with a disconcerting catch in it, like maybe she was drunk or stoned. But I learned she had stuttered as a kid, and overcame it by training herself to speak more slowly.

A rough, tough cream puff was Barbara Cicarelli; overly hardened in order to deal with all the crap of Nam. Used gutter language, and acted like she hated every wounded GI that happened to her care. "Oh for crissakes," I'd hear her snap, "look at this asshole gork. His chest is sucking wind, he's got MFWs from his guggle to his zatch, even his stupid putz is blown off—why bring him to us? He belongs in a fucking Glad bag."

Translated, the statement meant look at this brain-dead geek with his open chest wound, multiple frag wounds from head to toe, and no dick—he belongs in a body bag.

Of course she had to keep a distance. We all did that in Nam. Why snuggle too close to anybody, get emotionally involved?— just made it that much more draining when they were torn apart by terrible swift swords. This Cicarelli, though: at first I was startled by her lingo. Later, given the nature of that surgical hospital, I merged right into it with her. We depersonalized dinks so we could off them; and we depersonalized each other so it wouldn't hurt so much, the myriad lacerations that re-created us as moron vegetables rapturously fondling our puny limpissimo privates.

Not for long—thanks God—did I languish in the main ward. But while on board, I made a personal study of the different types of wounds my cohorts sustained. I'd help Cicarelli—Sicko to her intimates—whenever she made her rounds: I carried stuff on a tray, compresses for the crispy critters, IV bags full of glucose and morphine, lap pads, scissors, tape, the blood pressure tool, you name it. And I'd ask her questions. It puzzled me how anybody could live through such physical violations.

Soldiers burnt from head to toe by willie peter or napalm dropped by our own planes, covered by slimy blue pseudomona infections; guys with legs blown off at the knees by Bouncing Bettys, shunts dribbling out of their arms and thighs; grunts that had been riddled by a thousand fléchettes from one of Victor Charlie's homemade Christmas presents; teenagers missing their lower jaws and breathing through trache tubes; doughboys pumped full of dopamine to keep their blood pressure up; former high-school jocks who'd had a hundred D&Is in a week and a half-dozen laparotomies and double enucleations; boys who'd lost all their bowels and had colostomies at age eighteen; klutzes with burr holes drilled in their shaved noggins; expectants full of ventricular shunts, so fucked up they weren't expected to last the night and just lay at the east end sucking up pure morphine, which made the trip into never-never land a tad more comfortable. GIs in shock, captains who'd had spleenectomies, COs pissing solid blood through catheters . . . men who would be paraplegics, gay dudes who would be quadriplegics, heterosexuals who would confront the world from a face that looked like a burnt marshmallow, wondering what female masochist would have the nerve to save them; big, overgrown kids who from now on would pick up objects with steel hooks and metal fingers; adventurous gadabouts who would be lumps for life; epicureans who would never be able to see or smell or talk again; iron pumpers who looked beautiful except they'd never more diddle a broad or lift a barbell; slobs who'd spend the rest of their lives in bed, in wheelchairs, on featherweight aluminum walkers, on crutches—violated, mutilated, amputated . . . guys who were royally bitched forever.

And tough, ugly Cicarelli weaving through it all, joking with the spastics, the macho bleeders, the deaf, the defeated, the dying. "Hey, soldier, I got some goodies here, whattayou wanna do—flip, flop, or fly?" "Hey, soldier, how's it hanging today—stiff and stale and ready for a piece of tail?" "Hey, soldier, do me a favor next time, and holler for the bedpan, would you? I got Ivory Snow hands, I hate to make them dirty."

She cleaned their embarrassments, swabbed their blood, tenderly changed their dressings, skillfully nudged them into more comfortable positions—and never lied, never told them everything would be all right, but rather said, "You poor fuckin' bozo," and, without being obvious about it, touched them, gave a noodgy squeeze, held their hand awhile, and proselytized sedition: "If I was you when I got out of this hellhole I'd sue the President of the United States, I'd sue Congress, I'd sue the Army and the Navy and the Marines and the Air Force, I'd sue—"

She'd sue the fucking world.

"How come you got such a foul mouth?" I asked one day.

"Who wants to know—J. Edgar Asshole?"

"I just don't think I've ever met another woman with even as remotely dirty a vocabulary."

When she frowned the thick dark brow line lowered so that her sunken, bruised eyes were almost obscured and she appeared uncommonly fierce.

"And I don't think I ever met another country with even as remotely foul a war."

22

We liked each other well enough. Perhaps she cottoned to me because physically, at least, I appeared relatively whole. Bit of relief in the old mayhem ward. In fact, "You're so damn beautiful," she once said, dismayed, "that inside of a week or two they'll send you back to get stultified for sure."

Stultified. Never could accurately predict her lingo.

Maybe my third day there I woke up extra-blurry because Sicko had dealt me some potent sopors the night before. A big shot in a spanking clean uniform plodded down the ward, passing out Purple Hearts. An Army photographer armed with a Polaroid took snapshots. At each bed the brass monkey said, "In the name of the President of the United States and the U.S. Army, I award you this Purple Heart—" or words to that effect. Then he leaned over, and half the time slipped the medal to Cicarelli, who pinned it carefully on a sleeve, or on some gauze: the medal monkey feared pressing too close, lest he touch a wrong place, causing unbearable pain. Then the photographer took his pic while Mr. Big shook a hand, or a stump, or nervously patted a shoulder.

They repeated the awkward procedure at every bed, until they reached me. The top-heavy boob muttered his spiel, and the camera buff immortalized the moment; and all the while, behind them, Sicko made goofy faces, grimaced stupidly, twitched her nose, stuck out her tongue—blah!—rolled her bloodshot eyeballs. It occurred to me that if the general caught her act she might wind up in deep shit. But she was a reckless breed and didn't care, as she mocked my moment of profound humiliation.

Didn't take long for a perspicacious bloke like me to realize that Sicko spent many hours stoned. Rarely in the operating room, I'll admit. But on rounds, even at 8:00 A.M., almost always she was floating. I discovered later she did cocaine, popped myriad pills to raise her up, cast her down, go sleepy-bye. And acid too, she had taken many trips, she revealed . . . and smack; sometimes she tried that, would smoke it, or shoot up, then vomit afterward, sleep it off, trundle back to work—any spike for a lift.

She boozed a lot, also. Almost everyone there did. When she was off we had beers together, sat outside on sandbags, glared at concertina wire, conversed, rambled on—endless chitchat.

Smoked dope together on occasion, got nice and buzzed, then talked, pontificated, shilly-shallied—nothing special. No desire to burrow too deeply into the war; or trade memories about the world. Basically, we kept a pretty tight rein.

Once, it all welled up so that I could hardly stay restrained. Mildly blotto on Cambodian weed, I waved my hands ineffectually before my babbling lips.

"Do you ever . . . do you ever just feel like crying, like sobbing over all . . . all this *shit*?" I blurted.

Sicko hesitated barely a split second before responding: "No."

So I asked, "What makes you so tough?" I quavered, really on the verge of losing it.

"I grind glass up in my twat every morning before work."

That stopped me. An ugly enough response to jolt everything back into perspective.

I hadn't dallied there for long, either, before I decided she was bent on killing herself. But she owned a hell of a constitution. When not in the wards or in ER or in surgery, she chain-smoked cigarettes. On top of everything else, she did that.

Naturally, I had to ask, "Why are you trying to kill yourself, Barbara?"

She laughed. "I'm not trying to kill myself, Michael. I'm just putting in my thirteen, keeping my act together."

I felt an attraction between us. But we never touched or snuggled. Never shook hands, or hugged, or laid a weary head on the other's shoulder. In all that death and dying, among all those agonized cripples, buffeted hourly by emergency tension and undiluted pain, we maintained an odd formality. Didn't rock the boat. Let it be.

Come time for adios, I tracked her down, found her camped on an overturned fuel drum in front of the barracks, smoking a cigarette. I said, "Chopper's leaving now; I'm going back."

She smiled, oozing fatigue, maybe stoned. And shrugged, gestured offhandedly, very cavalier. "Bye."

"Good-bye."

Our eyes met; hers stayed cool, smiley, negligently neutral, betrayed no feeling.

Eventually, I extended my hand, in it the Purple Heart. "I'd like you to have this."

"I don't want it."

That stunned me. "What do you mean you don't want it?"

"I got enough sweet memories without it."

"Well . . ." I was pretty flustered. "You could use it to remember me."

She snorted. "Would it mean we were going steady?"

That hurt deeply. I had figured us for closer pals. "People like you," I whined, angry that she could not summon a more caring demonstration, "are underneath full of emotion, and just once I wish you'd betray a little of it."

"And idealists like you, Michael," she replied gently, "are full of shit. Now, if you want to do something useful with that Purple Heart, why don't you shove it up your ass?"

Of all the people (on our side) that I met in Nam, I think Cicarelli was the only one who truly had a kind of honor.

So, back to the old day-to-day I went. And I had a reunion with your friend and mine, Thomas Carp.

Who was probably the most outrageous psychopath I ever met. Stood out head and shoulders above the rest of us. Nam was ideal for men like him. One night I was exhausted, asleep on my cot in the tent, when Carp thundered in and dumped a bag full of heads on my bed. VC heads, purple and swollen, drained of blood, maggot stinky. I shrieked, I went bananas, grappling out of the sack, heads bouncing all over the place. Must have been six or seven at least, I forget. I kicked one across the tent, slapped another under the cot, grabbed a third and winged it at Carp, who was doubled over nearby, laughing so hard he almost couldn't breathe. "You sonnuva bitch, you fucking dickless asshole, you sadistic lunatic—!" Christ, I was apoplectic. And he hooted and hollered and crossed his arms protectively over his head, weak with laughter as he protested, "Hey, cut it out! Those are my heads! Don't mess with my heads, Smith! I can sell 'em! Can't you take a joke?"

No sir, right at that point in time I couldn't take the joke. I slammed a VC head off his arms, and flipped over my cot, flipped over the cot he was sprawled against, kicking him as he tumbled onto the floor half-paralyzed from merriment, and I punted another head out the tent doorway, where it clattered among a stack of helmets pilfered from our dead boys. Then I tackled Carp, flailing away, shrieking, "You sick son of a bitch, where's a gun, I'll kill you, I'll blow your maniac brains out!" But I was so upset I couldn't locate my rifle, a .45, nothing—I was positively insane with anger. And kept tripping over my own feet, over the heads, the upturned cots, canteens, my rotten marching boots. And Carp, all joggled into a hooting fetalness of joviality, begged me to quiet down. "Hey, take it easy, Smith, can't you dig a little humor? Christ, man—don't be a douchebag!"

I collapsed finally atop a trunk, and glared at him wheezing, shaking, tears spattering from his eyes; the dingbat couldn't stop hee-hawing.

"Oh Christ," he moaned. "You shoulda seen the look on your face when you woke up! Shit in a canteen, I wish I had a picture of that!"

Pictures . . . Carp took pictures of everything. He had a Kodak Instamatic, and a seemingly endless supply of film. Plus a wild proclivity for sex and death as subjects, preferably both, preferably connected. I'll admit most GIs, including me, had similar cameras, and most of us recorded those things also. Myself, I always clicked the shutter feeling unclean, slimy, immoral, but, yes, I have the snapshots. Supposedly it was against regulations to thus undignify the dead, even more against the rules to smuggle the film out of country. But laws were mighty loose in Nam, and so we all openly played Robert Capa and David Douglas Duncan. And most of our amateurish efforts made it back to the world.

But in Carp resided a peculiar kind of repulsive gusto, extraordinarily obscene. Beats me how he got away with it. The man was a bona fide crackpot . . . and therefore a mascot of sorts, perhaps. Maybe how he acted openly was the way we all deemed ourselves inside, therefore we tolerated, even encouraged, his morbid ogling shenanigans. He was a war casualty, he mirrored the nightmare perfectly, spoke to the golem in us all—hideously off balance, totally corrupted, trigger happy and ghoulish. He was like an overgrown fraternity prankster in college, given a license to butcher. All-American boy zealot.

In a rank cantina once he pocketed over a hundred bucks from us for eating a live tarantula. Just grabbed the hairy spider, popped it in his mouth, chewed fast, and swallowed it down with relish—said it tasted somewhat like gook vagina.

Carp was an entrepreneur. When nobody else had money, he had dollars (or piasters) galore. He had dope. He had black-market booze. He had a connection for everything.

One day he and Thorpe cornered a few rats and jailed them in a wire cage. They collected more rats, adding them to the prison, and fed the rodents daily—garbage, old Cs, Post Toasties, maybe a rotten arm when nobody was looking. The rats grew plump and frisky. When they had trapped about twenty-five animals, Carp and Thorpe climbed onto the hustings. Told everybody they planned to kill the rats in a blaze of glory, and sold tickets for the event. You could get in for your beer ration that day, or for real money—dollars or piasters—for cigarettes, dope, whatever you had to barter. Of course, most of us attended the execution; wouldn't have missed it for the world. When about a hundred GIs had encircled the cage, Carp splashed gasoline over the vermin and sailed in a match.

Predictably, the rodents came unglued. They hopped, leaped, screamed, and twirled like frantic ballerinas. They jumped around inside the cage like—what was that stuff in a Walt Disney movie? Flubber, I think. A magic compound that rebounds double its height on every bounce, if I remember correctly. Or was Flubber a seal?—or a trained porpoise?—I forget. Well, anyway, call them chubby little fur balls made of Flubber, going nuts in that cage, frolicking up so high they slammed off the mesh ceiling. Boy, what peppy jive-ass death throes! Ricocheted squealing helter-skelter, banging into each other—it was incredibly funny, sadistically ridiculous. We cheered, razzed, giggled over their flaming frolic. A few puffed up and exploded, spraying us with rat giblets. Oh how they scrabbled about. "Rat popcorn!" a PFC chortled, and half of us toppled groaning to the ground. Strange popping farts punctuated their bleating immolation.

Carp sloshed on more fuel, and we had a ball, swigging beer, smoking doobies. Called it later the zaniest caper of the war. Money well spent, by George—it wasn't often, in Nam, that you truly got your dollar's worth.

Naturally, soon as all the rats were deceased and smoldering, some wisenheimer suggested it'd sure be a kick and a half to corral a few gooks in a cage and roast them alive. "Cut off their balls, butt-fuck 'em all, then set 'em on fire."

Of course.

Made perfect sense to us.

Just the next step up.

Most GIs had a negative perception of Vietnamese women, and Tom Carp personified that attitude. In particular, he couldn't stand the sight of a pregnant slant. To his way of thinking, that was just one more revolutionary guerrilla in there, who'd be born to whittle punji sticks and otherwise threaten the security of America as slant-eyed communist vermin expanded their domination of the world.

Who was it—one of our presidents, or a secretary of defense?—who claimed it was easier to kill a guerrilla in the womb than later, out in the boonies?

Guys like Carp took that pronouncement seriously. If he spotted a pregnant zip in the open, and thought he could get away with it, he'd bust a cap at her. And he wasn't the only one. We called it a Vietnamese abortion. Just blow their yellow heads off—"One less commie in the world." Along that vein, I recollect how once, after we had swept a hostile ville and offed maybe a dozen civilians, a grunt named Carter performed a cesarean on a pregnant bitch who'd caught a round in her forehead, skewered the embryo on his bayonet, and marched through the smoke and devastation cawing,

"Arise, ye prisoners of starvation!" His way of telling the reds to go screw themselves, I reckon.

When we indulged in philosophical discussions concerning All the Great Questions, men like Carp were prolife, against abortion, and supporters of the death penalty, of course. Carp probably would have blown up abortion clinics for Jesus back in the world. I think he claimed Catholicism, too. I never understood his principles, however. He bragged about balling and snuffing whores; yet if he happened to be bareback and ejaculated inside their boxes, he refused to put out their lights. After all, a Carp sperm might have penetrated an ovarian egg, meaning that already she carried his sacred "life." So he'd merely slap her around, boot her down the stairs. But he preferred to bugger his gook nooky, denying them all access to a glorious American offspring.

Occasionally, Carp humped the B-girls wearing a prophylactic, not for birth-control purposes or because he feared disease, but rather to implement a game he liked to play afterward. Peeling off the rubber, stretched and gloopy with jism, he'd tell the bitch to eat it. If she balked, he touched a gun upside her ear and suggested she better start noshing. So she ate it. And he described what happened then: "Next time that whore took a shit, a come-filled balloon would blow up out her ass!"

Amazing how nothing embarrassed the man. He owned a particular Vietnamese skull which he claimed had once been part of a female Cong, a whore. In the top he had drilled a hole, then lined the cavity with clay and wedged into it a rubber vagina—a Pocket Pussy—of the type available in American porn stores, and also popular in Nam. "All the fun with none of the danger," Carp leered. Hence, whenever he wished to jerk off, he merely slopped Vaseline into his Pocket Pussy'd skull, and had at it. "I come boatloads in a minute," he laughed, "'cause I just love to fuck her commie brains out."

During the war, I never dwelt overly long on these crude tête-à-têtes. Never had much time to ruminate over there. And besides, given the nature of our work, it almost seemed natural, fitting into the perverted context of Nam, a hell so distant from the world that the world had ceased to exist. It was the world, in fact, that almost freaked me out once when I found myself in Hong Kong on R and R. Almost suffered a breakdown in an air-conditioned hotel room, tangled among clean sheets under an antiseptic gentle chinkette sucking on my member. A blessed relief it was to scramble back to Nam, return to the line, get it all back into properly bloody perspective again. Just took care of my business, carried a heavy bag, kept out of trouble, avoided stupid gestures.

Toward the end of my time I was in a chopper, cruising over a free-fire zone. We spotted a sampan down on a river. From on high it appeared to carry three women, five kids, and many blue-and-pink bundles of laundry, or maybe rags to sell. I saw a bicycle also. Obviously civilians . . . though nothing was ever obvious in Nam. The CO told the door gunner to waste them. But the gunner was new in country, he balked. "But sir," he shouted, "those are just women and kids!" "I don't care what they are!" replied the sarge. "I want you to grease the monkeys!" The door gunner waxed indignant—"I didn't come over here to kill innocent people!"—and he actually backed off from his weapon. The CO immediately placed him under arrest, and ordered me to fire the gun. I obliged; I sighted in the dinks and popped their cherries. It took three passes in all, after the occupants were totaled, to sink the boat—especially that bicycle—as well. It was important we deny the enemy access to matériel whenever possible. We even shot elephants from the air because they could be workhorses for the NVA or the Cong. The original door gunner crouched in a corner under guard all the way back home, crying. He hadn't understood that the dinks in that sampan were going to eat it one way or another, no matter what his stupid stance. And now he'd be court-martialed and probably spend half his tour in the stockade.

Me, I just fondled the trigger like a savvy boy, and when my time expired, I packed my bags, my souvenirs, and headed for greener pastures.

Hard to describe my convoluted thoughts on the Freedom Bird when it revved up to leave Saigon. Never been so uptight in my life. My last week in country had been excruciating. Nothing happened, no action, I didn't even hear a gunshot during those last seven days, but I was stretched so taut I'm surprised I didn't leap out of my skin and run amok. With freedom that near, I finally wanted desperately to survive, go home, have a future. The problem is, I had let go a week early, allowed myself the luxury of hope too soon. I felt jinxed, couldn't sleep at night, carried a gun in my hand practically the whole time. If a motorcycle a half mile away backfired, I jangled like St. Vitus dancing. It was awful. I never experienced that kind of sucker fear before, not in firefights, not when I was wounded, not when I cowered in the slicks getting shot at, not when I was pinned behind a paddy dike, not when our platoon got ambushed—never before had I sweat it out like that in Nam.

God, how I agonized that our plane would never bounce aloft. Right up until takeoff I believed sappers would come crawling across the Ton Son Nhut tarmac, stick satchel charges under our belly, and blow us to kingdom come. Most of us were tensed, probably thinking the same thing. Scared silly that at this last interminable minute some crazy dink hiding in a bamboo grove would take a potshot with his AK-47, and hit an engine, derailing our escape.

Believe it or not, Tom Carp was on the plane; had drawn the same time, same departure date, same bird as me. And it was only Carp who seemed distraught at leaving Nam. Stared out the window right in front of me, biting his fingernails. "Dammit," he muttered under his breath as we waited . . . and waited to be gone. "Dammit, dammit, dammit." Elocution had never been his strong suit.

Finally he half-turned round to me and groaned, "Smith, didn't we teach them a lesson?"

But I chose to let it pass. I was in no mood to fraternize with my fellow golems on the launching ramp that aimed us back toward the world.

And then we were droning over the ocean. Gone, but not forgotten. We had made it. Most of us still couldn't encompass that fact. Such a grim silence on the plane. What had I expected—cheering, hugging and kissing, champagne cocktails? None of that for us. Powdered flight attendants plied the aisles, dishing out liquor hand over fist—one freebie after another to all us introspective killers destined for the world.

But nobody talked much. I peered out my window, waiting for relief to come, but when it did it wasn't really relief. All that happened is the focus shifted. Vietnam tailed away behind me, and America loomed up ahead, waiting with sharpened teeth to extend a welcome. Barely a hitch in the changeover from fear of Nam, fear of the Cong, fear of death, to a fear of being alive, fear of going home. Home, where people were civilized and watched ball games on TV, ogled the Dallas Cowboy cheerleaders, and strolled through parks where kids tossed Frisbees and licked ice-cream cones. The population spoke a familiar tongue, English, and you rarely spotted cripples on the sidewalks. And daddies mowed their neat lawns on Saturday mornings. And I don't know exactly what happened, but I started shaking. My teeth chattered. Yet what could be so scary about a place like *that*?

A fight erupted in the plane, between five guys waiting for the bathroom. Waiting to vomit, waiting to release their nervous diarrhea—someone tried to cut into line and it got nasty. Bad words, clumsy punches. Took two flight attendants and a captain to sort them out, quiet it down again.

Then a person sat in the empty seat beside me. I didn't even move my head to acknowledge their presence. Had no desire for conversation. I wanted to be instantly disassociated from everything related to Nam, from everyone I had ever known in country. Wanted to incinerate my clothes, bury my dog tags, blow off my "friends," burn all the bridges. Never have I experienced such a lust to be alone as on that plane, winging silently over the glittering South China Sea.

"Well, Michael, I guesss it's history now, huh?" A woman's hand offered me a toke from her joint. Barbara Cicarelli's hand. So at last I deigned a reply.

"What are *you* doing here?"

"I'm off to Montana for to throw the hoolihan."

I accepted a drag off her roach, gave it back, she inhaled deeply, eyes fixated on the ocean. A loss of words for a while, until she cracked the ice again.

"What are you gonna do, Michael?"

"Who knows? Hadn't given it much thought. What about yourself?—truthfully."

"Think I'll travel to Washington and cut the balls off that pig in the White House and eat them. Then I'll hit Arlington and shit on Kennedy's grave. I figure he's the one actually started it."

"It's over, Sicko. What's the point?"

"Sure it's over. We drop into their country for thirteen months, rape, defoliate, castrate, burn alive, scorch the earth, destroy the people, the social fabric, all the arable land, then hop onto a 747, order a dry martini, and start worrying about important things— like how to buy a car, and if Liz Taylor is getting divorced again this year or not."

"Hey, take it easy."

"*You* take it easy," she said. "Ever think about this? Your average grunt is in Nam thirteen months. Can't speak the language. Got no family, no friends in the Nam. The culture is totally alien. He knows nothing about the history. None of his people are buried in that earth. There's no way he can relate."

"We had no choice," I said uncomfortably.

"We could have gone to Canada. Or to jail."

I had no response, just left it quiet for a spell until her jag continued.

"I'm ashamed, Michael, I really am. I spent the last two months under arrest; there was supposed to be a court-martial. Somehow, it all got lost in paperwork. They busted me for drugs, dope, booze. But it should have been for fragging every American above the rank of private that I bumped into. Because that is how I felt. But I'm chickenshit at heart. Too drunk all the time. Too stoned. You still got that Purple Heart? Give it to me, I'll shove it up my own ass."

She embarrassed me then, starting to cry. Really lost it. Making little noise, of course, but the tears poured out of her eyes, waterfalled down her cheeks, dripped off her weak chin. A flood of salty wetness that bugged my strung-out solitude. I feared she was having a nervous breakdown, and I didn't want to deal.

"I hate all of it . . . everything," she blubbered quietly. "The whole ugly shooting match. The whole great big obscene ball of wax."

Then she fought it under control. Trained her eyes alongside mine out the oval window at glaring ocean—wide, empty, peaceful.

And the plane surged on toward the world.

After a passage of time, her head slumped against my shoulder. Finally asleep. I removed a cigarette stub from between her fingers. And tried not to move; it would have been a crime to disturb her.

Cicarelli departed in San Francisco; so did Carp. We all had to change planes, head off in different directions. Or at least, when I boarded a different 747, I thought I was leaving them behind. By the time this one finally landed, I was stewed to the gills, and angry and more discouraged than I'd ever been in Nam.

I guess the experience was like debarking off a boat after months at sea; you keep rocking even though the world isn't. I could barely navigate through the mammoth airport—kept listing to port, then over to starboard. The scene was too unreal. All those people, big and clean and healthy. Talk about rarefied atmospheres. Well-attired men and women, kids in fancy outfits; everything spotless. And me limping along, dragging a dirty duffel bag, shell-shocked and gawking. Course, there wasn't an actual hitch in my stride. But whatever the reasons, forever after Nam I always felt I was limping.

A shiny world, rich and perfect. And tons of American pussy on the hoof, *white* pussy, round-eyed cunt; red, white, and blond blue-eyed quiff adorned in sexy, colorful clothing—it knocked me for a loop. How crazy to sniff perfumed air instead of running sores and rotten underwear, bleeding gums and diesel fuel, napalm-singed landscape and festering mud. Just the odor of the world gave me a hard-on. Floors of polished tile and gleaming elevators that ran perfectly. I picked up amoebas in Nam, and had to enter an airport bathroom. Twenty white urinals greeted me; another twenty antiseptic toilet cubicles had fresh rolls of paper in their wall holders. I lowered gingerly on a seat afraid it might explode. At last, a pampered ass!

No relatives knew exactly when I was due home. Hence, my plan was to reenter slowly, take my own sweet time. Maybe hole up in a motel room for a day or two, buy a bottle of 101-proof Wild Turkey, and debrief myself like that. One by one, I'd telephone the important people, explain my frail transition state, allay their fear and trepidation. No need to leap into everything at once. Keep cool, lay low, let it happen slowly. And only when I felt more comfortable in quarantine would I take another step, and filter back into life again.

Those were my plans as I trundled through the airport, and nobody paid attention. I still wore my uniform, and realized soon that I wanted it off toot sweet. Step one, no more Army drab. So I needed an airport hotel quickly, but couldn't seem to function. My knees were terribly weak; the shakes were coming on.

Would that this next apparition had not approached me in my mood. Young guy, young broad, probably late teens, maybe early twenties. She was shapely, very voluptuous, and self-conscious about it. Had a tawny bouffant hairdo, and scads of makeup—Hollywood pink lips, garish false eyelashes. And quite large tits, especially for such a slim girl. A flimsy tight blue Dacron body shirt exposed every bump, every capillary, every pore of the prickled aureole around her temptingly hardened nipples. Her lower half was poured into designer jeans so tight that no ripple creased the denim, except for a plump pussy indentation at the crotch. Her feet were pinched into black stiletto heels that took bitty clacking steps. A frosty, tough, untouchable apparition, so fuckable I wanted to commit suicide because in the USA rape was against the law.

One hand gripped her boyfriend's muscled arm. He ran about her height, and was handsome in a hoodlum way. Swarthy skin, maybe Italian. Black hair swept back, moderately feathered, though closer to an old-fashioned DA. Nice body, probably pumped iron to make wide his shoulders, big his biceps, round his pecs, slim his waist. Wore jogging shoes, jeans almost as tight as hers, and one-way Acapulco shades.

But it was his T-shirt stopped me cold. A white, tight number on which a decal had been ironed, depicting a bloody machete embedded among a pile of fractured, grinning skulls. Beneath the skulls a logo said:

KILL 'EM ALL, LET GOD SORT 'EM OUT.

They sauntered past me redolent of egotistical disdain. I swiveled with them, stunned. I wanted her so bad I thought I might snap, go crazy with lust. Grab her, blow him away, do my business, then snuff her. I wanted to kill *all* Americans right then.

But instead I lowered the duffel bag, settled atop it, covered my face with my hands, and sobbed until the frustration died.

I found a hotel in the airport. Bought my bottles, candy bars, Coca-Colas, and tubes of crinkle-cut potato chips, plus *Playboy*, *Penthouse*, *Hustler*, and *Oui* magazines, *Esquire*, *Time* and *Newsweek*, even an *Easy Rider* featuring voluptuous round-eyed models in string bikinis crawling over glistening Honda 750s and Harley Hogs—you name it, I purchased it, and climbed up slowly to my room. Drew a deep, steaming bath, raided the ice machine for cubes, mixed a fiery drink, then removed the SEALED FOR YOUR PROTECTION paper from the toilet seat and enjoyed an hour-long readathon on the lid. After that I drained the tub, replenished it with steamy water, and slid into heaven on earth, where I sipped my drink, smoked a cigar, and perused my sexy magazines, jerking off, one eye cocked on the twenty-six-inch color TV blabbing in the background. Pure, unadulterated luxury. Around midnight, I lathered myself in perfumed soap, scrubbing until I had used up three little pink bars, until I was more pristine clean than ever before on earth. Finally, I slithered into the king-size bed; Rocky and Bullwinkle cavorted on TV; the air conditioner blasted cool artificial breezes against my cheeks as I drifted into deep sleep between ultraclean sheets . . . and began my wartime dreams.

The scene was a dusty field: could have been west Texas, West Virginia, or Vietnam. Strewn across the field were human parts, bodies blown apart, heads and tongues, feet and fingers, livers and splintered bones, breasts, eyeballs, kneecaps. All human beings scattered across that field had been thoroughly dismembered by explosives; they resembled a great big jigsaw puzzle.

Naked, I pushed a red wheelbarrow through the grisly landscape, looking for somebody, though I didn't know who. Soon as I gathered all the separate pieces and fitted them together the secret would be revealed. As I canvassed the littered terrain, I halted to gather up an arm or a leg, a head or a hand that seemed like they might go together, and I set them in my wheelbarrow. Then, when I thought I had amassed all the correct parts, I guided my barrow to the edge of the field, and began reassembling the body. A slow, frustrating task. Sometimes the body was almost together when I realized I had two left legs, so I reentered the field, hunting for the proper appendage. Then I noticed one blue and one green eye in a face, and, thoroughly exasperated, I traipsed out there again, seeking another blue eye, or green eye, depending.

Despite hours of painstaking reconstruction, I never created a complete or recognizable human being. It was always a Vietnamese kid, a total stranger; or some fat American truck driver; or a bizarre woman who *almost* looked familiar; or a black GI resembling a buddy of mine who'd bought the farm in Chu Lai—but it wasn't really him, wasn't really anybody. Yet I was stubbornly obsessed, and always returned to the mangled bodies, pushing my wheelbarrow, seeking the exact parts that would create the person I sought.

It continued, my fruitless labor, never ending, into the fabled wee small hours of the morning. When I awoke at dawn, it was not with any sense of consolation that the war at last had ended. But rather, I greeted the day in a sweat-drenched terror, convinced that the sadism and the horror would permanently torment my new life in the world.

Awake at last.

2

BACK IN THE WORLD

Sad to say, I was a bona fide cliché. Couldn't get untracked. It was 1970 (or 1972?—I disremember time a lot), and I was twenty-three years old (I think), had no idea how to run my life. 'Course, everybody around me, Mom and Dad, aunts and uncles, the bosom of the well-bred nuclear family, had it all figured out for me. Back to college, Michael, bag that degree, then you can *be* somebody. Well, I'm not the Ford Motor Company, I hadn't a better idea, so what the hell?—okay. Trotted down to the community college and registered for classes. Fifteen minutes rid of the U.S. Army, and I was all signed up on another dotted line, meeting a schedule, taking orders again.

I sat at a little wooden desk harking to the rap of some dude wore leather elbow patches on his tweeds and pontificated about Wystan Hugh Auden, or "The Love Song of J. Alfred Prufrock." Surrounded by blond, blue-eyed ponytails who swooned over the Bee Gees and the Beach Boys. Between classes I walked cross campus among long-haired peace freaks jangling keys to Chevy Corvettes and Ford Thunderbirds in their pockets. I felt like Peter Pan and Tinker Bell all rolled into one, oodles of pixie dust stashed up my bleeding rectum. Sometimes, in classes, I lost the thread; smell of cordite kept insinuating itself through the open windows. Odor of death, too, caused my nostrils to wrinkle. Often some squeaky-clean underclassman in a charcoal-green sweater and carrying a lacrosse stick would be walking toward me on the main quadrangle, or a dazzling nubile cheerleader type wearing a Yogi Maharishi button would turn the corner . . . and all of a sudden I'd picture bloodstains across their sweater or pink blouse, and their faces would blossom into skulls. My urge was to knock them down, kick in a few ribs, pull out the trusty old K-bar, and perform a standard mutilation, renovating their prissy, complacent bodies. In this country they'd blame it on flying saucers, call in an exorcist, make a mint with a series of cheapo movies.

"Extraterrestrials, Spock—what'll we do about this?"

"I dunno. Us Vulcans can't compute."

"Beam me up, Scotty—these people are nuts!"

I went all goose bumpy, limping around in that depressed frame of mind. My heart started fibrillating. A rash appeared all over my calves and forearms. It itched uncomfortably and was diagnosed as numismatic dermatosis. "Probably just a reaction from some crud I picked up in Nam," I told the doctor. "Bugs, slugs, drugs."

"Actually," he replied, "nerves probably have a lot to do with it."

Einsteins I was dealing with. "Take two aspirins, Michael, and wear warm pants."

A social life held no intrigue for me. And anyway, people seemed to shy away, communication was not my strong point. Clothes, records, relationships, men on the moon, the Beatles' breakup, or Timothy Leary—they didn't light my fire. Truth is, I was stretched pretty taut and wanted mostly to be left alone. Needed time, frankly, to metamorphose from killer back to Johnny Frat.

Especially I wanted no truck with the subject of Nam. Let sleeping dogs lie, I figured—I had my fill of punji pits, Bouncing Bettys, and booby traps in my head. Nam scared me silly, all the ways it could surface in my dreams: God forbid I should talk about it to boot. I saw a dentist to get some caps because I ground my teeth at night while sleeping, and woke up to enamel sand dunes on the pillow.

And I was horny all the time, not normal horny; I mean I had a lust, a sexual anguish burning, but dared not ask a woman for a date. No doubt she'd start to pry, take one look at my scars and bleat, "Oh you poor boy," wanting all the juicy details. But I did not wish to rap about it. Afraid if I did I'd go crazy, become a werewolf or something, sprout fangs and crack her head open with a cinder block, cut her to pieces, pack them into three suitcases, and deposit them in downtown bus station storage lockers.

But I felt such a need to humiliate flesh—theirs, my own. I wanted whores and junkies; I fantasized about hurting buxom broads so whacked out on speed or mescaline that they shivered with deathly chills in my cruel arms. I conjured up cocaine floozies who would do anything to me, with me, for just another toot. I invented S and M freaks whose pale legs I could bend back to tie their ankles against their wrists behind their spines—

Cruising the ville late at night, I almost picked up a tall peroxide nigger in a black leather micro-mini, and deposited her whimpering in a trash can after the semen deluge. I almost lured cocky obnoxious teenagers into cheap motel rooms and cut them down to size with all my black-and-blue aberrations. I ogled them in the sleazy parts of town, outfitted in purple body shirts and red spandex short-shorts, black-seamed hosiery and Dacron pants so tight the material seemed to have been painted across the ripples of their pitted skin. I pictured how it would be to yank their chins backward with bent coat hangers, shove their own high heels up their bleeding rectums while they begged me not to hurt them more. . . .

And I spoke to them of Nam. While they arched in pain I remembered my friend Carp. While I caressed their hog-tied bodies with my guns, I told them about the pig that ate a boy alive, the prisoners who died in Conex boxes, and all those naked NVAs who fell from the sky—oh, my buddy Carp was always present, wasn't he? Goading me to perform.

They panicked as I spoke to them of Bien Hoa and Nha Trang and Da Nang. I read to them newspaper articles from the daily blats, stories abounding in demented killers who might have been myself. Here's one, baby, about a teen angel thrown naked from a fifth-story Los Angeles balcony last night, ankles wired together behind her head. Her arms had both been broken before the fall, her body burned in over a hundred places by cigarettes.

"The devil," I hissed at my groaning captives. "The devil made me do it."

I gimped around so electrified I'm amazed my heart didn't explode. And had a constant hard-on. Seems I jerked off one, two, maybe even three times daily. My cock grew sore afraid of my fevered right fist. I'd be seated at the dinner table, tickling my erection underneath Mom's Irish linen tablecloth, downing pot roast and potatoes and gravy, sipping a glass of Lancer's rosé, stroking myself to the image of Carp's final play on that doomed dinkette in the helicopter, while Dad chatted about the advantages of whole life versus term insurance, or Mom tittered on about installing the latest grand poohbah in her chapter of the Daughters of the Eastern Star. Then Mom said, "Please pass the lima beans, Michael," and I did that, my eyes glazed as I heard choking female gurgles in my mind . . . or was that just the Mr. Coffee in the kitchen, brewing the after-dinner Medaglia d'Oro demitasses with which Mom liked to top off our meals?

The TV cart always sat in the dining room while we ate. They loved programs like "All in the Family," reruns of "Star Trek" and "The Honeymooners."

Books tell me that when most shell-shocked boys limp clear of carnage, they tend to hang up their guns forever. Minute they don themselves in mufti they scurry directly to the gun closet and throw out all the deer rifles and shotguns, all the pistols and commemorative derringers and other assorted utensils of mayhem that had been used in their childhoods mostly to decapitate bunny rabbits, knock down deer, or blast apart wigeons or pigeons.

But not yours truly. I was a different kind of vet, used to guns, and considered them an extension of, an outlet for, my anger. Down to Grady's Gun Range I drove three, four times a week, where I clapped on the old Hear Guard earmuffs, and tattered assorted targets with my weapons. I grew up hunting, and had three shotguns—an old Stevens side-by-side 16-gauger, and a fancier Richland Arms double-barreled 12-gauge, made in Spain. Also owned a workhorse Browning automatic 12-gauge with a twenty-eight-inch barrel, ventilated rib, et al. Aside from that, of course, I had one of your basic Colt .45 MK IV, Series '70 government-model automatics, and a .357 Smith & Wesson combat Magnum with a six-inch barrel. My long-range needs were taken care of by a nice little Weatherby Mark V 30-06 to which was clamped a 3X to 9X variable scope on a Buehler mount. Not a very large or diverse arsenal, but it was a decent civilian starter kit for a guy like me, who wasn't quite sure in what direction his antagonisms lay, and who resisted strongly his folks' efforts to get him to a shrink so he could babble his way clear of the depression.

Mom kept dropping little hints, like, "Michael, Michael, why don't you go out with *girls*?" But how could I explain I was afraid "girls" would be afraid of me? I mean, what was I supposed to do? Transport Sherry or Pammy or Brenda to the drive-in for a double feature like *The Apple Dumpling Gang* and *The Love Bug*, then go scarf a malt and a bun at the local Cozy Corner? After which off to the obligatory parking scene at the reservoir we'd toddle, where I might twine groping fingers up under her cashmere sweater for a titillating handful of plump jugs? Or—God forbid, my lucky night!—suppose I could actually sneak the Big Fella between her hairless dumpling thighs for a taste of the promised land? Then what?—we'd start planning marriage, buying a house on time, settling into steady jobs, anticipating *children*?

No, better that I just moseyed over to Grady's whenever the urge hit, and used up a dozen boxes of ammunition shredding paper targets that offered silhouettes of rabbits, deer, or human beings to aim at.

After a fashion I enjoyed the gun range, the assorted noises.

Reassuring, perhaps, was the gaggle of schnooks like me down there, blasting away in anger or paranoia, letting their aggressive American genes get off in a properly controlled manner. All the women who showed up attired in tight jeans and Day-Glo pink curlers tickled my fuzzy. Earmuffed and relentless, fingernails lovingly painted, they gripped huge pistols and fired away at imaginary rapists and burglars and child molesters.

But I never socialized. Why wallow in conversations about guns, or crime in America, or the Nam? Steer clear of *this* jackal, everybody; no friendships, please, no commiseration from redneck NRA freaks, bloodthirsty hunters, or triple-K groupies. Once I deigned to palaver with a stoned auto mechanic who raced quarter-mile funny cars at the local drag strip on weekends, and about halfway into our chat about ballistics, "niggers" and "wops" and "gooks" began sprinkling into the dialogue, so I cut it short. Had enough of that crap in Nam to last a dozen lifetimes. Far as I was concerned, Jane Fonda and John Wayne could *both* go fuck themselves.

Still, I patronized the range. Drew odd comfort from my cohorts there, and stayed anonymous. Kept secret my contradictory ruminations; and wanted no truck with their poignant imaginations either. I read the newspapers; I knew the score out there.

Indeed, I dug into the papers avidly. All of a sudden I had an interest in the world. Why all the social, economic, political upheavals? How come Vietnam? I suppose my travel adventures overseas had whetted a latent curiosity about the workings of history. Nam plunged me into something bigger that had been floundering for millenniums.

I initiated the quest by sort of randomly devouring the *Times-Herald*, the *News-Dispatch*, the *Daily Freedom*. Ah, such a condom-curdling epic of distress out there . . . how had I grown up so unaware of its dimensions? America, my country 'tis of thee, home of the star-spangled milk shake, Doris Day and Sandra Dee, was really a pretty violent nation. In fact, if you truly followed the papers, read between the lines, checked out police blotters, and added up the crime, you could be amazed by the extraordinary savagery going on out there, just around the corner, even right here in River City.

I began a scrapbook. Years ago I had gathered mementos, sports-oriented photographs, articles and line scores: football, baseball, basketball, same shtick. Mom probably still treasures those records, up in the attic, down in the basement, in one old trunk or another. This time around, however, my clippings described a naughtier score. Violent crime, car accidents, rape, and armed robbery; I snipped and pasted daily, and stashed my products in an Army footlocker beneath my bed. Read the stories, gazed at lurid photographs, mused on the people involved, their life stories, what made them snap.

Every day gung-ho Yankees flipped, went on mass-murder rampages. Scions of Howard Unruh, Charles Starkweather, that Charley Whitman character who climbed the Texas Tower and offed sixteen people. My Nam pal, Tom Carp, had nothing on the Nebraska farm boy who robbed a bank, lined up seven tellers and loan officers on the floor, then executed each with one shot apiece in the back of the brain. Three gangsters robbed a Cleveland hamburger joint, then herded the employees and seven customers into a freeze locker and opened up with sawed-off shotguns. A Florida maniac tied the hands of seven coeds behind their backs to their ankles, cooled 'em cold bloodedly, committed necrophilia, severed their heads, and dumped them into Everglades drainage ditches.

Daily stuff, small potatoes, six to eight column inches. More famous perverts triggered books I could buy and read: the Boston Strangler, the Hillside Strangler, and Charley Manson's demented band of creepy-crawlers. I lay in bed nights, reliving (in Technicolor and Panavision) those dire minutes during which Sharon Tate and her friends bought the farm. Or that Kansas family from *In Cold Blood.* I'd be gooning at a crucial football game with Mom, Dad, the neighbors, Dallas owning the ball, third and five on the Washington twelve-yard line, when all of a sudden there was Sharon Tate, Hollywood jugs, blond hair, eight months pregnant, whimpering *"Please don't"* as the knives punctured her bloated abdomen.

You get the drift.

"If you ban guns, only criminals will have guns."

"Guns don't kill people, people kill people."

"Guns, Guts, and Glory are what made America great."

"Kill 'em all, let God sort 'em out."

The proud litany of a democratic land.

Seeking relief, some days, I lugged my basketball over to a city playground and executed jump shots during the hours before dusk. I enjoyed that. Dribbling through dim, moist air, lofting turn-around jumpers, long set shots, right- and left-handed sky hooks. But one evening some pimpled Joe Blows interfered, suggesting a game—three on three—and against my better judgment, I acquiesced. Game heated up right away, of course, but I was flat, my moves lethargic: bets were laid on the outcome, play to 50. I soon resented their intrusion, had no hunger for the competition. So when a jackass elbowed me roughly under the basket, I didn't hesitate, but swung on him instantly, catching him below the ear, and kicked at his chest as he went down.

"Hey, what the fuck—?"

The others stopped, completely surprised. "What'd you do *that* for?"

"Give me the ball, I'm splitting."

"Fuck you and your ball," their leader said, and he flung it at me so forcefully all I could do was ward it off.

Then they jumped me, and I went insane. If I'd been armed, I would have slain them all. As it was I let out a bloodcurdling scream that scared even me, and embraced the beef with open arms. In the end, they broke two of my ribs, but it cost them dearly. I was still standing, one eye puffed shut, lips spurting blood, when they backed off. "He's crazy!" the leader coughed. "Let's get out of here."

Of course, they took along my ball.

In the car careening home my heart suddenly *K-thumped!* then banged against my chest wall like a jackhammer trying to blast out. Simultaneously, my body went as cold and damp as ice, nausea attacked my stomach, and wild shiny jiggles of electricity danced before my eyes. Dizziness zoomed in, and I hit my brakes, veering curbward onto the sidewalk, knocking over a caution sign, stopping against a tree. Slumping sideways, I gasped for air, desperately struggling to stay conscious. Incredibly, I never passed out. I was upright again in ten seconds, and my heart quit going bananas, the cold sweat faded. Scared stiff, I waited for another blow. But none materialized, not right then. I tarried a moment longer, then surmised I'd better make tracks before a cop poked his nose into my dirty linen; not in *this* mood should I tangle with the fuzz.

Cautiously, I backed onto the street and crept off in the correct direction, steering a hesitant path toward home, convinced that my heart would explode again and it'd be Sayonara City for Michael Smith.

The whole flapdoodle must have been a nightmare for Mom and Dad. How could they resurrect their darling boy? Dial 911? Drop back ten yards and punt? Ask Dear Abby for her snotty trenchant wisdom on the subject? They had no idea how to right the wrong. Who was this monster, shaped like their all-American child, who dwelled all jittery and sullen in their split-level ranch estate with a double garage and a Chris-Craft on a boat trailer beside the driveway? It probably knocked their socks for loops to observe me standing in such pain before the mantel which held my football, baseball, bowling, and putt-putt trophies. My dumb dejection must have angered and confused the poor doting imbeciles. What had Vietnam wrought? They fuddled through it, all thumbs, and prayed their tails off on Sunday, I suppose, begging the clouds to part and make sunny again their world.

Off to school, down to the shooting range. In between I piloted my '65 Chevy around town aimlessly, my guns heavy on the backseat, a camera in my hand (old hobby, school newspaper, things like that). I drove willy-nilly, landscape a blur, seething inside. I imagined destroying wealthy neighborhoods, and photographed the mansions, row on row. Cruised through the ghetto, snapping pics, and conjured a flamethrower ending all that misery. Stopped at McDonald's and Wendy's and Lota Burger and secretly captured on film the other blubbery patrons while I ate. *Kill 'em all, let God sort 'em out.* You bet, why not? Made perfect sense to me.

America was daffy, our home absurd. We had a power lawn mower—*click!*—to cut the grass, an electric Weed Eater—*click!*—to trim the walks, a leaf bag—*click!*—that attached behind the lawn mower, a Vacu-Leaf—*click! click!*—to suck all the deciduous residue from the pecan trees out front, and a sprinkler system embedded in the lawn—*click!* once more. Each vehicle carried a remote-control device for opening the electronic garage door. Our kitchen boasted a huge self-defrosting refrigerator, a dishwasher, a microwave oven. In the utility room?—a washer-dryer, a freezer full of sea bass, venison, doves, ducks, geese, pig meat, sirloin steaks. A color TV console dominated the wall-to-wall-carpeted living room. Had another TV in my parents' bedroom, a third in my room, and a fourth down in the basement rec room near the bar and another refrigerator. Dad put Odor-Eaters in his shoes; Mom douched with Lily of the Valley twice a day; Airwicks occupied half the counters and window ledges, making certain that nothing smelled.

If I farted, one or the other of them struck a match.

I whiled away many an hour in the rec room, drinking before the tube after Mom and Dad had crashed early: it was always "a busy day tomorrow." Jack Daniel's Black Label suited my mood. Whatever the TV program didn't matter. I punched remote buttons, switching channels at will, blap, blap, bleep. Rarely viewed whole sitcoms, or a complete ball game, or an entire advertisement. I jumped nervously around, blipping from one vapid show to one vapid singer to another vapid entertainment. Ann-Margret, Robert Blake, Archie Bunker, Bill Cosby. None of it, viewed in such a fractured manner, made any sense. Which, I suppose, was the point.

Sometimes I labored in my old high-school darkroom until

dawn, developing all the aimless photographs I'd taken—of neighborhoods and complacent people on the street, and the gizmos, gadgets, and toys that filled our happy home. And stared at them—like a moron—I stared and stared and stared.

Then tore them all to shreds.

Drunk is how I stayed at night; drunk and stoned. Before Nam, I had a few dope contacts; and I checked in again on my return. At first I merely scored a lid here, bag there—personal acquisitions. Like Nam, carried a heavy bag. Then I agreed to help move some stuff, because I needed the bread. But that part of it stayed small. Why be in hock to any thug? And I steered clear of H and toot.

Sleep at night?—very funny. After that initial attack, my heart got pretty quirky, and sometimes, usually late at night, it started acting futzy, lost all rhythm, thumped, bumped, kicked, and bobbled behind my sternum, acting mighty queer. Then it would slide into a long fibrillation that left me queasy, but wouldn't knock me out. I learned to gasp in deep breaths, and sit upright to control it. Or I strained down as if constipated in what I've since learned is called the Valsalva maneuver.

Came to pass I couldn't lie prone at night, because soon as I stretched out it would commence again. So I propped up pillows, and drowsed in a sitting position, light-headed and nauseous from the constant fibrillations. Obviously, I should have quit the weeds and dope and liquor. Eat healthy and exercise for a better life—good advice. But I seemed bent on becoming a gork.

Compare me to Rothstein's Yiddish Vietnam golem casting a dark shadow through our handsomely equitized lives. Perhaps I resembled a hockey-masked Jason from the *Friday the Thirteenth* movies to those poor souls, who just waited for me to pull a chain-saw massacre on their lives. "Viet Vet Goes Berserk, Fillets Mom and Dad, Then Cuts Off Own Head and Flushes It Down Toilet." While refrigerators and other appliances hummed, and the air conditioning clicked on and off automatically, and the sprinkler system doused the thick rug of a flawless lawn surrounding our impeccable suburban home.

Late one night, Barbara Cicarelli phoned. Suddenly, a voice out of the already distant past. "Hey, Michael, how you doin'?" Drunk or stoned, wiped out, wasted, going down fast, she coughed, a terrible hacker's choking.

"Oh, I'm fair to middlin', Sicko—how 'bout yourself?"

"Can't complain, you know how it is," she rasped jauntily. "Sure is great back here in the world, ain't it, Michael?"

"Things could be worse."

The line seemed dead for a space before she asked, "*How* could they be worse?"

I didn't have an answer. There followed a "pregnant pause," during which I sensed that she was weeping. Finally, I said, "Hey, Sicko—lighten up. Are you okay?"

"Sure, I'm fine. I already told you that. How about yourself?"

"I'm fine, too. I already told *you* that."

"Well, what are you up to?"

"Little bit of this, little bit of that. You know, I go to school, play some ball, get out with the family from time to time—we hunt together. Go to movies off and on. Watch TV. Smoke a little weed."

"How's the weather down there, Michael?"

"Pretty good, pretty good. It rained the other day, but mostly the sun is shining."

"It's not bad up here, either. Though they claim it'll be an early winter."

"Well, you better wrap tight. You're practically living at the North Pole."

"No I'm not. This is only Montana, for crissakes. The North Pole is a million miles away from here."

She sounded pissed off. "It was only a figure of speech, Sicko. Don't take it so personal."

Another pause; nothing from her end. So I asked, "What are you up to? Did you go back to school, find a job, get married?"

"Yeah, I work. Gotta pay the rent, you know. In an emergency room up here. Sometimes I ride the ambulance. I do my turn in the

Air Aid chopper, flying people in from the boonies. Drunken Indians with bowie knives stuck in their bowels, or windshield splinters protruding from their foreheads."

I said, "Maybe you shouldn't have gone into that stuff so soon after Nam."

"What am I supposed to do, Michael, sit around scratching my ass, waiting for Mr. Right on a white charger to carry me off to the little white cottage, picket fence, birdbath on the front lawn, and rose trellises? I have to eat, you know. Gotta keep busy. Busy fingers are happy fingers. Idle hands are the playthings of the devil."

I waited until the end of her coughing fit before I ventured, "Sicko, you don't sound so hot."

"I hate being the one to break the news to you," she replied defensively, "but you aren't exactly coming through like a barrel of laughs, either."

"Well, it's hard," I said.

"What is, your dick?"

"Getting acclimated again."

"Oh? Hey, not me, I feel right at home. The emergency room is a war zone. You wouldn't believe what people do to each other around here. Yesterday we had a three-year-old kid in, his momma got drunk, pitched him out a three-story window. He landed in a pickup truck. Last week they brought in an Indian had one ear cut off; he got in a bar fight with a Vietnam vet. Couple days ago I helped scrape off the road seven Indians who'd been riding in the cab of a pickup that collided with an eighteen-wheeler full of Coors beer. Michael, it never stops. I put time in at the rape crisis center on my days off; there must be a half-dozen rapes every day. They just opened a battered women's project, and there's poor little black-and-blue girls with two kids and a bun in the oven crawling in and out of there night and day. I even hold down a three-hour time slot at the suicide prevention office once a week, and the goddam phone is *always* ringing."

Her voice had risen a few decibels, beginning to sound hysterical. Nervously I changed the subject.

"Hey, Sicko—enough of that garbage. How's your love life?"

"Great. I got a vibrator. Call him Mr. Bill. He does a good clean job, requires minimum upkeep, and always respects me in the morning. How about yourself, Michael, knockin' 'em dead on Saturday night?"

"Sure. Life is a bowl of cherries."

"Ha ha." She really sounded ugly. "What's that supposed to be, a sense of humor?"

Enough, already; we both caved in. The bottom fell out and I realized I couldn't take it from her, not like this.

"Sicko, I don't want to fight with you. I'm sorry. Not with you or anybody else, I'm pooped."

Silence.

"You still there?"

"You mean corporeally or spiritually? You mean is my body still alive and functioning? Or was that a more metaphorical question—like is my brain still here, am I still sane and rational?—I dunno. Can't answer. You tell me."

After another pause I suggested, "Maybe you need a vacation."

"Where do I go—Miami Beach? Watch Cuban drug hoodlums machine-gun each other? Count the bodies of Haitian boat people washed ashore on the pretty beaches?"

"Sicko, I gotta hang up. You're making me depressed. How come you called in the first place?"

"Oh, just checking in, you know. Say hi. Wish you a Merry Christmas. My horoscope said a friend from the past would lift my spirits. So, you know, I think of you as a friend from the past. We shared so many good times together."

I let that sarcasm dribble off my back. "Do you have any friends up there? A guy, a woman?—I'm not talking sex or anything like that. I mean, just somebody you can talk to?"

"Do you?"

Ask a question, receive an answer. Another dead space on the line, until finally I admonished her:

"You got to keep it together, Sicko. You can't blow it. You have to take care of yourself. Stay off the dope, stay off the booze, stay off the pills. You can't just waste yourself for nothing."

"Why?"

"I don't know why, but you can't. If you hang on, things will get better, they'll change. The war will go away."

"Where will it go away to?"

"I don't know. But you should stop murdering yourself. There's no point."

"Sounds like you got it all under control, buddy boy."

"Yup, that's me: Mr. Under Control."

"Well, screw you, Mr. Under Control," she said, and hung up.

Barely had I pondered *that* happy life, than the old reach-out-and-touch-someone jangled again: Tom Carp, if you please; boy maniac, Angel of Death, Mr. Double Veteran himself. "Hey, old buddy—how they hangin'?"

"Who's this?"

"Me—Tom. Jesus, you forget old friends fast."

Emily Post believes that you never ask, "Tom *Who?*" But I was feeling pretty blunt by then, so I bypassed the amenities. "Tom who?"

"Carp, for crissakes! Remember, Nam?"

That had a certain ring to it—remember Nam? No, I'm sorry, can't say as I recall—

"Oh, you."

"Yeah, me." And then he took off. In his cups, I reckon, or stoned, or who knows what anymore these days: pilled, chilled, chemically thrilled. Cheerful, though: and the spiel, believe it or not, touted a Peace-Love-Groovy Kingdom in northern New Mexico. Free dope, free ginch, so why not crank my lard-ass in gear and mosey on up? "Be just like old times." Sure . . . Together Again. On he rambled for half an hour, describing all the meat at his disposal. "Hey, I've just about worked Mr. America to the bone, old buddy—I need some help!" And in the end he re-emphasized the invitation, even waxed poetical. "You should see this place! Mountains, rivers, horses, little farms, cows all over the place—it's just like Nam, only nobody's shooting back at you. All the food you can eat, all the hot-to-trots you could possibly desire, and nothin' to do except have at it with a fifty-caliber dong! I'd known it was like this, I never would have signed for the Nam!"

Good-bye.

Click.

Buzzzzzzzzzz.

Well, who could resist a tourist brochure of that ilk? It was time to leave town, anyway, hit the road, launch a journey of discovery, take a powder. No more of my gloom and doom reflected at me from my parents' morose bewildered eyes. Why continue like a cancer gnawing at their obscene cheerfulness? Too much silence reverberated in our beautiful home. My despair must have clung to the purified walls like moss, like slimy jungle vines, like Southeast Asian mildew. I had a vision of that silence in countless elaborately coiffed high-tech houses all across the land. I mean, radios blaring, woofers and tweeters crackling, the TV chattering twenty-four hours a day—but all that jabber disguised a monumental silence enveloping all our perfect dwellings, all our picture-book communities with their shiny downtown malls and opulent shopping centers, it crushed everything and everybody under its vast weightless moodiness.

So—hi ho, hi ho—Michael's moth toward Tom Carp's flame . . . it was off to New Mexico. Land of enchantment, land of the fabled communes. Freaks wallowing in trust funds. Why not make a run up there, take along some dope, kill two birds with one stone? Plenty of free sex compliments of hippie nymphomaniacs— hot dog (warm puppy, cold frank)! Plus ten thousand square miles of luxurious country—the healthy outdoor life. Climb a mountain, mount a maiden, catch a trout, shoot a bear, tryst a trollop (catch a dollop). Brown saffron rice and gorgeous sunsets viewed from the tops of snowcapped peaks in that wonderful Peaceable Kingdom.

Fair enough. Albeit belatedly, I decided to turn on, tune in, drop out. Dad cosigned a loan for me, releasing the bread to buy weed. I also owned a small bundle, stashed in various institutions, that had been accumulating since age twelve. Dad trained me early in the selection of stocks and bonds, investing money wisely. I actually owned a portfolio of CDs, treasury notes, blue-chip stocks. It all started way back when I ran a paper route and Dad drove me downtown to meet his banker. And there I sat in scuffed jeans, ankle-high Keds, learning arithmetic. Later, the old man opened a newspaper and explained stock quotations so I could follow my investments. His broker was also my broker, a corpulent good-time Charlie named Dan Mott, who labored for an outfit called Quinn and Company.

Now I ordered Dan Mott to unload everything, I wanted dollars. Next, I turned over my life insurance policy, pocketing the cash value . . . and I had liquidated my assets. Still had a stereo, TV set, and other odds and ends to sell—but I fenced them quickly for rock-bottom prices. Just putting together the vigorish, boys. Committing the crime, in my father's eyes, of living off my capital.

A mechanic friend cleaned up my heap, changed the oil, polished the points and plugs, replaced fan belts, tuned her up real cherry. And I was ready to make tracks. The folks fumfered, at a loss for comments. Relieved, no doubt, that the golem was skedaddling; scared stiff I might blow a fuse and disappear for good.

Our last supper together. Linen tablecloth, bayberry candles, a bottle of Lancer's. Dad liked a highball before dinner; Mom favored manhattans. The TV on a cart occupied the background, laugh tracks muttering through another spate of addled nonsense. We ate cold gazpacho, lamb chops, asparagus in hollandaise sauce. Not much relevant conversation. Dad, the stoical patriarch, Mom the nervous Nellie—she talked too much, female chitchat. "Write when you get there . . . don't forget the laundry bag . . . what about a raincoat?" Her pink frilly apron declared I AM THE BOSS. She jumped up and down, to clear stuff out, cart other stuff back in, heat the Brown 'n Serve rolls in the microwave: the sound of its timer chiming had punctuated all our meals.

We made it through, scarfed Häagen-Dazs ice-cream sundaes for dessert, sipped demitasses of Medaglia d'Oro, and concluded with tiny crystal glasses of Grand Marnier. Then I folded my green-linen napkin back into its silver ring, kissed Mom good-bye, shook Dad's hand, and accelerated into the darkness. I had two suitcases of clothes, four G's of passable bush in a flight satchel, my scrapbooks, and all my weapons.

Seemed like a typical way, for a typical joker like myself, to enter the vast American night.

Mr. Under Control, indeed.

I zoomed across prairie land, hill country, the sagebrush desert. Many a dead jackrabbit and squashed armadillo marked the route. Scrawny cows meandered lethargically in parched arroyos. I tailgated stinking cattle trucks and huge semis toting mountains of hay bales, and eighteen-wheeled tankers lugging tons of oil and gas from here to there. The radio I kept fixed to WBAP, "Bill Mack's Open Road Show," and jiggled my legs nervously to the honky tunes of Waylon and Willie, Tammy and Tanya. In all-nite diners and twenty-four-hour truck stop cafés, I drank black coffee, filled my thermos, and hit the road again, mainlining boxes of caffeine-filled raisins, Hershey bars, chain-smoked cigarettes; and drank Coke after Coke to soothe my throat. The diet guaranteed a burnt-out sensation at the bottom of my gullet, but I ignored the heartburn and kept on truckin'. I was so wired I might never sleep again until my eyes lurched out of my skull, my heart wrenched clear of my chest, and my tired old Chevy nose-dived off the road, catapulting end over end into the greasewood desert, there to explode in a typically panoramic (and Technicolor) conclusion.

On the front seat lay wads of money and beer cans, the Weatherby and the Magnum, the Colt .45 and the 12-gauge Browning automatic. And I felt death closing in as I motored across the searing desert valleys. After awhile only inches, half-inches, *millimeters* seemed to separate me from a final rampage that might go down in American annals alongside Charley Starkweather, Ted Bundy, Juan Castro, or that madman who, in the not too distant future, would waste all those spic children in a San Diego McDonald's.

Make no bones, death whispered in my ears all the time now,

58

licked my fevered lobes with its darling tongue; the hour approached. Often, as midnight headlights closed in on the desert roadways, I contemplated a fatal veer, ending it all in a joyous cataclysm of buckling metal and flaming gas tanks—Hollywood, by Christ! Yet I wanted to savor my transition to the gates of hell, I needed to terrorize the living earth before I died, let the world know just who was to blame for my derangement. Enough ego remained, I suppose, for me to require a more self-conscious and publicized conclusion.

So I didn't swerve. And refused to pull over onto the sandy shoulder, blowing my brains to smithereens. No, I intended to go out in a richer blaze of anger and frustration. If it had to happen, let it be a statement that nobody could forget, a fiery memorial, at least, to Nam. Let all the presidents and movie stars flinch a bit over their morning newspapers, pausing if only for a second with their lips touched against the rich pulpy taste of freshly squeezed OJ.

Hour after hour I headed north, through the desolate night. Past sandstone buttes and eroded mesas, and dry washes full of aching stones and glittering bones, and the occasional ramshackle dwellings of desert people, ghostly under the stars.

I never halted, except at weary little gas stations or convenience stores with self-serve pumps where I replenished oil and gas, and amplified my larder of Twinkies and Hydrox cookies, taco chips and baloney sandwiches. Handfuls of uppers and downers descended through my aching esophagus, chased by the smoke of a hundred cigarettes, and the sugary fumes from my stash of homegrown weed. My eyes stayed permanently open, in a fixed and glassy stare. And my brain might never snooze or awaken again. My veins and arteries were scorched by negative chemical reactions; my heart fibrillated almost constantly.

Weak-kneed and dizzy, I was parched and frightened and on edge; keyed up, insanely alert. Guns beside me, guns in my lap, guns on the dashboard, guns in my hands—their cool blind metal soothed my fingers. I rubbed their barrels against my crotch. I popped two, three .45 bullets in my mouth at once and sucked on them like jelly beans or throat lozenges. They took the place of gum, and eased the tension.

I was headed for a rendezvous with Thomas Carp.

When cop cars came toward me, I raised the Magnum, aimed it through my windshield, and pretended to squeeze one off. They never seemed to notice. I went five miles, ten miles, twenty miles over the speed limit, daring them to try and catch and bust me. I laughed, picturing the resultant scene. Me resting quietly in my cab with a cocked .45 in my lap, while some big dumbbell dressed in black, wearing knee-high SS boots and one-way shades, sauntered toward his own extermination flipping the pages of a citation book.

But nothing happened. North I continued, droning along in the rut and routine of deserted landscape, with only a stray Injun here and there amoldering in his grave. The vast, heartbreaking desolation suited my mood to a tee. Then I grew appalled by such impersonal width, and for a moment almost wept.

Pretty soon, however, I grew accustomed to the space. It danced off my shoulders like the awful white energy of atomic bombs. A fierceness invisible in the ever-unfolding air knocked my argyle socks off. Graceful antelopes grazed like rabbits or moocows upon the open range. At first, lulled by the hum of the road and the whine of my tires, I ignored them. I had long since quit playing the radio: why let music jar the great unbending monotony of this landscape which kowtowed to nobody? Even ceased drinking for a while, and grew less extravagant with my pills, ignored the roaches in my ashtray; just grooved on the icy summer silence.

But suddenly I hit the brakes and slewed dramatically onto the shoulder. Close by a herd of fifteen antelopes grazed. I leaned against the hood sighting in the Weatherby, squeezed off a shot, and watched the nearest pronghorn go down poleaxed. The others scattered, I fired three times in quick succession, another buck dropped, a bullet up his ass. He kicked erect again, then skidded as if both front legs were broken. Struggled up gallantly, but then did a jerky flip as my last bullet creamed his brain.

I kept the K-bar knife honed sharp enough to shave with. Discovered in the garbage on my floorboards a Styrofoam cup. I marched through softly falling dusk-light to my first kill. Slit his throat and held the cup under the flow; it filled up in no time, hot blood draining quickly, glassy eyes sightless, a scallop of green foam around the lips.

Over my kill I crouched drinking the blood, remembering Carp again, his fantasies of eating dinks, force-feeding rubbers into whores, burning rats alive. Drank the blood, feeling warm and crazy. If I imbibed enough of it, if I shot enough antelope, then perhaps nothing or no one could stop me from perpetrating my mission on earth, whatever it might be.

The other animal, still alive, breathed stertorously. Again I slit the throat, filled my drinking gourd, downed the elixir, and licked my lips. Then clicked another aimless photograph for posterity. In all the universe no weak tick of compassion dented the endless sagebrush plain. Hadn't seen a car on the highway in hours. The land had hushed the way frogs always clammed when I had stalked close to them on summer boyhood nights. Shh, frogs, shh crickets, shh little children hiding in your gingerbread houses in dark forest realms teeming with witches, poisoned apples, and big bad wolves—shh *everybody*—hear those footsteps?

A giant killer is on the loose, seeking brains to savor.

Toward noon, second day, I chugged into a small desert town, and spied the neon brightness of a 7-Eleven sign. I needed gas, beer, and more substantial nourishment, like a microwave burrito, or a hot sloppy joe. I did not even snap that the Magnum was in my hand until it clacked against the cooler door when I reached for a Mickey's Bigmouth.

Well, okay, why not? thinks I. This is America, and I'm patronizing a convenience store, the most oft-robbed institution in our great land—might as well go for it. "No guts, no glory," Tom Carp always said. So I laid my beer, cigarettes, and Slim Jims on the counter, and leveled the gun at the checkout clerk. He was a pimpled teenager with a little Nazi cross dangling off his ear, and a round yellow Smilie button—HAVE A NICE DAY—clipped to his shirt pocket.

I said, "I want a bag for this stuff, and whatever bread you got in the register."

He didn't believe it. Checked my eyes, then the .357, then my eyes again. And smiled, almost as if realizing that he'd become a movie actor, and I could make him famous. And he blurted, "You're kidding."

I followed the usual script, thumbing back the hammer. "No, I'm not kidding. Now give me a bag and the money and make it quick."

He still glanced at me with a disbelieving smirk as he produced a bag, and dreamily shoveled in my loot. Then handed over the sack.

"Mister, you're not even wearing a mask."

"The money, you dumb gork."

"Hey, okay, take it easy . . ."

He clanged open the register, still smile-smirking—Holy moly, it was really happening, what an adventure, wait'll he told the guys! And scooped out all the paper.

"You want coins too?"

"No thanks. Lift up the drawer; I need the big bills under there."

He affected a look of stupid, transparent ingenuity. "We don't keep anything under the drawer."

I emphasized my need by touching the muzzle to his chest. "Lift the drawer, boy, and let me see."

"Hey, hey, okay, okay." He was actually annoyed, still didn't truly feel the danger. Probably had watched a million deaths and mutilations in TV movies, always plastic, never relevant or real. So I was probably exactly like a movie.

Under the drawer?—a dozen checks, and several twenty-, fifty-, and hundred-dollar bills. Quite a haul. I separated the cash from the bullshit, while he grinned foolishly, not in the least bit worried. Fact is, he stared at me, wondering was I a TV actor, or in movies—? Charles Bronson, Clint Eastwood, Chuck Norris.

Then he chose to be a wise guy. Couldn't resist one more crack. *Look at me, Mom, no hands!*

"While you're at it"—he gestured toward a cardboard stand next to the register—"why don't you steal a pack of gum?" He had big ears, very cute Norman Rockwell jug handles on either side of his head.

As I reached for the gum, he added cockily: "You're bullshitting me, mister. That isn't even a real gun."

He needed an attitude adjustment. So I raised the hog and shot him at point-blank range: *G-blom!* The whole store shivered, plate glass rattled, a coffeepot jiggled on its hot plate. The bullet punched right through the Smilie button and the kid and shattered a Wesson oil bottle on a shelf next to some Bunny bread twenty feet beyond. The wise apple vented a kind of *glurg* sound, and was probably tap city even before the slug reached the cooking oil. He dropped straight onto his knees—*twang!* Then keeled sideways. His head snapped over, catching the gray edge of a metal waste-basket lined with a green plastic bag. And as he slumped to the floor that wastebasket tipped over, engulfing his head in crumpled cash register tapes, candy bar wrappers, empty Frito Bandido bags, and aluminum soda cans.

When I glanced up, I saw the woman. Apparently she had entered the store during a robbery in progress, but failed to notice. My shot woke her up at the cooler compartments, sliding door open, a Diet Pepsi clutched in one hand. Kind of a flaccid broad, not very sexy. Pink curlers, and heavy mascara surrounding tired eyes. Under a nondescript white blouse her floppy, shapeless bosom bulged in many directions. Tight elastic pedal pushers accented a lumpy belly, spreading thighs. Probably just dashed over from a nearby Laundromat. Too bad she had witnessed the killing, and might remember my evil face.

She remained in the same position, mouth dropped open, as I approached. Oh dear, oh dear. Why had she chanced in here for a Diet Pepsi at exactly this moment? Was there no just God on high? I pressed the hot muzzle of my Betsy directly between her badly plucked eyebrows.

"Let go of the door, please."

She obeyed the command.

"Now you and me are going back there." I nodded at an open doorway beyond the coolers. Very carefully, she stepped in that direction, and I followed, the gun poked between her shoulder blades. The door led to a storage and warehousing area, cardboard boxes, couple of dollies, splintered wooden crates that once held apples, oranges, grapefruits. And two rest rooms—one said BRAVES, the other SQUAWS. When we got there I told her to choose the BRAVES door, and she hesitated.

"But that's the men's room." Fastidious bitch. I jabbed the gun.

"It doesn't matter."

She opened the door onto the usual stench: piss, and damp cigarette butts in the urinal. Crumpled paper towels overflowed from the wastebasket onto the floor. Water faucet dribbled with a hissing sound. A chipped Vend-a-matic on the wall dispensed SEXY SURPRISES. Another machine offered scented condoms, French ticklers. A picture on it showed a bikinied babelet, all rump roast and humongous mams. Some horny fool had drawn a huge cock spurting droplets of inky come all over this sexy glamour girl. The toilet beside the urinal was clogged up; hadn't been flushed in weeks.

"Turn around slowly." Like an automaton, a good little Barbie doll, she obeyed and faced me. I thrilled to this power, it took me right back to Nam. Blood rushed into my head and elsewhere. "Okay, now, take off your blouse."

Her eyes begged for mercy. She put the soda pop on the washbasin, and her hands rose and methodically unbuttoned the blouse. She let it slip down her arms behind her onto the floor.

"The bra goes too."

Yes sir, yes bwana, yes memsahib, yes GI, you number-one, you number-one GI—what a good American gook. Droopy tits with big tarnished dugs and skeins of ugly stretch marks unrolled down to her waist.

"Now drop to your knees and blow me."

Very carefully she sank onto the floor. My free hand unzipped my fly and worked it free for her.

"If you bite me, if you hurt me in any way, you're dead. Make it good."

How does somebody that terrified make it good? Her tongue was so dehydrated from panic it rasped like a cat's tongue against my head. She tried munching a little, but couldn't make her mouth work. She gagged, backing off, caught her breath, and tried again. Tears rolled down her cheeks. It felt to me like being sucked in sawdust. She choked again, and, pulling off, murmured desperately, "I'm sorry . . ."

But I was disgusted by her fumbling. Time for serious business. Visions of Tom Carp in that helicopter with the NVA prisoner spurred me on.

"Stop. That's enough. Turn around. Crawl over to the toilet."

That completed, there followed a thoughtful moment. My slave kneeled before the rancid commode, tears streaming down her cheeks.

"Pull your pants down to your knees." She hooked fingers under the elastic waistband, and tugged the toreadors over puckered buttocks and thighs misshapen with cellulitis.

"Bend over and stick your head in the toilet."

She balked.

"Do it, please."

She gripped the edge of the bowl, started to bend down, and puked. Gagged and upchucked, entire body jerking as all the sour gunk splashed out. Not a pretty sight, so I allowed my eyes to wander until she had calmed down. Then I kneeled behind her and demanded she poke her head in there again, as, with my other hand, I spittled up my fingers, lubricated between her legs, and shoved it in—*Bingo!*

"Oh God," she moaned, "Ted will kill me." She barfed again, dry heaves, and her inner convulsions made me climax instantly. So I withdrew and, all in the same motion, placed the Magnum barrel against her rectum and pulled the trigger, rending her life asunder.

Then I straightened up, and I left that dirty bathroom.

The jug-eared kid was happily ensconced at his register, ringing up my victim's Diet Pepsi. I walked past them both, pressing the Magnum tightly to my far side, like Roger Staubach after a fake on a rollout. The kid called after me, "Come back and see us again—have a nice day."

Well, I might return to that 7-Eleven again, who knows? Me, or somebody like me with less control over their rage. In this diverse and fascinating life you never can tell about things, what's real, what's made up, whose invention of the world (of the war) holds water.

But anyway, up to a point fantasy can only get you (off) so far. And I might just want to start a scrapbook on *myself* one day.

Toward the end of my trip I achieved a mountain range, edged over it slowly, descended into a baking valley, followed a muddy river north. Soon I entered the Rio Grande Gorge and trailed its suicide curves up toward a high plateau. How disappointing. The journey had passed too quickly. Old legends had suggested I'd be on the road for days and days, crossing time zones, land zones, emotional zones, covering a fantastic distance which lay between me and a new life—pioneering America, Conestoga bound, restlessly plodding westward into the last great myth on earth. Instead, I reached my destination in almost the same mood and condition as I had departed my former home. What a distressing anticlimax.

Somehow, the country had lost a bit of the old mystery from its spaces between places.

3

NEW LIFE, NEW PLACES, SAME OLD SONG

There ensued my "psychedelic period." Sad to say, I made a lousy hippie. I couldn't seem to mellow out; I was afraid to fuck for fear I'd kill instead. Yet I tried the life-style for a while, figuring What the hell? At least the bizarre commune scene was a good place to hide for a spell. My first day in town I located Tom Carp—twenty pounds heavier, Fu Manchu mustached, and loaded for bear. Greeted me like a long-lost bro' and wasted little time in introductions. He handed me over a mayonnaise jar full of penicillin and said, "Let's go get laid; Mr. America needs a workout."

We wound up south of the ville at a hot springs where twenty kids bathed nude, smoked dope, and stood guard, brandishing rifles, shotguns, pistols—I'm surprised they didn't have bazookas, M-79s, or flamethrowers. Things had changed in just weeks since Carp had extolled to me the placid virtues of the Peaceable Kingdom. The war featured local Chicanos versus longhairs. The freaks were uptight, self-righteous, into God, vegetarian diets, Nubian goats, and anti-Chicano ballistic missiles . . . and Carp was their playground director.

Tom seemed uneager to drop his pants, but I shed my clothes in a jiffy and went swimming . . . for about ten minutes. Then an old Mercury chock-full of locals parked above the hot springs and sizzled there; they drank beer, their stereo blasted mariachi songs. Uncomfortably, bathers left the water and dressed. Armed to the teeth, my pal Carp and five other hirsutes emerged from a tilting shack and lounged around, waiting for the locals to split. Clash of values, here; the drug generation meets four hundred years of inbreeding. Or was that vice versa? Carp said, "I just dare one of those greasers to even *squeak.*" He packed an AR-15 that had been converted to automatic using one of those git-kits you can send away for in *Soldier of Fortune* magazine. "Thirty rounds a second," Carp informed me, grinning. "One of those nerds gets uppity, I can turn him into Swiss cheese."

Well, some things never change: Welcome Back to Nam. Two nonplussed women led me across a ravine to a large two-story ramshackle house called the Tree Star Barn. Outside on a wood fire supper bubbled in a large caldron. Two blond, tan, naked guys and a woman in a purple sack dress squatted beside it, adding ingredients, tasting their gruel. Only furniture inside the house was a dozen bunk beds, and dirty mattresses on the floors of various rooms. Other junk included grimy backpacks, muddy hiking boots, tattered sleeping bags, warped guitars.

A crash pad for roadies. The Tree Star Barn had little rhyme or reason, no electricity, no windowpanes, no running water. Carp rented a place in town, but I sort of liked the anarchy there, and aimed to scope it for a while. What we drank, bathed in, or used for cooking issued from the hot springs. No gardens, no fruit trees, no chickens or other animals tempted permanency. Just scads of dope, as Carp had said, and a sexual promiscuity. Guys and gals rutted together at night, sliding casually among each other. Nobody cared who you were, or if you had a name. I turned away three women the first night, and awoke at dawn because a petite chick was trying to blow me. "Hey," she carped, "go back to sleep, I'm a succubus." Somehow I refrained from bashing in her face.

"By the way, Tom," I asked my Vietnam buddy when he returned in the morning, "what's a succubus?"

"A chick who eats the tail pipes of Greyhounds," he replied toot sweet.

So I knew I had found again my comrade of intellectual dimensions.

Later each morning, somebody less zonked than the others would scuffle around, collecting bread for a town run, for supplies, for the evening repast. Which we ate plopped around that caldron, dipping food into wooden bowls, slurping it up with our mouths or fingers, or sucking it off smooth sticks. Sometimes Carp attended meals, sometimes not. But when present he affected an incongruous fastidious bent: his own bowl, his own spoon. "This is America," he joked when I queried. "You're supposed to be civilized, at least."

Beyond that, nobody had much responsibility. We lived in filth, though our bodies—thanks to swimming—remained fairly clean. I didn't care: nothing much mattered anymore. I was a man on automatic pilot, I guess. Plus I savored the suspension of morals and social values; it had a nostalgic beat. After a couple of nights nobody teased me much for not banging my ass off with all the ginch at hand. They almost admired me when I said I was holding out for "love." If people had food, drugs, money, they shared, they were generous. Except me. My stash remained a secret, a security blanket for the future. Everybody understood it was a summer place, the Tree Star Barn, which would collapse in frosty weather. Meantime, better live it up. Lots of grasshoppers stroking their fiddles. We had acid, and enough mushrooms to keep it interesting. A group dabbled in Native American church rites, gobbling peyote all night whenever an odd old Pueblo Indian emerged from the surrounding piñon forest to lead them. My liquor habit most Star Barn denizens found decadent, although one woman named Shangri La (she had a kid, Shanti, a dog, Anonda) could not wean herself from Southern Comfort—we made the booze runs together.

I figured screw the Hippie-Chicano War: I felt too dangerous for amateur theatricals like that. Carp blew the cover on my Nam experience, but I stayed mum about the armory in my car: I really might need it to be a surprise one day. Those who fancied themselves warriors, let them protect the rest of us. The lads and lassies trusted Carp to seal their perimeters at night, and he and his rag-gedy-ass crew of Carpettes were happy in the job. They wielded shotguns, deer rifles, a Mini-14, that AR-15, a couple of .45s. Only Carp knew the violence score, but truth to tell I noticed a change in him. He liked responsibility, being the chief toady, deploying his men. And he did it with a qualified calm I'd never observed in Nam. Call it a restraint bred of maturity? Or simply a proper cau-tion given that our country had rules? In any case, his professional attitude added stability, it mitigated the possible mayhem. Women remained a trifle edgy, however; apparently he slapped them around a bit too much back in his town pad, during their conjugal furies.

While Thomas Carp and company kept an eternal vigil, this little werewolf disported quietly in the hot springs, trying to figure it out before I made a move. People floated around languorously, bumped lazily into each other, dreamily commenced their dirty deeds: an original manifestation of Peace-Love-Groovy. If they all fucked each other, nobody would own another human being, jeal-ousy could not occur. I tended to simply spectate from a marijuana haze while others indulged their sexual habits before me. In my head, however, I invented crude ways to violate these unself-conscious nymphs and satyrs. In my head, I say; I had no trust that I could act anything out and avoid the electric chair. Push came to shove, I was terrified to let my golem off his leash.

Well, it was all pretty laid back, and after awhile not even very erotic, thanks to a lack of sexual tension, I suppose. Guys could hit on a bitch the way they reached for a cigarette. Just walk up be-hind her at 11:00 A.M., lift her skirt, shove it in, pump a few times and come, then dawdle away pleasantly dazed while she continued pinning up damp clothes.

Murphy's law clearly indicates that all idylls must end, how-ever. So some locals eventually grabbed one of our female mem-bers off a town street, raped her, of course, then flayed her pretty badly. In return, our bozos attacked an old adobe house belonging to one rapist, and riddled it good, seriously wounding a seventeen-year-old tecato inside. I steered clear of it all—let the amateurs bungle it proper, I was saving myself for bigger things, biding my time. In droves, cops landed on the Tree Star Barn, arresting freaks, confiscating weapons. Somehow, Carp eluded the drag-net—in fact, he disappeared an hour before it went down, return-ing only when the coast had cleared.

Next, about thirty Hell's Angels roared into the hot springs on a quiet Monday morning, beat up two guys, and gang-banged a pregnant woman who'd been in the water; subsequently she lost her baby.

A heavy paranoia crept in. Peace-Love-Groovy wasn't all that much fun anymore. Our numbers were half depleted; roadies avoided the place, word was out. The final blow occurred at 4:00 A.M. on a cool September day, when members of the local Chamber of Commerce dynamited the main hot pool: our social center was destroyed.

Even flashback cripples could read that much writing on the wall; we packed it in. Freaks dressed, shouldered their knapsacks and bedrolls, and assembled outside the Tree Star Barn for a fare-well ceremony. It included a Hopi blessing, an Indonesian rattle, a Tibetan prayer wheel. Then my friend Carp, an expert on such matters, tossed a match into the gasoline-soaked front room and effectively Zippoed the crumbling edifice. I expected gooks to scramble out screaming, but only a skinny cat leaped to freedom in the nearby ditch.

Time to plod on toward darker pastures. Carp invited me to camp at his digs if I wanted, but something much too slippery characterized the man. In the final analysis, I had no soul I wished to share with him; I wanted no confidant for my Asian nightmares; I didn't like reminiscing about the Good Old Days—flaming rats and pinko whores in helicopters, the Pig Boy and that old squat-ting geezer in our path. We were too close in arms to the sizzling fires of hell: I feared every word, every suggestion that issued from his smiling mouth.

It just wasn't enough merely to have genocide in common.

Put another way (absurd as it may seem), I felt I was better than him.

But I kind of liked the area, and stuck around for a while—who knows why we choose to keep on playing? Hope for the future?—don't make me laugh. Yet the mountains were high and wild; the sagebrush mesa surrounding town was dry, empty, beautiful. The prehistoric Rio Grande Gorge passed by ten miles west of the plaza. A dozen small rivers full of brown trout and cutthroats trickled out of the Sangre de Cristos. Deer and elk and bear and beavers populated the forests. I could put my guns to work, steer clear of people, grow a beard, be eccentric, live and let the poisons drain.

Of course, my angers rarely died away. Whatever my outward display of calm, inside apocalypse and catastrophe rode always close beside me—in my nightmares, over morning coffee, throughout the day wherever I traveled. Yet nothing truly focused. In one fantasy I strapped dynamite around my body and marched into a police station (or the White House, or the Pentagon) and accomplished a worthwhile eradication during my final desperate act. But I never put a coherent plan in action; too dulled, too wishy-washy, too torn between the hallelujahs and the grave.

Perhaps I awaited a signal from God or from Thomas Carp. A burning bush or a stone tablet to point the way. THOU SHALT COMMIT GENOCIDE. THOU SHALT DISMEMBER THY NEIGHBOR'S WIFE. THOU SHALT BURN ALL THE LITTLE CHILDREN. THOU SHALT SOW THE COUNTRYSIDE WITH BUTTERFLY BOMBS. THOU SHALT COMMIT A VIETNAMESE ABORTION—

I wound up leasing a one-room studio pad overlooking a seedy town park. A single mattress on the floor and two dilapidated wooden chairs. But it had a cable TV hookup with access to—Holy moly!—twenty-seven channels. Money was departing hand over fist with nothing returning to my pockets, so I landed a job at a local flower shop–landscaping outfit, and tried to hobble onto my feet again. And, though nobody out there gave a royal hoot, I thought a telephone might add a patina of civilization to my sleazy scene, so one day I checked in at the local Ma Bell office to place an order.

74

Four women at desks up front handled service calls and bill payments. The frontmost lackey took my breath away. She was tall, skinny, beautiful; silky blond hair hung halfway down her back. She wore a paisley print shirtwaist dress with padded shoulders. Had a slightly pug nose, pale blue eyes, full lips. And delicate creamy skin. She seemed shiny, like an angel; vague, a bit ethereal. When she called my turn, her voice was weak, tremulous— the kind you wanted to protect. She embodied everything I didn't. I perched tensely in a blue plastic chair while she wrote up my order, flipped a transparent card onto her computer viewer, and shifted it around, absorbed in the numbers depicted on her screen. When I cracked a joke, she smiled wanly, slightly pained. A desktop nameplate identified her as one Noelle Johnson. I ached to own the woman.

She concluded the order, then summoned a man from in back, an actual lineman named Bob. He looked the part in a red-checkered MacGregor shirt, clean Lee jeans, polished work boots. Our town was mostly dirt lanes without names or addresses, so I explained the route to my apartment. He nodded. "Oh, it's that condo behind the park that just filed a Chapter 11."

By the time I split I felt much better about things; I had Noelle Johnson on my mind. It was time at last to ball a woman; she seemed like my kind of victim.

But how did you capture a bitch like that, so fragile and rare among all the world's assholes?

An anger burned inside me like willie peter, never going out. I couldn't seem to snuff it enough so that my intended, Noelle Johnson, would never tip if I roused the guts to make a play. I worked hard all day, excavating gladiolus, transplanting trees, delivering flowers. Kept to myself a lot, never encouraged communication. But I worked hard and they kept me on. My body trembled constantly. I chain-smoked, mainlined coffee, ate stupidly, ate unhealthy. In the morning coffee and juice, maybe a bowl of Wheaties— Breakfast of Champions . . . vestigial eats from my athletic days. Took peanut-butter sandwiches to work. Evening meals were a joint, four or five shots of Jack Black, a baloney-and-cheese sandwich, heavy on the mustard and mayo, a bag of taco chips. I chased the bourbon with beer, smoked another joint, sat cross-legged on the living-room floor, watching TV, hating it, fascinated by the pap. Car crashes, melodramatic cops, murders and kidnappings, tits and asses on female detectives. I sat there glued, coming unglued, zonked out of my skull, permeated with fear and loathing—hey, this was no way to prepare for the capture of a frail maiden like Noelle! But sometimes I just abided in a pool of my weapons, aiming guns at the squeaky-clean neutered Fausts who hawked new cars, floor cleaners, and designer jeans between bouts of Tinkertoy macho mayhem and sitcom pabulum lunacies. Every bit of the fluffy hype insulted my intelligence and my experience in the Nam. I wanted to waste the culture, drape it in flaming napalm, eradicate all the hysterical puffy *cheerfulness*. Who created such cruel buffoonery? I pictured the first Pilgrims on Plymouth Rock looking around hungrily for Indians to bugger, smiling like Howdy Doody.

I knew indeed that it was time to get my shit together, clean up my act, fight for life. For whatever reasons, though, I seemed to lack resolve, even with Noelle Johnson as the prize. Michael Smith, journeyman sleepwalker. Couldn't tone down the anger, or halt the drinking, or quit the dope. Or see a doctor.

'Course, I had to, finally; that last—check out a sawbones. His brilliant diagnosis?—my nerves were shot, my blood pressure atrociously high, my heart dangerously erratic. He prescribed digitoxin for the heart, no salt and diuretics for the blood pressure, and informed me I also had a bleeding ulcer.

"What about the constant depression, Doc? Half the time I can't breathe. I want to cry. I need a release. I want some rest at night."

He referred me to his friend George the Shrink. George the Shrink explained that often depression is physical—a chemical imbalance—not mental. The solution?—antidepressants: Pertofrane was one, Elavil another. He scripted me enough Valium to eat like

jelly beans, gobble like candy. For the heavy jobs he prescribed a
real blockbuster veggifier, Thorazine. Thenceforth I traveled
around with a bottle of Maalox and a half dozen baby-proof plastic
jars of chemical Twinkies in my old kit bag.

Seeking normality, I joined the greenhouse slow-pitch softball
team. Town leagues were a big deal that summer. I liked the game,
but engaged in it too fiercely. On a close play I'd trample the first
baseman to dislodge the ball, or spike the shortstop even though he
missed the throw. You go looking for fights, you get them. The
league was competitive, macho, dusty. We drank beer incessantly
and wore sleeveless T-shirts on hard dirt fields surrounded by
noisy spectators in pickup trucks. I kept glancing in vain for a
sighting of Noelle Johnson, miraculously perched on a fender, eagerly rooting me on. One day a ball careened off my shoulder as I
slid into second, and I charged the man guilty of the errant peg,
fully intending to dismember him. Both benches emptied into one
hell of a free-for-all. I lost two teeth, and quit playing ball, spooked
by what might happen next.

But how to help myself? I lacked hope, and puttered in my
empty apartment plotting murders. Especially, I wanted to clob-
ber Noelle Johnson, whom I saw from time to time floating around
town like a buttered lamb. Kill her not for any transgression I
could name, but simply because she remained so unattainable that
I couldn't make a move.

I sold the Chevy, bought an old Dodge truck. Upon occasion I
revved up my new beater at night and drove across the Rio Grande
Gorge Bridge, out to the western mesa. There I fitfully communed
with an absolutely silent sagebrush world. Above me I could *feel*
the entire panoply of stars. Coyotes howled and I loved them—I
howled back . . . and laughed . . . and howled some more. Across
the gorge, town lights twinkled in a thin line beneath the dark
humps of mountains. A world at rest out there. But not me. I
always traveled with my guns. And occupied a cushion in the bed,
slurping my bourbon, puffing my dope, humming to myself, talk-

ing aloud to my fantasy Noelle, eternal nonsense. Occasionally I cut loose a few Magnum rounds, or fired a shotgun at the stars. The coyotes shut up. I adored the noise, how it rang my clock, reverberated across the misty open spaces afterward. Eventually, I dozed off in a stupor. Might awaken at 5:00 A.M. to an early summer sprinkle, or covered head to toe by chilly dewdrops. Or maybe the terrible relentless sun would broil me alert spare minutes after dawn, parked in the middle of nowhere—as if on the ocean—head aching, mouth swollen, lips cracked, heart doing a jivey bebop routine between my ribs.

One morning out there, when I slowly pried open sticky eyelids, Noelle Johnson, all slippery white and sensuous, was hunched on the tailgate, sizing me up. But she flapped away before I could grab the Magnum.

I knew how to fly-fish for trout, and went after them on the Rio Grande. Each weekend, if the river was low and clear, I hiked the gorge, casting for rainbows and browns. In my backpack I carried beef jerky, candy bars, chewing gum, cigarettes, blackberry brandy, Jack Black, joints, pills, boxes of Magnum ammunition for my favorite hog. Never required a sleeping bag, just curled up in this nook or that cranny when it grew dark, jacket draped around my shoulders. The river's white-water roar blotted out my thoughts. High sheer walls towered over me, leaving exposed only a skinny splash of stars. I liked the bats fluttering around me, although occasionally, just for joyless kicks, I fired the Magnum at them, never hit a one.

I could be alone in that crevasse, more alone than anywhere else in the world. I chose bajadas, narrow old sheep trails, that few sojourners used nowadays. Too hidden, mighty difficult. It was a solitude I craved. I loved rocks, the beige-yellow cliffs, the talus slopes, the huge basalt boulders lining the river. Though it was dangerous to hop from boulder to boulder, I appreciated the exercise. It was the best place to die I could think of.

Such a river, such a wild beauty. I danced along with all the manic skill and crafty deliberation of a werewolf, gleaning trout from the turbulent waters. Stashed them in a burlap sack twisted into one of the pack straps across my back. And concentrated more on catching fish than I may have concentrated on enemy gooks in Nam. I howled in execration if, once hooked, a trout escaped. And kept every fish I caught, unhooked it, slithered it into my sack. Twenty-inch lunkers, or six-inch babies—all of them died. I had no fishing license, no wish to obey the rules. And barely paused from one trout to the next. I moved through that canyon in a blur of keyed-up hunting tension, feverishly building up my body count. Weighty piles of fish squirming against my hip, gasping out their slippery lives, jogged no compassion in me. I liked the destruction, taking all those lives.

When my sack weighed too heavily, I stopped. Dumped them onto the sand, or onto a wide smooth stone. And smoked a cigarette, pensively assessing my accumulations. An almost calm moment that rarely endured for long. Idle, I was wasting time. I had so many more trout to catch and fight, so many fast swimmers to watch rocketing clear of the water, helpless at the end of my line, bursting out of their skins with life . . . how I detested the ones that got away.

Always left my piles wherever I dumped them; for the muskrats, the gophers and birds, whoever had a hunger. Didn't like to fry them up myself. Catching them was the point, their frenzied struggle at the end of my leader. Then to feel their dying squirms in the sack against my hip. And finally to sit tight, admiring their sweet dead bodies, silvery sleek and innocent, just like cool Noelle. Somehow, by its utter senselessness, their lovely stillness momentarily silenced my rage.

So in my own demented way, I courted that ethereal woman.

Tell me, how much loneliness is too lonely? When does companionship become imperative? I only had a single friend in town. His name was Willie, Willie Pacheco; on weekends we gathered wood together. Willie had returned from Nam three years before I did my time in Southeast Asia. Though only twenty-eight, he had a ravaged face, a crippled body—he resembled a man prematurely fifty. He kept his long greasy hair tied back in a ponytail. And walked with a limp—his back ached all the time. Twice wounded in Nam, he received monthly an 80 percent disability check to prove it. The bread bolstered him up, after a fashion. Laboriously, he split wood by hand; we sold it for eighty bucks a cord. Smoked dope incessantly, did Willie, and dealt a bit of my dwindling stash for me—all else aside, the man could be trusted. He hauled around a veritable drugstore of painkillers to keep him perpetually foggy. He had departed Nam a junkie, and so tabs of legally prescribed methadone were an addition to his self-destructive arsenal. I had watched him split wood until his arms dangled inertly, and the glaze overtaking his eyes seemed like the veil of death itself.

Two like peas in a frazzled pod, we foraged together in our trucks. His ramshackle '53 Chevy had no headlights or taillights, and an impossibly spiderwebbed windshield. An expert mechanic, somehow he kept it running. Willie's daughter, Mariangela, never left his side, a scrawny eight-year-old, silent as a tomb. An inseparable pair. Local welfare honchos were always filing papers to grab her for a foster home where a real family could "love" her. Passionately, Willie confronted the authorities. Legal aid lawyers battled back on his behalf at every opportunity. Willie packed a nickel-plated .38—in his pocket, or on the dashboard of his heap. He drank, too, forever tugging vinegar from a bottle of cheap dago red, the best he could afford. Mariangela, in dirty dresses, wrinkled socks, and rummage-sale shoes, never protested; she cared the world for her daddy.

Willie had local family: cousins, aunts, uncles. They hated his guts, always feuding. Willie, the tecato, the wasted carnal, the black sheep had been court-martialed out of Nam, dismissed with dishonor. Never could get it together. Attended countless therapy sessions, drug programs, AA for veterans, and graduated with half his screws loose, a brooding, violent intensity, an inability to make it in the straight world. Top it all off in this Catholic hierarchy, he told the church to take a douche by fathering a daughter out of wedlock, with a Filipino woman who subsequently OD'd.

I liked Willie and his daughter: they made more sense than many other dingbats. Our two-truck caravan puttered into the mountains or across the mesa to the piñon forest, and there spent Saturdays and Sundays together, collecting wood for winter. Willie hated chain saws, couldn't abide the racket, and so he invested hours of back-breaking labor to smash it all by hand, utilizing a double-bladed ax as sharply honed as a razor. I paused often to watch him crawl over dead trees, punching them apart with unerring blows that always landed perfect. When he discarded his shirt, working bare to the waist, I was touched by the fierce energy of his scarred and emaciated body; the ribs stuck out, the head looked mammoth atop his attenuated torso.

Beside him darted the dirty grasshopper waif in shapeless dresses, clambering effortlessly among trunks and sagging branches, gathering up the wood chunks and stacking them expertly, like pieces of a puzzle, in the bed of their dilapidated Chevy.

I always bought two six-packs and threw them in my cooler. We paused to eat when the trucks were laden, drank a few beers, talked a little. Willie had grown taciturn in old age, tired of attempting to figure things out. Mariangela never spoke, always hunkered off by herself, fearful of intrusion as she hungrily wolfed the sandwiches. Willie was intelligent, thoughtful, always in pain, rarely complained. We shared a joint; he grinned, allowing as how he liked the land, liked working with his hands. Loved the smell of sagebrush, piñon, juniper, greasy engines, gathering rainstorms. Why stop drinking or smoking, he asked; why save his withered body? The only fight worth diddley-shit was for his daughter. I mentioned Nam a few times; Willie shrugged, scratched his knee, probed his rotten teeth with a toothpick.

"Let them grease it, Mike. Let them destroy the world. Who cares? I'll dance at the funeral."

They had been living in a one-room house, no running water: it belonged to a brother-in-law. After a quarrel, they threw out Willie and his daughter. I lost track, and we missed a couple of piñon-hunting weekends together. I asked around, and finally discovered that they were camping on the mesa south of town, not far from the new sewage plant, on the banks of the Pueblo River. I drove out on a cool dusk when southwest winds had started to ruffle the sagebrush. Chill sunshine reflected off a few newly white peaks of close-by mountains. They had arranged rocks in a circle, and were cooking stew in a pot over the camp fire. Neither of them rose when I descended. Willie flicked a cigarette into the glowing embers, uptipped his bottle, and offered me a hit I declined. Mariangela quietly tended their supper, flames reflecting off her wizened eyeballs.

"I'm sorry," I said.

Willie's grin was already minus half its teeth. "I'm sure the world acknowledges your sorrow, Mike."

"What are you gonna do?"

"Well, we kind of like it here."

"Where do you sleep?"

"She sleeps in the cab, I crash in the bed."

"What happens when it rains?"

"I sleep under the truck."

"You can come to my pad. I'll put you up until you find a place."

He grinned softly again. "No. It's not our style to be a burden."

"It isn't a burden."

But he had dismissed the offer from consideration. Mariangela removed the pot, testing it with her finger; then she tasted the concoction.

"You got a line on another place?" I asked.

"You got any stuff?" he countered.

"Sure." I extended a Marlboro package holding a half-dozen joints.

"Listen, Willie, I brought some money." I started to remove two hundred dollars from my wallet. But he raised a hand. "Save your bread, Mike, we don't need it."

Anything else would push his pride, so I dropped it; we shared a joint. Mariangela poured the stew, handed a tin cup to her father—I rejected the other. She sipped slowly, staring into flames. We all felt lonely, and sort of together, but Willie was through talking. Finally I gave a Hershey bar to his daughter and drove away.

My only friend in town.

A couple of times, I'll admit, I dwelled on Thomas Carp. Maybe, after all, my desperation hungered for even that kind of pal. Opened a phone book once, but chickened out. And despite the smallness of our town, I never spotted him around. Apparently, we moved in different rhythms, parallel but never intersecting nightmares. Perhaps he had already pulled up stakes and located another hippie kingdom that needed beefy exterminators in exchange for unlimited chicks to plunder. Whatever, I chose not to languish for long on our missed connection. Still, he hung fire in the back of my mind, promising lurid adventure.

Instead, at last, inevitably, I locked in for real on my true prey. At work that day we had yanked several carnation beds, re-steamed and fertilized the earth. Toward noon I left with a pickup bed chock-full of pretty flowers, invaded the phone company front lobby, and spread armfuls of redolent color across her desk. Wide-eyed as a wounded deer, Noelle was flabbergasted. Her pale cheeks flushed crimson when I introduced myself, thrusting a hand through the bouquet to shake her long delicate fingers. I wonder, could she intuit murder in my grip—who knows? She gave me a sweet smile, and out of charity, perhaps, agreed to a date. I thanked her too profusely, and left her in pink majestic puzzlement, softly inundated by carnations.

Spiffy in a sport coat, sixty-dollar Haggar slacks, and a pair of Justin boots, I picked her up at seven in my washed and vacuumed truck. Noelle lived alone in a tidy three-room house, with her four-year-old son, Merlin, a somber child framed in bright blond curls. The plump teenage baby-sitter was all breasts and bulging haunches sheathed in a pink sweater and skintight yellow pants; I wanted to bend her over the couch even as I helped Noelle into a satin patchwork cardigan of many colors, and escorted her out the door.

Long time since yours truly had tried to be civilized in such a well-appointed restaurant perusing the wine list while trying to select between escargot or a half-dozen salty oysters. A blue candle flickered inside a smoky float bowl; a yellow rose in a silver bud vase decorated our table. Noelle sat primly upright, shoulders squared, reserved, untouchable; her sad eyes demurred half the time, or else suddenly stared directly at me, plaintive and gut wrenching. She had recently endured a rotten divorce, but didn't want to discuss it. I had recently endured a rotten war, but chose not to mention it. We spoke of weather, TV movies, her problems with Merlin. I played up the aesthetics of Rio Grande trout fishing, gathering wood with Willie. She kept in shape by attending Jazzercise at the Tennis Ranch twice a week; and also rode a bicycle, swam at the Spa, played a little tennis. I asked about her hair— "How do you keep it so silky?" She laughed—nervous and deferential—tossed her head self-consciously, and mentioned herbal shampoos, jojoba creams, and other conditioners. Watched her diet, counted calories, was terrified of flab, cellulose, fat. Her rap bored me; her beauty stung like a thorn. A man could twist that long hair in his fist and yank back her head, press apart her unresisting thighs, and shoot her full of his impregnating pollutants.

For dessert we shared a plate of chocolate mousse. She dipped up careful bites at the end of a silver spoon, slipping them cautiously beween her full lips with a deliberate mincingness I found terribly sexy. And pictured my cock between her lips, those sad eyes staring up at me, her lovely hair on fire. Suddenly, her skull leaped across the table, and it cackled like a witch, admitting to the same corruptions as me. But outwardly in real life she was so prim, slim, and remotely glossy that no one would ever know.

They brought coffee, a cheese board, a sorbet of sherbet, a fragrant mint wrapped in green paper, a tangy, syrupy liqueur. She'd only downed a glass of wine or two, and must have noticed that I'd consumed a half dozen Johnnie Blacks and a six-pack of Dos Equis, but she never said a word.

We toasted her new life, my new life, and blue skies from now on. When we split, I asked if she'd like to see my digs; it caught her off guard. "Oh, okay—but only for a minute . . . I have to be home soon." She checked her miniwatch: "The baby-sitter." Oh yes, the succulent baby-sitter.

I could tell the visit scared her. The emptiness of my palatial manse, its spare undecorated walls. Loneliness in that one cold room, in the mattress and the sleeping bag, in the TV set and VHS machine beside it on which were stacked a half-dozen X-rated cassettes. And the guns lying around that I wished I had concealed.

"It's so empty, Michael."

"I haven't had much time, yet. Been so busy—"

My voice cracked; inside my skin every muscle shivered. I expected my teeth would start clacking. My hands gripped stiffly at my sides might fuse against my upper thighs. The tension felt unbearable. Hit the bitch, Michael, break her jaw, knock her stuffings into the scattered guns. Then pounce with a werewolf howl, shred apart her pleated skirt and yank down the panty hose. Then scuttle her promised land, and break her swan-graceful neck for good measure. Next, heave her body through the plate-glass window and jump out after her onto a lawn covered by leaves of bloody glass. And kick in her perfect teeth, then spray the white length of her twisted torso with an awful flowering of pent-up jism.

"I have to go now, Michael."

"All right, Noelle." She scarcely heard my "I'm sorry." I should have begged her to stay and talk. Wanted at least to pat her shoulder or an elbow on the way out, but knew that if she recoiled in alarm, I'd kill her for being afraid.

We drove to her home in near total silence. I commented on the moon; almost round, right purty. "The gorge trout don't bite as well when the moon is full."

"Why is that?"

"I don't know. Gravity pressures on the water. Maybe even rivers have a tide."

The baby-sitter needed a ride; I offered. Noelle balked, then reconsidered, grateful. Merlin slept, why leave him alone if I could do the job? She paid the high-school honey, and the bouncy girl hopped aboard my truck. We drove sluggishly into the night.

She cracked gum, smoked a weed, clicked on the radio to a heavy-metal station. "Not too loud," I said. The screeching, feedback-shrill music reminded me of Nam, head-hunting, getting high, the rotten spoils of a firefight, hallucinogenic death.

I smoked along to be polite. Her dime-store perfume bored into my brain like an electric drill. I was so hard I thought it might split the fabric of my tasteful slacks. I knew exactly what came next. Pull onto a dead-end road that meandered toward the National Forest, then address my cock-teasing passenger, and explain the deal: "If you fight me, you're dead. If you tell anyone afterwards, I'll come hunting for you before they get to me. I'll barge into your classroom and blow away every kid with shotgun blasts and automatic rifle fire until I reach you, hiding under a desk or crouched in a cloakroom—do you understand? If you tell anybody, I'll butcher your parents, I'll slaughter your brothers and sisters, I'll set your home on fire—"

We reached her house without incident. She landed on her feet, flipped a butt into the weeds, gave thanks, and casually tossed her head, then skipped off to her oak-paneled front door, disappeared inside.

My first official date in the world.

A brand-new life in store.

In desperation I called my pal, that hard-ass, going-down-fast, ugly nurse from Nam. I needed some advice for the lovelorn. Instead, she answered like a ghost from all the graves that were ever exhumed by war. In the background, after I'd identified myself, I heard a child gurgling and asked, "Who's that?"

"It's Johnny. He's almost one."

"Oh." The incongruity left me speechless.

"I needed a kid," she explained. "Somebody innocent and simple. I wanted to be around something alive and expanding, instead of always dying."

"You're married? You live with a guy?"

"God no. Mr. Bill is still my main squeeze. He always respects me in the morning. Any other intimacy feels like violation."

"And Johnny's pop?"

"He belonged to a friend who didn't want him anymore. I adopted the little bugger."

"I still don't understand the kid."

"I thought maybe he would save me," she replied, "but instead it's a day-night struggle just to keep him healthy and alive. I feed him the best of everything—we're in a co-op, so only organic passes between his lips. But even there you can't be sure, so I wash all his food. I peel his cucumbers and apples so there won't be herbicides, insecticides. I'm so afraid of cancer. The damn tomatoes, they radiate 'em to make 'em look rosy. Same with bananas—that yellow is arsenic pestilence. He loves chicken—you ought to hear the artificial venom they inject into capons and pullets. Even lettuce—they zap some kind of Freon gunk on it to make it look crisp and delicious. All food is toxic."

Well, that was a conversation stopper, though I fumfered ineffectually for a reply. She cut my confusion short by saying:

"You sound in great shape, Michael. Hell must agree with you. Why the call?"

"I don't know, exactly. I'm lonely. I feel scared."

"Saigon fell," she said. Perhaps she thought I'd missed it. I didn't miss it, though. Just couldn't remember had it been a year ago, or half a decade? Those events had merged, time had waffled; drugs do funny things to your average veteran.

"Yeah, Saigon fell." Like Icarus, into a lake of fire. Brimstone, Revelation, Hiroshima. "At least that's over."

"You know what Yogi Berra said?" I could almost hear her, through her coughing, cracking a faint sardonic grin.

"What?"

"It's never over till it's over.'"

"For me it ended long ago," I lied. "Thank God."

"I envy you, Michael. At least that's one of us."

Then she took off like a crippled racehorse, babbling about atrocities, the hospital emergency room she worked in, the ambulance she rode, the rape crisis center, the battered women's project. A passionate litany of human beings wounded by domestic war. Three white men had castrated an Indian in a bar. They operated on a three-year-old tot sodomized by her father; it necessitated a colostomy. A woman shot her husband after he knocked her down in the driveway and ran over her with a new half-ton GMC; she did a month in jail, received a twelve-year sentence for manslaughter, wound up in a cross-state psychiatric hospital. A young rakehell promiscuous husband caught his wife cheating, just once, and beat her so badly with a steel wastebasket that she'd been in a coma for three months.

"I visit her every day," Sicko said. "I hold her hand and talk to her. I say, 'Come on, Eleanor, you can do it. I love you, Eleanor, please wake up.'"

"Why do you want her to wake up?"

She snorted. "Because where there's life there's hope."

"Who says?"

"You know something, Michael? I think you need an attitude adjustment."

I smiled warily, lost again for words. So Sicko prattled on. She was reading tons of books about the war. I asked, "Why do you want to steep yourself in all that gore—haven't you had enough?"

"I want to understand."

"What's to understand? It began with the first Pilgrims four hundred years ago."

"Do you ever want to atone?"

"For what?"

"For all the boys whose lives I helped to save."

I had to think about it for a minute. What dangers lay on the underside of *that* iceberg? Shouldn't sleeping dogs be allowed forever to lie?

Apparently not. It seems she could recall every crippled person who'd entered that ER she'd worked in Nam. So much blood had soaked her sneakers that they squeak-squished when she walked away. Vividly imprinted on her brain was every enucleation and intubation, every laparotomy and lobotomy, every nephrectomy and all the ghastly pseudomonas, every shunt and spurting aorta, every spleenectomy, every colostomy, every crispy critter, every intravenous bag of dopamine, every gork, every tourniquet, every amputated leg, hand, finger, psyche. Every lap pad soaking up blood in an open chest cavity, every collapsed lung, every abscess from an overlooked frag wound, every bowel that had to be run again and again, picking out bits of metal, every ruptured peritoneum, every case of gangrene, every baby delivered by cesarean, shrapnel in its half-a-head.

She had a photographic memory for those things, those broken boys and half-melted civilians, those castrated grunts and tubercular dinks missing their lower jaws. They occupied her waking hours, and mesmerized her hapless dreams.

She remembered a three-year-old Vietnamese boy with an arm blown off at the shoulder. She remembered an eighteen-year-old Chicano soldier with pieces of flak jacket sticking out backward through his shoulder blades. She remembered an all-American soccer player who'd arrived at the morgue in a Glad bag, his testicles and prick in a plastic Baggie taped to his right thigh. She remembered them going into shock, she remembered helping to kill the hopeless ones by driving extra doses of morphine home, because "snowing them" to death was more merciful—

"My country 'tis of carnage, sweet land of ruptured bowels, of thee I hate." Cicarelli toked deeply on a weed, coughed lightly, gasped for breathing room.

"Let go of it, Sicko. It's an old tape."

"No, it's a way of life, Michael. Never stops. It's going on out there all the time, right under the peppy surface. There's dead bodies lying under the stage at the Miss America pageant. And Bert Parks sleeps with vampires."

"Hey, take it easy. What's the point?"

"Sometimes I look at Johnny, sleeping in his crib," she said wearily. "All pink and chubby, and I want to slit his throat. Other times I think I'll raise him to be an exterminator. A whole damn Dirty Dozen rolled into a single human being. Then I'll turn him loose on Washington, DC."

Funny how perceptions change. From myself, I had been taking it for ages. From her it was boring, dulled my senses, pissed me off.

"Leave it alone, Sicko. The war is over."

"Who says?"

Well, I had thought perhaps to connect with a sympathetic kindred spirit. But I could tell the effort was in vain. And so I said, "I'm going to hang up now, Barbara. I'm sorry, but we're no good for each other. We don't make any sense."

"Makes sense to me." She sounded like a robot.

"You take good care of Johnny."

"I always do, Michael. He's my pride and joy. Hope of the future."

"You take good care of everybody."

"Always do that, too. It's my mission in life. I give great care."

"Well . . . okay . . . good-bye."

She had no answer, not for me, at least—I'd never mentioned Noelle. It looked as if I'd have to save myself, and win the lady on my own. Ain't that ever the truth?

It was as simple as ABC.

Instead, who to my wondering eyes should appear but my old buddy, Thomas Carp. Gone was the Fu Manchu and the greasy globs of almost Rastafarian hair; in fact, at least outwardly, the man had cleaned up his act. A bit more portly the belly, of course, befitting a resurrection. A button-down shirt and a floppy tie complemented the rumpled seersucker that flapped nervously around his hips as he strode a Safeway aisle to greet me. Looked prosperous, almost, neatly shaved and coiffed in the manner of the day. I almost didn't recognize him, that killer in sheep's clothing; but then he snagged my hand and crushed my knuckles until I winced aloud. The voice boomed out of that transformed Beelzebub true enough to form:

"Michael, you old cunt hound, where the hell you been *hiding*? I missed your ass, buddy, I been looking everywhere. What happened? Hey, didn't we have some times?"

Carp feinted sideways, acknowledging a woman who'd infiltrated the background, a lean and weasel-faced lass of smoky eyes and a grim but teasing mouth. She wore a flouncy shirtwaist dress and heels so high they seemed to tilt her aggressively forward. "Mike, meet Shirley," Carp effusively proclaimed. Her greeting lips seemed like a hazy dare, and though I couldn't tell for sure, her pupils seemed dilated. In her arms she balanced a bottle of Importers vodka and two cartons of Kools. Ugly, docile, sexy—no thanks, I could do without their scene.

But as we exited into the macadam parking lot, Carp teased me with all the grace of a grisly killer born.

"Hey, bro', you look like a man in need of a healthy workout. Follow us home and I'll let her crank you up, I promise. We can ball her together, if you want. She loves the muddy road."

Graciously, I declined. Wasn't feeling up to snuff, had chores to do, the usual. Yet I tarried beside Carp's old Volvo for a moment; he regaled me with his tales of success in the real estate market. "Hey, this burg's great right now. Six months ago the market was soft as molasses, but now it's going great guns—I scored three closings last week, I'm almost rich!"

While he talked, Shirley lounged back against the vehicle, sulky, gazing dispiritedly across a sea of cars. And I'll have to admit she tempted my unrequited gonads. But an alliance with Carp was too fearful to imagine. Yet there she lingered, a defeated bitch who promised hours of fun and games. How long, how *long* had it been since I'd unloaded my crippled sperm into such a tempting vehicle?

Just before we parted, Carp performed a nasty little trick. Exactly in the middle of a dissertation on interest rates and money markets, he leaned down a bit, running his hand up under Shirley's dress, and, raising the fabric almost to her waist, he wriggled his social finger up between her thighs—she didn't budge. Carp straightened and sniffed his finger, eyes closed, pantomiming bliss. Then thrust the finger under my nose. "Get a whiff of that, pal—sure you don't want a sample? Go ahead, be my guest."

Shirley eyed me neither here nor there while I backed off from Carp's undainty cruelty, shaking my head. "No, no, I'm sorry—" Why apologize to the goon? But Carp replied, "Hey, no problem, I understand—maybe next time when you're feeling horny." He employed a familiar harshness when he gripped her chin between thumb and forefinger and displayed her head at a provocative angle. "Shirley's always ready, aren't you, baby?"

I turned and skedaddled, shaky as all get-out. Puffy and white clouds hung in a pale blue sky. Chirpy deodorized housewives pushing kids in overloaded shopping carts gossiped among the cars. A pink, helium-filled balloon, touting this bargain or that one, sailed high, triggering faint wisps of fantasizing in us morons down below.

From behind my steering wheel I watched Carp's yellow Volvo enter the flow of traffic heading south. I pictured me up her muddy road while she gave him head. Then, screaming inside at the effort, I switched it to Post Toasties and Froot Loops, and gamboling infants on Sunday morning. Noelle Johnson leaned over and delivered a steamy cup of coffee, chicory fragrant.

Forget Tom Carp: if I truly wanted to save my soul (and my ass) it was time at last—come hell or highest water—to insist on a real romantic connection.

So off to the phone company I traipsed again, eager to see the girl of my dreams.

Unfortunately, things had changed at Ma Bell. Redid the entire office. No more could you deal with one of the girls at a front desk. A new partition blocked off the lobby so that now, when I trundled through the front door, expecting to meet my beloved Noelle, I was greeted instead by a wall and a single desk, behind which sat a bland receptionist, alone and cracking gum.

"I want to talk with Noelle Johnson," I explained. "It's about hooking up another phone."

"Sir, you can place that order with me." She flipped a form out of a basket, poised her Bic above it.

"What happened to all the people?" Her curt style offended me.

"We're modernizing. This way is more efficient. It's all computerized these days. Centralizing the operation. The town is growing. After awhile they won't even need an office here, it'll all be automated."

"Look, I really want to see Noelle Johnson."

"They're not allowed to meet directly with the customers, sir. Now, if you'll just give me all the information, I promise we'll get on it right away."

Baffled, I supplied the information. Then strode angrily up the street to a gas station and telephoned Ma Bell, asking for Noelle. "I'm sorry," Ms. Efficiency declared, "but she's on a call right now. I'll refer you to Abigail."

"I don't *want* Abigail!" I shouted. *"I want Noelle Johnson!"*

"Sir, let me connect you with a supervisor—"

I banged down the receiver, banged it hard. In fact, I slammed it repeatedly until the plastic shattered, then I left it dangling and kicked out a glass panel in the booth and stormed outside almost insanely frustrated, about to flip and head for my guns. A shotgun blast or two at Ma Bell's glass doorways and automated receptionist would knock apart their stuffy partition, and expose my beauty at last.

Instead, I heard a police siren, and when the patrol car braked just as I reached my truck, I halted. Two local bluesuits debarked, right fists clenched around their clubs, left fingers fluttering nervously above their holstered pizzolovers.

"No trouble, buddy," one said. "Just stay calm. Let's keep this civilized."

"You come any closer," I told him, "and I'll go berserk. I warn you, I'm dangerous."

I must have had a no-nonsense gleam in my bloodshot eyes, because they hesitated, and we faced each other. The leader pointed his club, speaking as if to a child. "Okay, man, I want you to turn around, real slow, and place your palms against the hood of that truck. Lay 'em out flat, spread your legs a little, now come on, we don't want any more trouble."

"You advance one step closer," I warned, "and you'll have to off me to arrest me. I'm a Vietnam vet, and I've killed more gooks than you assholes ever dreamed could be murdered. So keep your distance and leave me be, I'm going home."

And I reached for the door handle. Perhaps I actually thought the menace had curbed them, but the minute I turned, they pounced, and the first blow caught me upside the ear—I went down hard, ending that petty contretemps. I woke up in their greasy little jail, facing two bamboozled Indians and a bedraggled Chicano morosely staring at me; blood caked my nostrils and I could hardly breathe.

In due course, however, all things come to those who wait. A miracle, shaped like a fat, lethargic jailer, unlocked the cell door and called my name. I followed him down a mildewed corridor to the front room, where another lackey said, "Here's your stuff, Mr. War Hero." He flipped over an envelope containing my belt and wallet (relieved of twenty dollars), keys, and pieces of small change. "Now get out of here before somebody changes their mind."

America, it never ceases to amaze me: democracy in action. I kept my mouth shut—no questions from this golem. Through no doing of my own, there I was, a free man, out on the streets, ready to kill again. I stumbled into the light of day, blinked my eyes a dozen times, then, with a gnawing hunger it seemed important to assuage, I veered in at a local greasy spoon . . . and changed my life forever.

4

JANINE

The Chuck Wagon Café was as nice a slice of rural culture as had ever come down the pike. A sloppy, comfortable joint that abjured cuteness, going for the utilitarian jugular instead. Formica tables covered by red-and-white checkered oilcloths, attended by rickety plastic chairs, their legs splayed by so many fat bottoms. Salt and pepper, catsup bottle, a ceramic cup of sugar packets, and a Coors beer ashtray for a centerpiece. Along the counter was a row of squeaky twirling stools. And on the counter stood one display case for stale pies—a gluey cherry and sticky lemon meringue. Another plastic cake safe held three-day-old lemon and pineapple Danishes. Greasy home fries accompanied every order, and the waitress automatically poured a cup of lethal black coffee the minute you grabbed a seat . . . then waited forever to take your order. In back a single harried cook, old cleft-palate Mary, tried to keep it rolling. But it was the waitress who grabbed my attention, eventually changed my life, obliterated Noelle (who?), and catered to my sickest passions.

Janine: Janine Tarr. What a cock-teasing bundle of voluptuous pulchritude. Curly, kinky, tawdry bleached-blond hair flared out like carnival neon. She stood five foot two on tiptoes, and that first time I saw her she wore a faded pink jumpsuit with a zipper up the front. A diminutive floozy who probably weighed no more than a hundred pounds, yet she had wide shoulders and was outrageously top-heavy. Her breasts strained against that zipper. She had a tiny waist, no hips to speak of, not much butt at all. Both ears were pierced numerous times, and she wore gold buttons in a few holes, imitation gold gypsy hoops in her lobes.

Forgetting all about my recent escapades, I watched her for a while. Whenever a break occurred in the action, Janine smoked like a chimney, standing down by the counter's end, fiddling with an ashtray, all her weight on one leg, the other slippered foot rubbing up and down one shin. She moved in a curious fashion, shoulders slumped forward aggressively, legs kind of drawling after—difficult to describe. She had lousy, slump-shouldered posture that was endearing and sexy; it accented her bosom, which always, no matter how restrained, was lasciviously jouncing. She radiated a world-wise, yet perky and almost innocent energy.

Strange face on that doll. Not exactly pretty, but intriguing. Half childlike, half tired and old, getting wrinkled. And provocative. Small eyes, a trifle slanted and catlike, which she widened with mascara and eye shadow that made her look cheap, almost whorish. Rest of her features seemed a bit gaunt—high cheekbones created that effect. She wore too much powder or liquid makeup, and fat splashes of rouge. Nose?—not quite button, not quite straight—rather a slightly rounded little snout. And her mouth? A bit too wide, yet with enticingly plump lips. The full lips seemed drawn down in sorrow or contemplation because of cute jowls parenthesizing them. And not much chin to speak of.

Turned out later, as I got to know her better, that the only age she admitted to was "thirty-nine and holding." But when she smiled, which was often, her face lit up mischievously, peeling years off her age. She beamed like a teenage honky-tonk waiflet. And laughed easily—it was merry and sassy and gay. Made me want to squeeze her like a plump little dumpling, and sink in my eager teeth.

Like many a savvy waitress, she wore a wedding ring, but was not married. I also learned that about her later. "This ring holds the animals at bay," she would tell me. "Helps keep all those eager peckers down to a dull roar. Saves wear and tear on my bottom."

Her voice killed me. Knocked me for a loop the first time she sauntered over to my table like a pint-sized Mae West, placed one hand on her narrow hip, and, while pouring my coffee, said, "Hi, soldier, whatcha know good?" She didn't realize I'd been a grunt, it was just her typical bantering howdy. Delivered on a husky, quavering southern accent that reeked of black-eyed peas and hominy grits. Until used to it, you had to listen twice to most every word she uttered. When I commented on the accent, asking where did she hail from, Janine actually winked and said, "I come from three hundred years of the best racist, gothic, Baptist inbreeding in America, and don't you ever forget it." Then she flounced away without even scribbling my order.

Instantly, she placed a knife of hunger into the dead smack center of my chest. I can't explain it rationally, I just wanted *this* lady, now; I knew she was my special "other"; simple as that she held my answers; we were destined to be a pair.

I stroked myself cautiously under the table, fantasizing about our erotic escapades. I trussed her up right proper, bound hands behind her back, bent her legs rearward and twisted ropes around her ankles. Took her for a ride on a hot summer day, pulled over to the side of a deserted road, stripped her naked, then pressed her over against the broiling tin of the front fender and did my eager business while her tits sizzled against the hot metal—

While I thus envisioned our "relationship," innocent, provocative Janine went about her sultry business, "hottening up" the diners' java, clearing plates and swabbing the tables, plunking ice cubes into water glasses, and slinging out hamburgers and BLTs, burritos and bowls of chili. "Waitin' on the tables," she joked, quoting a country-and-western tune, "just waitin' for the tables to turn."

Before I could approach Janine, however, I needed to be in more control. Yet though I doubled my intake of Pertofrane and

Elavil, began sipping Maalox by the quart, and chewed Tums and Rolaids like Life Savers, my stirring devils kicked and clawed like kittens in a sack held underwater, desperate to escape from drowning. Naked NVA bodies twirled out of the muggy Asian sky like manna from a US heaven; and fat hogs rooted in the empty rib cages of casually slaughtered boys. Cicarelli's drear lament punctuated little Johnny's dreams—

During the most placid days of bee-droning August, I battled against the elements, leaning into fierce arctic winds full of nasty particles that stung my eyes, abraded my cheeks, drove sharp winter knives into my belly, rapped my ankles with tiny iron hammers. I needed all my strength to push forward, keep on working, or make even a halfhearted attempt at pretending to be awed by the miracles of life.

My teeth seemed to change shape, growing sharper. My nostrils flared, sensitive to the layers of rotten smells around me. Dizzy spells came and went—I heard voices; dying kids cried for help; Vietnamese mothers wailed; radios crackled for dust-offs, air cover, reinforcements.

At the café, Janine was friendly but remote. I was embarrassed, afraid of myself, and knew not how to broach the tempting broad. So at first, idle chitchat is all we ever mustered. But when her back was turned I touched a crowbar to the crease between her buttocks . . . and rammed it all the way to China.

For a while I had avoided newspapers. Now I started buying them again. A good reason to dawdle in the eatery, feigning indifference—*qué no?* In Chicago three men grabbed a woman off the street at random, and ferried her to a house where eleven men raped her, then they dumped her in a vacant lot. In Milwaukee, a husband and wife and their three kids perished in a house fire set by an arsonist, their eldest daughter's ex-boyfriend. In Cincinnati, a man wearing a flak jacket and crossed bandoliers of 9.6-mm ammunition invaded a first-grade classroom carrying two shotguns and a Mannlicher carbine, and held the children, their teacher, and an assistant principal hostage for eleven hours. Eventually, a police SWAT team stormed the building; a six-year-old black student, the assistant principal, and the crazy died in the exchange of gunfire.

Oh dear. Like waves of nausea it chugged up my throat and into my mouth while Janine delivered combination plates, or smoked a sultry cigarette during break. I wanted to cry out all the time. In our own rustic ville the golems were having a field day impossible to ignore. A youngster at the local Indian pueblo was murdered; his dismembered body was discovered by dogs in a field. Every week our newspaper reported a rape, a battered wife, a child molestation. Down the road a piece from my condo heaven a long-standing feud between neighbors finally erupted in violence. A dog belonging to Polcyk waggled home one day half-skewered by a hunting arrow fired by García. Polcyk loaded up his shotgun and planted both barrels of double-aught buckshot in the center of García's chest. A jury called it manslaughter, and remanded Polcyk to the state pen. He left behind a befuddled wife and six hungry kids to feed.

Oh Janine, I want your great big tits—and your Heart of Gold—in my hands, in my mouth . . . to keep away the cold!

I needed a way to approach the bitch, but right then seductive elocution was not my strong point. Nevertheless, for one so obsessed, an opportunity was bound to present itself. And soon I found my opening—Janine was a sucker for kids. One day, at the table next to mine, a smiling couple sat down, accompanied by two darling little offspring, a boy named Josh, and a baby—Rachel. Janine's face lit up when they appeared. She swung a kiddie seat out from under the counter, toodled right over, plopped it down, snatched the baby out of her momma's arms, and strapped her in.

"Well, what have we got *here*?" she laughed in that syrupy southern voice. And then with a fingernail painted electric pink she poked the plump tyke in the belly to elicit a smile. "Now, if that ain't a healthy-looking fritter. Cute as a bug in a rug. C'mon, darlin', gimme a big happy!"

Me, I damn near swooned, awash in Janine's faint perfume and

101

erotic softness. She had tied a lavender ribbon in the left side of her hair. And it was all I could do not to reach out as she swished obliviously by and cup one of her full breasts, heavy behind the stretchy material of a beige blouse.

The boy she treated with more deference. "How's it goin', slugger?" was her greeting as she ruffled his cowlicked hair. "Been out there swatting fungoes with your daddy?" Apparently, she knew that sports were a passion with the kid, and she had a reference in that field to make him feel at home. "You watch the game last night? I heard that Brett hit two home runs, now ain't that man a gas?" She even pinched his bicep as she scooted about her tasks. "I bet you'll follow in his footsteps one of these days."

Then back to the baby girl. "Golly," Janine crowed, planting a smack on Rachel's silky head. "What an adorable little cherub. Wish I had one like that."

So when she approached my table, I said, "You have kids?" I tried to be nonchalant.

"Just one, but she's a handful. Cathie, my ever-lovin' devil's daughter. Only sixteen, but pushing forty. Know what I mean?"

"You don't look old enough," I said.

"Aw, come on, gimme a break, soldier. I'm old enough to be your mother." She giggled coquettishly. "I been around the block so many times, I don't know anymore if I'm going or coming." Then she was off in a swirl, piling up the platters, scraping tips off tables and clinking them into a mug behind the counter.

The Chuck Wagon closed at 4:00 P.M. I decided to tarry late, and nursed my coffee forever. Pretended to be immersed in the newspaper long after Janine had flipped the cardboard CLOSED sign, and was putting the operation to bed.

"Do you need a ride?" I asked, after the chores were finished. She had exchanged her waitress slippers for high-heeled slingbacks, and wore a tight black skirt and that beige blouse was veined, by her plump chest, with a thousand heartbreaking wrinkles. A skinny golden chain dangled around her throat.

"No thanks." She tugged on a faded dungaree jacket, and lit a Kool Filter King. "I ain't got much in life, but I got wheels."

She slung a colorful ragbag purse over one shoulder, and I followed her outside. Enthralled at the door of my Dodge, I watched her tiptoe clumsily through dirt and gravel toward a maroon Chrysler Imperial that I had observed before, and figured must have belonged to an oil-rich Texan. But I'll be damned, it was her vehicle—or her boyfriend's behemoth: a bumper sticker read STRANGE, DERANGED, CAN'T BE CHANGED. She clunked her purse on the hood and rummaged around for keys. "Goddam keys!" The cigarette drooped like Bogie's from her carmine lips, wafting smoke up toward frowning, squinted eyes. "I oughtta have my dumb head examined."

"Is something the matter?" I called over. She glanced up, irritated, surprised I still hung fire.

"You bet something's the matter. I need a good brain surgeon. Perform a radical lobotomy!" And she began to scoop garbage out of her purse, slamming things down on the hood, hissing and spitting about those errant keys. Envelopes, a fat paperback book, lipstick, compact, hand mirror, cigarettes, packs of gum and Chloramints and other candied breath fresheners, and then a gun— bang! Clopped down on the hood with all the other jive; a nickel-plated .38 from where I stood.

Janine ransacked a minute more, then dumped the entire contents of her oriole nest onto that mammoth status-mobile.

Still no keys.

Okay—what now? Last resort time: she peered through the frosted window and discovered the objects of her quest idling in the ignition, where she'd left them.

"Oh fuck Christ piss cunt cock!" She banged her forehead with one fist, leaning back against the door. "That's the third time this month I've locked those keys inside. Umpteen thousand dollars for a car, and the warning buzzer doesn't work!"

I had sauntered casually over by then. "I have a coat hanger. I've done this lots of times." The gun was an old cheap .38, loaded too, judging by the bullet snouts visible in the chamber. The book was a James Herriot best-seller, *All Creatures Great and Small*.

While I fished for the lock knob, I asked about the luxury

womb. "You'll pardon my curiosity, but how's a nice little hash slinger like you driving a car like this?"

"I got it in the divorce," she grumbled, sulking, arms crossed, smoking a third cigarette. "It's *all* I got, the bum. But I figure it's better than zero. These heaps are equity, I already negotiated a bank loan on it."

"How many miles to the gallon—six?"

"Who wants to know?" She tilted her belligerent head suspiciously.

"Well, no offense, but there can't be that many bucks in waiting on tables. I'd turn this in on a Datsun that got thirty-five miles a gallon, and pocket the difference."

"Oh you would, would you?"

"Makes sense."

"Maybe I like this car." She crammed stuff back in the purse. "Gives me stature. And I could use a little stature these days."

"Why the gun?" I asked.

"What are you writing, a novel?"

"Nope. Just curious."

"I use it to shoot men." She released a glint of her mischievous smile. "They get sassy, I just blow them to smithereens."

"Guess I won't be sassy, then." I hiccuped triumphantly as the lock button popped up, and I opened the driver's-side door.

She swung impatiently inside, remarking, "You *better* not." But as the starter cranked she glanced up gratefully. "Hey, thanks a lot, Michael. You ain't a bad egg. Gimme some sugar."

I'd never heard that expression before, but understood instinctively it meant a kiss. So I bowed for a cursory peck on the lips; then she prepared to launch the spaceship, wiggling her rump into a comfortable position on her pillow—the seat was hiked up to its forwardmost position.

"Would you like to go for a drink, Janine?"

A startled amused expression came over her face. She reached up, giving me a pat, and said, "Not now, sweetie." Then she smirked. "Go home, Michael; dry the wet from behind your ears. Take off those rose-colored glasses."

The door closed—"You be good now, hear?"—and the elec-

tronic window whirred up. She backed around suddenly, maneuvering the wheel like a pro, and surged forward, head craning to
see over the steering wheel and beyond that football-field-sized
front hood. She left behind a man dazed and palpitating, determined to have her ass.

Oh Janine, my Sweet Janine!

I lay curled up on my dirty mattress, sucking on her prodigious
mams. I made her into a gook, yes I did, forcing her to devour
sperm-filled prophylactics; I explained in glowing detail the nature
of a Vietnamese abortion, and threatened to roast and eat her because she wasn't really a human being. How I loved to abuse her
soft atomic explosions of chub, my dick, my guns, my head enveloped by her sumptuous tits, athletic snatch, bottomless rever-
berating throat. She squealed if I just barely touched her, and
begged me to defile at will. I greased up her cloaca and twisted in
the Magnum barrel while she spread wide her buttocks for me, her
groans muffled by the duct tape stretched across her mouth: that's
how we silenced Cong in Nam.

At times I removed the tape and jammed the gun barrel into
her froggy mouth, and she sucked on it while I coolly fucked her.
And I couldn't get enough. I loved to watch her with my weapons
stuck in her mouth, between her legs. I loved to watch her eating
her own tits, licking bananas, and with my dong between her lips.
I loved to watch her in every style and suggestive pose of depreda-
tion we could think up. And Janine the erotic blimp stared into my
eyes, begging me for death, I think. Ordered me to cock the Magnum, and fuck her with my finger on the trigger of that loaded gun
between her teeth. She came, and came again, biting the blue steel,
and each time her voice blurped urgently up along that shaft, im-
ploring me to shoot—but I ignored her pleadings, I didn't want to
lose this voluptuous aberration in my life—

I woke up drenched in sweat, my cracked lips bleeding, tears
splashing from swollen eyes. I wanted that cunt in my life, upon
my dick, and I would not be denied.

Creepy little hobgoblins were everywhere, daily more blatant than the night before. Heading for work, I clicked on the truck radio, and before I could snap the dial to music I heard a news blivet about three unfortunate Florida coeds who had been found in an abandoned house, "one strangled, one stabbed, one shot in the head." That phrase stuck with me for days like the refrain of a popular song; "One strangled, one stabbed, one shot in the head." In the Chuck Wagon Café, as I followed every one of Janine's luscious moves over the top of my newspaper, that lilting rhythm made perfect sense: "One strangled, one stabbed, one shot in the head."

Another time, late afternoon, I clicked on the TV and caught the tail end of a news program. A camera was panning through a well-appointed suburban neighborhood. As it passed a primly landscaped ranch-style home, the commentator revealed that two girls and a boy, aged eleven through fourteen, had been murdered on film in the air-conditioned dwelling by a gang of pornographers fashioning a snuff movie.

Such nuggets of information stayed with me always. That decorous American dream house and the snuff movie; those three dead Florida coeds. And the Chicago woman grabbed at random off the street . . . and my neighbors Polcyk and García . . . and the murdered Pueblo boy—

Plus Janine Tarr, who dangled from a meat hook on my apartment wall, grinning garishly as blood dribbled from her ruby lips, from deep between her thighs. . . .

Cicarelli's next call roused me from bed at 3:00 A.M. She sounded awful, on the verge of nervous collapse. "Hey, Michael, how you doin' way down there?"

"I'm okay, Sicko—how about yourself?"

She coughed, a real spasm. "'Scuse me, gotta light another cigarette." I heard her fumbling with paraphernalia, striking a match, exhaling a deathlike rattle. "God," she murmured gratefully, "that's real coffee." And laughed, a mirthless sound.

"How's Johnny?" I asked when things had quieted down.

"Johnny? Who's Johnny? What are you talking about?"

"Your Johnny, Sicko. Christ, are you all right?"

"Oh, *my* Johnny. Why didn't you say so? Had me confused there for a while. *My* Johnny. Sure, can't forget about him, can we?"

"What's wrong? Something's really wrong, isn't it?"

"Do you mean with the world?" she asked sarcastically. "Like, do you mean the possibility of nuclear war, the environmental destruction of the planet, illiteracy in America, starvation in Africa, the crime rate in New York City and Los Angeles—is that what you're talking about?"

She pissed me off. "I'm talking about you personally, Sicko. What are you taking, what are you on? You dropped a tab before you called?"

"Oh, hey, listen to Mr. Self-Righteous. Mr. Under Control. Mr. Big Man with All His Guns. Don't give me any of that Christer shit, Michael, I don't need it. What are you, Mr. Clean, these days, Mr. Born-Again Asshole? Well, fuck you if that happened, fuck Jesus Christ and all the horses he rode in on!"

When she had settled down again, I tried a different tack. I apologized. "Hey, I'm sorry, I didn't mean to be nasty. I'm only concerned—"

"Yeah, you and every other bleeding heart out there, reeking with good intentions. I'm impressed, I really am." Ice cubes rattled as she drank something. "I'm grateful for all the sympathy. You know, that's something I really gotta admire about this country, it's full of people with heart. Honest and truly. It's really big of you to worry about me. Why don't you send me one of those pink embossed sympathy cards, Michael? You know, you can buy 'em at the card racks in Safeway, they only cost a buck. 'To a Swell Friend: Roses are red, violets are blue, the shit in the toilet reminds me of you.'"

How does a person respond to that? The ice tinkled again.

"You still there?" she asked.

"Just barely."

"I'm not keeping you from anything important, am I?"

"Sicko, it's three o'clock in the morning."

"You gotta get up early for work tomorrow?"

I nodded. "Yeah, I'm afraid so."

"Not me," she said gaily. "Not anymore. I'm retired. No more emergency room, no more auto accidents, no more gut-shot Indians, no more battered women—good-bye to all that. I took a vacation."

"Well, you probably could use one."

"I didn't *ask* for a vacation, Michael. They just gave it to me."

"I don't understand."

"They *fired* me, dingdong. Revoked my license to heal. They put me out to pasture."

"I still don't understand."

"Big C, baby. I'm riddled with it. They shot me full of radiation, and now I glow in the dark like a Christmas tree. I'm beautiful. Every two weeks I go in and eat about a hundred pounds of chemicals, then I vomit for a week. All my hair fell out. You should see me now, if you thought I was ugly before."

"I never thought you were ugly."

"Well, you gotta laugh, Michael. Have a sense of humor, remember? Only way to make it through the holocaust."

"Look, I'm sorry. I mean . . . oh, what about Johnny?"

"He's not here," she muttered drunkenly.

"Where is he?"

"They put him in a foster home. Took him away last week. Couple Nazis in black boots just walked in and grabbed him. Served me a whole portfolio of legal papers. I'm incompetent, did you know that? They said he was malnourished. Of *course* he was malnourished. Where am I supposed to find the bread to keep him healthy? They said he was unhappy. *Course* he was unhappy, what's so much fun about watching your momma crouch over a toilet bowl puking her guts out day and night? Huh? What's so funny about that?"

"Jesus," I said, "you sound horrible. You gotta get some help."

"From who? From where? I go to a clinic, I got a card, it pays for the treatments, period. It doesn't pay food, doesn't pay mortgage. The bank is already on a high horse, talking foreclosure. I told 'em to come ahead, throw me into the street, get it over with."

"I'm talking about friends. I'm—"

"What friends? The only friend I had is a vegetable in a coma down on the county ward. Who'd want me for a friend, Michael? I'm skinny as lizard shit, I cough out my lungs by the hour, and I'm defoliated and blotchy all over—hey, I look just like Vietnam."

"I'll send you some money. I've got a little saved."

"Send me some weed instead. That'd be nice. I tried to enter one of those programs for cancer victims where they let you smoke it, but I was denied. This state is too uptight."

"Okay, I'll do that. Listen, as soon as you're better, they'll let Johnny come home."

"Yeah, sure." Her voice changed abruptly, gone listless, stripped of all its venom. "Soon as I'm better again, everything will be hunky-dory. The Welcome Wagon will show up at our door every morning, full of ham and baloney and broccoli and big quarts of thick creamy milk. I can't wait. Maybe they'll even fly us to Hollywood so we can be contestants on 'Dialing for Dollars,' win a million bucks. It's something to look forward to. You watch that program?"

"I'll mail some weed, and a check for a hundred bucks tomorrow. I'll make it Express Mail."

"Yeah, you do that, Michael. That way it might arrive before I keel over."

And she hung up, left me holding the receiver, staring out the window at moonlight on the park where two wild cats wrestled with each other.

From the halcyon days of our youthful adventures overseas, the bloody chorus never stopped.

In desperation I made a decision to fight fire with fire, meet the problem head on; if I couldn't beat 'em, join 'em. The town's weekly newspaper was looking for a photographer. I applied for the job and got it, ditched the greenhouse, and geared up for my new métier. To face the world was my purpose; deal if I hoped to survive. It seemed like a positive endeavor.

Once again my rhythms changed. Much of the work was garden clubs and Bank Employee of the Month awards, corral fires and the Episcopal Church Glee Club, and a record rainbow trout landed by a Texas tourist. But of course the darker side of life cropped up from time to time, and therein I found my challenge.

It began with the victim of a motorcycle accident, sprawled in a weedy gutter, shirt unceremoniously yanked half over his head, one ankle twisted haywire.

Next, I covered a three-vehicle accident that caused two deaths and rendered one infant a vegetable. Five other family members survived in various stages of mutilation. The late-model Camaro had accordioned back to the windshield; the pickup cab was severed off at door handle level. The teenage couple inside had been *novios*, slated for marriage in November.

After that they sent me to a trailer park where a young local teacher sat quietly behind the wheel of his truck. A star-shaped 30-30 bullet hole marred the windshield. The slug had snuffed the driver instantly. Nearby, crumpled against the stoop of a pink-and-white trailer, was the body of the assassin, who in turn had been clobbered by a Saturday Night Special wielded by the trailer's occupant, the ex-wife (divorced three years) of the rifleman, and the lover (until a few minutes ago) of the teacher in the pickup. I took action photographs of the cops handcuffing the distraught woman, muscling her off to jail while ambulance personnel prepared both stiffs for transportation to a funeral home.

Come Saturday, I rode in the wailing ambulance thirteen miles north of town, along bumpy dirt roads to an adobe farmhouse set beyond a field where sheep and horses grazed. A satellite dish antenna was situated beside the house. A Chevy Blazer, late-model pickup, and a Toyota Corolla were parked in the yard. Four police cars awaited our arrival. A quiet bearded man sat in the back of one cruiser, guarded by an officer holding a riot shotgun—I took

110

their picture, then followed the technician's parade into the immaculate house.

Portraits of Jesus on the hallway wall, and a framed sampler that actually beamed GOD BLESS OUR HAPPY HOME. In the spotless kitchen were cheerful Formica counters, a dishwasher, a microwave oven. The rest of the house had wall-to-wall carpeting, air conditioners, frilly yellow window curtains. A handsome brick fireplace dominated the living room; a vase of tulips stood on the glass coffee table; to a large, cabinet-style color TV was attached a VCR taping machine. An oak bookcase contained the latest in stereo equipment, and an extensive record collection.

Lined up in perfect order side by side on their bellies six feet away from the TV, were the five children, ages three, five, six, nine, and twelve. All had been executed in the back of the head by a single shot from a 22-caliber pistol. The wife, wearing an odd pair of leathery reindeer slippers with upturned toes and a soft beige robe, lolled in a nearby armchair, head tilted sideways, mouth open, glassy eyed.

I raised my camera and began to record it all for posterity—Mr. In Control.

Not long after that, made almost heady by my new, responsible persona, I toddled off to insist that Janine Tarr have at least the courtesy to grant me a date.

No sooner had I settled down at a corner table, however, than a tall baboon moseyed into the Chuck Wagon, passing out cards for the Ku Klux Klan. His thin face atop a lanky frame had no chin. He wore a plaid shirt, cuffed-up dungarees, and well-oiled work boots. A watch on his wrist looked too fancy for the outfit. Underneath, thought I in my infinite wisdom, dwelled a Born Again member of the Moral Majority, here to preach against the sins of all kikes, spics, wops, atheists, and niggers. The card featured a pen-and-ink drawing of a robed disciple, the Klan cross in a red circle displayed over his heart. Black headlines spelled out: "Invisible Empire: Knights of the Ku Klux Klan." Under that, large red letters exhorted:

111

The fine print offered an address in Denham Springs, Louisiana, to which an interested party could write for free information. Back of the card was like the Bible on the head of a pin. "There are thousands of organizations working for the interests of blacks. How many groups stand up for the cultural values and ideals of the White Majority? Not many. As a result we are faced with reverse discrimination in jobs, promotions, and scholarships—" And so on and so forth, self-righteous racist venom to the nth degree.

I said, "Hey, buddy, come here a minute."

He approached my table, mellow and friendly, all set to uncork the spiel.

I waggled the card at him. "What is this racist shit?"

He seemed hurt. How dared I impugn his integrity? "It's not 'racist shit,' sir," he protested, a trifle too timidly for the organization he represented. "If you'd like to write away to that address there, they'll be real happy to send you a free brochure—"

"No, wait a minute." The burn was rising, spreading, starting to make me crazy. "I know racist shit when I see it. So what gives scumbags like you the right to enter a nice clean town like ours, and start perpetrating this garbage? Who paid you to do this dirty work?"

A fatso at another table, sporting a yellow John Deere headpiece, said, "Hey, take it easy, man. He's got a right. This is a free country."

"'Free'—?" I whirled on him. "What are you talking about, 'free'? You don't even know what 'free' means. Free to burn a cross on the lawn of every black family tries to move into a middle-class white neighborhood? Free to dump two billion tons of napalm on gooks so poor they got a life expectancy of thirty-six, and never even heard of plumbing? That's freedom, free speech, free country? Christ on a crutch! I'm a Vietnam veteran, and I'm ashamed of what I did! I went ten thousand miles away from home—"

"Okay." John Deere was not the sort of bigot to mince words

112

over a cup of joe in some penny-ante café full of squeamish hay-seeds. He pushed back, heaved up, and got down. I somersaulted floorward, ducking to avoid his initial swing. For emphasis, he tipped over my table, which careened off the kneecaps of Mr. Klan Organizer. Then John Deere bent over to grab me, obviously forgetting the Viet vet part of my rap, and the next thing anybody knew, the fat aggie was pedaling ass-backward through a plate-glass window, just like in a Hollywood movie. And as for the Imperial Wizard flunky?—well, he had the lay of the land in fairly graphic detail already, and couldn't split fast enough. But I caught up halfway to the exit, swinging a catsup bottle at the back of his skull—it glanced off his right shoulder, spraying tomato crud across the café of ducking diners. Probably my next haymaker would have decked him, if not for two sudden imponderables. The first was Janine Tarr, opulent corn-pone waitress, who materialized directly in front of me, her entire scrumptious bosom heaving sideways as she started to swing an orange plastic chair in my direction. The other was those two town cops I'd forgotten about, seated at a corner table; they leaped up soon as the fracas started, and were right now bent on my subjugation.

Janine's chair beat them to me. Maybe the cops deflected my attention; certainly, I never saw Janine's chair coming. So it struck like a proverbial bolt of lightning out of the blue—blindsided, booby-trapped, fragged cold handed—and the lights died just long enough for the bluesuits to scramble all over me, yanking my arms together so hard my shoulder bones almost screeched clear of their sockets. And, knees threatening to dislocate my spine, they clapped on the cuffs, then held me still a moment longer, waiting for the feathers to settle.

"Holy mackerel," her raspy southern voice proclaimed. "That boy's a real handful!"

Jail again; it was getting to be a habit with me.

But what an inept way to arrive in this banal purgatory, not even a decent drop of blood—only catsup!—on my hands. I felt doomed and weary and stupid, and I figured this time to cool my heels awhile. Surprise surprise, then, when that pudgy jailer opened my iron door, grumbling, "Move it, buster, they went your bail."

"Who went my bail?"

"Some twat looks like Dolly Parton."

"Who you calling a 'twat'?"

He halted, very dramatic, back to me, shoulders hunched from a world-weariness caused by too many grubby ciphers like yours truly giving him guff. Just paused, very silent, two beats, making sure I had the message . . . then he proceeded forward again.

She was standing there: I couldn't believe it. Hands jammed high into the tiny pockets of a fox-fur chubby. A flower, a pretty lily that must have cost a buck ninety-eight at Safeway, but resembled an orchid, was stuck in her hair. Her loose and silky Goodwill skirt was cut across the knees. The tired eyes seemed trapped in too much dark mascara; naturally, a cigarette dangled toughly.

Women. Explain their self-destructive natures to me, if you can.

"What are *you* doing here?"

"This is Save an Asshole Week. I raised the money to go your bail. I'll expect it back at eleven and a half percent interest in two months. I'm *serious*. I can't afford not to get that money back."

While they tapped my belongings from a manila envelope onto the counter, I asked, "Why?"

She shrugged. "I figure maybe you needed a friend. I feel guilty about my part in it. I'm just naturally the nurturing type."

"I'm okay. I can take care of myself."

"I noticed."

I was stuffing doodlets into my pockets, threading the belt through my loops, checking my wallet. To the creep behind the counter, I said, "A ten is missing."

He didn't even glance up. "File a report."

Janine said, "Well, that's everything? Then let's go. This place gives me the willies."

Obediently, I trailed her out to the Chrysler. Only then did I snap that one of my cheeks was twice as large as the other, and the

eye above it was puffed completely shut. After ushering me in on
the passenger side, she circled the car, dropped behind the wheel
onto her cushion, and lit a fresh cigarette. During the process, her
chubby opened. Her white blouse was low-cut peasant style, with
a pink ribbon woven through the décolletage. Revealed was a
cleavage deep and round; her rising breasts seemed poised to float
out of the blouse like runaway dirigibles. God, I wanted to grab
her. She exhaled, gazing studiously beyond the windshield.

"Where do you live, soldier? I'll take you home."

"You don't have to. I appreciate—"

"I know I don't *have* to. Just gimme the fucking directions."

"You always talk with such a foul mouth?"

"Ever since I disremember."

We cruised through the nighttime quiet town. She seemed uneager to talk, and I was too weary and full of aches to be much of a
blabbermouth, though I felt woozy from sexual longing with her
beside me. In a few minutes we reached my apartment building.
She parked in the shadow of a stairwell leading up to my pad, and
kept the motor idling. Never had a dashboard so many low-key
lights, glowing digits and dials; faintly, the radio played a pop-
Motown-disco medley. Janine torched a new cigarette from the
butt of her old one.

I asked, "What are you trying to do, kill yourself?"

"I thought of asking you that same question."

"The answer is 'yes' and 'no.' Not like this afternoon, though.
That was stupid. Ku Klux Klan—Jesus."

"Coming from where I do I'm not much of a Klan supporter.
My ex used to give them money. He was too chicken to put on a
robe, though."

"Coming from where you do?"

She tightened her lips, refusing to look at me. "What about
you, Michael? Why the rage—lousy marriage? Divorce? Vietnam?"

"Perhaps that last, I guess." I fiddled with the glove compartment button, no oomph . . . all worn out . . . and crazy about this broad.

"Well," she exhaled sadly, "I'm sorry. Life doesn't get any easier."

She jiggled her right leg nervously, smoked, kept her eyes fixed on darkness beyond the windshield. I gazed down between my knees at the furry floorboard. The silence became almost uncomfortable before I broke it.

"You know, Janine—I want you. I think I'll go crazy if we don't make love."

"You and the rest of the world," she mumbled, real demoralized. "Take a ticket and get in line."

Okay, what now—plan two? Punch her jaw, jam her arm down through the steering wheel, twist her around, flip up the skirt, pull down the panty hose, and charge?

"Let me tell you something, Michael," she began evenly. "I may look like your average sleazy street slut, but it's only a game I play. Feels like fun to me. Jews have a word—they call it 'chutzpah,' correct? And I figure I got a right to my style, without having to beat back every male chauvinist pig on the block, understand? My image makes me feel peppy, but it sure doesn't mean I spread my legs for bottle caps. Am I getting through?"

Sure. What the hell. Defenseless, I nodded, trying to keep control.

"I don't like bullies," she said. "I've had it with men whose idea of a good time is to put me through a wringer."

From somewhere, a spark of humor: "Is that a proposal? Or are you just teasing me?"

She bit her bottom lip and faded into the smoke; I punched a button, rolling down the window.

Janine said, "I reckon I'm tired of doing all the work. I need TLC myself. I wish just once somebody would give in return to me."

But then perhaps she heard herself whining, and quickly ditched the self-pity. "Hey, whoa, easy. That's enough gloom and doom. Get out, soldier, I'm going home. It's been a long day."

"Do you want to come up to my place?"

"No thank you, Michael."

"Do you want to stay here and make love in the front seat?"

Her face, confronting my insistence, was old and sad, almost ugly, minus every inch of sparkle that gave her a youthful bloom.

"Really—what would be the point? I'm in lousy shape, and I kind of get the feeling you are too."

"I guess so. Maybe. Yeah."

"I haven't fucked anybody in a long time." Her hands shook as she fired up another weed. "I don't even know if I *want* to fuck anybody, now, or even forever. For years in a terrible marriage I walked around like a zombie. Ran away from home at sixteen, and married the first son of a bitch that ogled my tits. I had my first-born when I was seventeen. Later, Buddy died, so I had another. I hated my husband's guts, but I loved that new child, and I was scared, so I kept my mouth shut. Didn't have no education, didn't know how to earn a living. I knew if I left him he had all the money, he'd get the lawyers, he'd win custody of Cathie. We lived in a big house with a bunch of color TVs, and dishwashers, and washer-dryers, and the best stereo money could buy, and wall-to-wall carpeting, and central air conditioning, and a king-size water-bed, and china from Limoges, France. And the kid attended good private schools all the time so she wouldn't have to rub elbows with blacks. Shoot, every time I opened the damn refrigerator, half of southern California and Hawaii tumbled out on top of me. Yet all I thought about for many years was suicide. Or I was numb. Or I made plans to escape but I was too scared. I guess finally I decided to wait until Cathie was grown, then I'd make my move. So finally I summoned the guts. Just me and her and this big stupid automobile and the clothes on our backs. I waited until Jack was at an overnight conference, then we quickly packed the car and hauled ass. I never been so scared in all my days. We drove all the way here, nonstop, a thousand miles from that big old air-conditioned mansion. That was nine months ago. And we live in a little adobe shack, the roof leaks, the toilet backs up half the time, and it's *cold* 'cause there ain't no heaters, only wood stoves. But I

117

learned to chop wood and feed those stoves. Cathie bangs around half the time bitching at me. 'Why'd you leave Daddy? I hate it here! I wanna go home!' But I ain't going back, no way, not on your life, no sir, never. That was no home, there; I *am* home here. I got nothing, but this is the happiest I ever been. And I aim to be mighty careful before I let down my guard with another man. I got a lot of sorting out to do. I'm just learning how to *feel* again. And how do I *want* to feel? I'm not ready to hassle big things. Hey, every day I wake up drowning. I couldn't even work the self-serve pump at the gas stations so I'd save a nickel a gallon. So it's small things I'm doing right now, the old day to day. Get up, get dressed, put on makeup, see Cathie off to school, feed the cats, go to work, try and look sexy and be perky so I'll get bigger tips. Now, does that make any sense to you?"

She stabbed out the cigarette, and folded her arms defiantly across her chest. The spiel had fatigued me, and all I could do was nod.

"Tell you something else, Michael. I haven't had an orgasm because of a man in, oh, I dunno, too many years. So I'm real good with my own hand. I even own a vibrator. I always hid it from Jack, terrified he'd go nuts if he discovered it. So I don't even *know* about sex. Guess you might say I'm pretty gun-shy. I dream of romance, yes I do, but I figure there's work to do on myself before that happens. First, I want to be tough. And every day I'm getting tougher, so if I keep at it, well, the rest won't be no hill for a stepper. And I aim to be a stepper. I *am* a stepper in fact." She gave a snort, a caustic half-laugh. "I got a late start, is all."

Ruefully, I smiled. "I guess that answers my question."

"Yeah, I reckon it does."

"Well . . ." Nothing else to say. "I guess I'll be running along now."

She leaned toward me. "Good night, Michael—gimme a Yankee dime."

Though I wanted to attack, batter, grab, instead I gave her a chaste little kiss and backed out of the car.

"You take care of yourself," she called, slamming the yacht into drive. "You hear?"

I heard, and waved so long. Then I couldn't make it up the stairs. Instead, I slumped onto the bottom step, and instantly went to sleep.

Yet the second I closed my weary eyes, a fearful dream returned. That field of body parts and pale faces drained of life and connection, a listless crowd of nameless victims in a setting so remote it seemed like a fantasy from Antarctica. I pushed my wheelbarrow through that drab scene, gathering up bits and pieces of grisly flesh. Across the plain nothing stirred, no legs, no fingers on any bloody hand, no smiles on any faces. As always, I made it to the edge of the field, unloaded my cargo, and labored to fit the pieces together. But nothing worked, of course. I might have been a mental patient working some simplistic kiddie puzzle, poking square pegs futilely at round holes. My unsteady hands repeatedly flubbed the process. Big heads on tiny torsos, left wrists on right arms, female breasts above a dangling penis. Even when all the parts complemented each other, they remained out of kilter, oozing a Frankensteinian horror.

And never more than a half-life stirred in my creatures. Maybe they shivered and launched feeble squirms; their mouths and eyes opened and closed, stiff and herky-jerky . . . like sci-fi automatons. They could never speak or walk, but rather arched helplessly, tapping their paraplegic hands against black-and-blue thighs, or raising their gawky legs into odd, suppliant positions, like weird embryos in damp dark places writhing blindly around—like moronic mushroom people.

In my arms at last I held one creation, a frail blind girl, limp and dreadfully inarticulate; she had no teeth, her tongue had been ripped from the mouth. Beautiful developed breasts lay behind arms which jutted out crazily like baby-turkey legs. The feet I had mistakenly glued on backward.

No matter: I extended her out as an offering to the supernatural landscape, to that mute world of plundered human beings, deaf to all entreaties of the heart.

When I woke up, the editor of our paper stood before my desk. "Some weirdo's parked in the sagebrush over by the highway bypass, sniping at State Police Headquarters."

I grabbed my camera pack and hurried over. They had the bypass barricaded off at the main highway going south, so I had to walk a quarter mile up to the scene. Police vehicles were scattered along the road; tense men, armed to the teeth, crouched behind them; radios squawked. Dozens of other cops, posse members, and assorted deputized gun freaks crept around the arroyos.

Matter-of-factly, cool as a ghoulish cucumber, Thomas Carp greeted me with a big "Hello," and asked me how they were hanging. He had just materialized at my elbow. The seersucker suit had been replaced by a flak jacket, a web belt toting a polished .38, and he carried the converted AR-15 I recalled from our hippie days. "Just another loony," he said with almost deprecatory charm. "Couple of Lurps could smoke him out in no time."

The flasher lights of an ambulance standing by were blinking. And about five hundred yards away, parked in the sagebrush near an old green water tank, was Willie Pacheco's truck. "Oh no," I cried. "That's my friend. Lemme go and talk to him."

"No way," said an officer in charge. "He's got a girl with him. He's crazy. We tried to approach with a bullhorn fifteen minutes ago, and he wounded an officer in the hip."

"He won't shoot me. The girl is his daughter."

"Sorry, Mike. His own brother tried to coax him out, and he nearly blew *his* head off. Just take your pictures, but stay back and keep your head down."

It was a major story, I guess. I tried on different lenses, made some photographs. The sun was hot for drear November, not a cloud adorned the sky. The operation sputtered, seemed desultory at best, a carnival in slow motion. Agents of the law rustled in the arroyos, edging closer; others simply waited around for a conclusion. Carp smoked one cigarette after another, hobnobbed with other deputies, and seemed in no hurry to finish the job. Once he

120

actually winked at me and said, "This is amateur stuff, this is peanuts," as he strolled on by.

Peanuts. A Forest Service helicopter made a single pass over the truck, and, unmistakably, a rifle barrel poked out the Chevy window and fired a shot. In response, several gully-bound dodos unloaded their weapons at the truck, until a bullhorn blared: "*Cut it out, you assholes!*"

Silence.

Mingle, mingle, talk, joke, smoke, pee: the ambulance lights continued blipping. Carp landed beside me again, commenting wryly: "Shirley's still around if you've got a taste for kinky ginch. I get her so coked up she goes crazy. Three nights ago she almost sucked my dick off." Then he trotted off again to confer with the muckety-mucks, making plans, no doubt, on how to respond if the rabbit bolted.

Maybe a half hour passed in boredom; no action from the police, no shot from the truck. Meantime, skilled members of the local SWAT squad bellied through the sagebrush ever closer to Willie and his kid. I tracked them with a 400-mm lens. They wore helmets and flak jackets, and carried canisters of tear gas.

For a small town, we could sure corral a lot of fuzz. I was amazed. Must have been every state police officer and county sheriff deputy and local town flatfoot on the books. Stretching the imagination, our little ville counted maybe twenty thousand inhabitants. But the army of cops and posse buffs dawdling on the road or in the sagebrush must have numbered a hundred. Packing riot guns, sawed-off 12-gauge shotguns, Mini-14s, and a slew of other rifles, including a few M-16s—well, that last surprised me. I hadn't seen one of those motherfuckers since Nam.

Finally, the SWAT crew inched within a stone's throw of Willie's truck. Though I repeatedly scanned the truck with glasses, I could distinguish no movement inside. Eventually, some brave character pitched a tear gas canister under the Chevy; instantly, the truck was enveloped in stinging fumes. With that, half the concealed army jumped erect, training their bazookas on the battered vehicle, waiting for Willie and the kid to stumble out. Oh

Lord, I thought, they're going to waste the poor boob as soon as he pops in view, echoes of Bonnie and Clyde. And in the process, no doubt, given their formation around the truck, they'd probably perforate each other to boot.

But nothing happened. No Willie, no daughter. Carp sidled over and grinned laconically. "Bunch of helpless dorks." Then he drifted away again.

The truck was immersed in lachrymose smoke, then breezes dispersed it all. After that, nobody knew exactly what to do. They all stood there, as exposed as penguins on an ice floe, aiming their modern instruments of destruction at that poor relic of a truck. Until some particularly astute guerrilla got the bright idea that if Willie was still alive, he might come up blasting again, so they all ducked down to cover in the sage. I heard Carp joking with another spectator; he seemed to know that the drama was over—no combat jollies today, folks. Not like the Cong, no sirree; this flustered vet was just another wimp on the asshole of petty crime.

The silence endured too long, and it was too quiet. Ultimately, a few brave souls duck-waddled up to the rear of the truck. Through glasses, I watched them inch along the sides until they reached the open driver's-side window. Then abruptly they straightened, stabbed their gun barrels into the cab . . . and re-laxed. They opened both doors. One of the guys faced our crowd, grinning from ear to ear, and held up his hand in the V for victory sign—or was it a V for peace? From my vantage point it was diffi-cult to make out details; seemed like a bundle of rumpled clothing was humped on the floorboards. As the rest of us began a general surge toward the ancient pickup, Carp fell in stride beside me, muttering, "All's well that ends well," and he offered me a weed that I refused; I wanted to accept nothing from the man.

Willie lay crouched over Mariangela, protecting her with his body. The coronor decided they had been dead for at least an hour. The girl had a single head wound, up close; apparently he had killed her. Willie himself had caught three rounds—in the hip, under the left rib, in his right shoulder: police bullets fired who knew how long ago.

Apparently, he had bled to death.

"Well shit," said Thomas Carp. "Another nigger bites the dust."

One December night I left my sterile digs at nine, gassed up at an all-night station, scored a dozen shooters of Johnnie Black. Then an illuminated phone booth caught my eye. Pulling over, I dialed Cicarelli, punched in my credit-card number, and listened to it ring. Her gravelly voice was so low, drugged, sleepy that it could have been a record playing at half speed.

"Sicko—can you hear me?"

"Who's this?"

"Me. Michael. Michael Smith. Mr. Under Control."

Pause . . . total befuddlement. Finally that slow, slurred voice managed to say: "I don't know who this is."

"Michael *Smith*! Vietnam, remember? I offered you a Purple Heart. Christ, woman, what's the matter with you?"

"Dying," she mumbled. "*Who* did you say this was?"

"Me, Michael." I kicked the booth in frustration. "Hey, Sicko—I just called to say 'Merry Christmas,' that's all. How are you?"

"Christmas?" Her voice picked up a little edge.

"Yeah," I shouted. "Merry Christmas! Peace on Earth, goodwill toward men. Kill 'em all, let God sort 'em out!"

"Is it *Christmas*?" Lord, from what a deep place she dragged those painful syllables.

"Not quite, but almost. Haven't you been out shopping?" The tears began now, bursting out, splashing all over the place, sloppy as hell. I felt I was trying to resuscitate a human being a thousand miles away, using only the sound of my voice.

"Christmas can go . . . hump a rolling doughnut," she finally managed.

"You better believe it."

"Michael . . . *Smith*?"

"Yeah, Michael Smith. C'mon, Sicko, what is the matter with you?"

"Dying," she repeated. "Took a . . . pills. Why did you call? Who *is* this?"

"What do you mean, 'pills'?"

"Whole bunch," the slurring thick voice said, fading back toward a stupor. "Hundred footballs. G'bye cruel world." Then she woke up a tad. *"Don't call the cops!"*

Silence, then, until finally I agreed. "Okay, I won't call the cops."

"Good." Then of a sudden she came alert, and spoke a clear sentence. "Michael? Oh yeah, I got the dope, thanks a lot, it was very helpful."

"Sicko, you didn't really take those pills?"

But she faded again, going going gone. "G'bye," she said in a very tiny voice. And after a longer lapse: "I love you."

"I love you too." Then I listened to nothing at the other end. I listened to nothing way up north in Montana. I couldn't hear any breathing. Faint voices argued in Spanish somewhere along the line. Things crackled. I called into my mouthpiece: "Sicko. Hey *Sicko!*" So we reach out to touch across the miles. But nobody responded. There was just that hum of the open line.

I drove around drinking, plotting mayhem, weeping for the world. As I drove north of town on the deserted highway big snowflakes began to fall. Winter, winter; winter in my blood. I hurried past a dimmed 7-Eleven, a garish Lota Burger, gas stations and drive-in liquor stores, a lumberyard and an organic food co-op, the Feed Bin, a bank, a couple of greasy-spoon cafés. Then I was out on the lonely highway, going north; mountains faded on my right; the sagebrush mesa stretched left, whitening from the snow.

At the blinking light five miles north of town, I turned west: snow came down more fitfully. One car passed in the other direction, then I had the blurry universe to myself. Turned on the wipers, clicked on the radio, but all the country music and all the mariachi songs were devoured in the storm's static. So I flicked off the radio, and proceeded silently into the whirling white darkness.

Other side of the gorge I hung a Louie down a dirt road and headed south of the mesa. No rhyme, no reason. Deck the halls with hunks of holly. I pictured the White House Christmas tree, all lit up for the president. Only instead of your normal decorations, Vietnamese arms, legs, and tongues hung from the fabled branches; Cambodian ears and testicles dangled instead of candy canes. Oh someday, I thought, the chickens will come home to roost, gouge out the president's eyes, punch in all his teeth.

I parked and sat still, enveloped by snowstorm. Michael P. Smith, Vietnam vet, sterling news photographer, all-American schizo, and qualified professional killer, contemplated his navel a million miles from civilization, a full moon rising in his heart, Janine Tarr ever gentle on his mind.

The road turned white; sage branches gathered crystals; it seemed I should leave before I was marooned, maybe frozen. Then that captured my fancy for a spell. Get out of the truck, Michael, strip off all your clothes, and march off onto the mesa, disappear into the dancing tempest, never wake up again—Peary heading north.

Instead, I cranked it into gear, heading south once more. The road was frozen, hence undangerous. I thought of Cicarelli, another anonymous victim, a dedicated nurse whose most heartfelt regret was that she had saved so many boys. Patched them up, sutured their stumps, sewed shut their detesticled scrotums, fixed their spines so they could live out their days as happy quads—I thought of her in bed, touched by the night-light's blue gloom, and the telephone beside her lifeless hand, while snow softly coated her roof, and carolers galumphed from door to door, hyping Good King Wenceslas.

Cicarelli.

Michael P. Smith.

Janine Tarr.

Willie Pacheco.

Two million gooks.

Shirley of the weasel face and lifted skirt.

A communist woman in a helicopter.

Thomas Carp. . . .
Oooooommmmmmmmmmmmmmmmmmmmmmmmmm.

I was trucking carefully home at dawn, taking the long way around, the scenic, still semirural back route that circled south of town, when I spotted a figure on the snowy pavement ahead. I stopped the truck, descended, and approached the man. A large shepherd mutt, which had been patiently on guard in the nearby ditch, whimpered and got up stiffly, limped over and licked my hand. The man was old, perhaps in his midseventies; had gaunt cheeks covered by a white beard stubble. He was dressed in a Levi's jacket, work gloves, a pair of old galoshes. His seedy cowboy hat, weighted by a four-inch cone of snow, lay down the road about twenty feet away. The man was dead. I brushed snow off his face, revealing speckles of blood around his lips. Then I swept away snow around his body, and discovered bits of thick glass from a busted headlight. Hit-and-run, no doubt, sometime earlier in the evening. The dog whimpered again, sniffing at the man's head; then it sat down bewilderedly, asking me for an answer.

My response?—I got real wary. Stood up, checked both ways to see if anyone was watching. Then I backed up to the Dodge, scuffling a toe through my tracks, smudging away telltale footprints. I swung the truck around the victim; the dog gave a plaintive bark as I swerved by, but I was no fool. I avoided the hat, and kept on accelerating, confident that enough snow would fall before the next passerby to obliterate my tread marks.

I knew how the system worked. If I reported the hit-and-run to the local cops, they'd jump my ass when I claimed I didn't do it. They'd arrest me, throw me in the hoosegow for a drunk, take Breathalyzers and blood tests, even kick in my own headlight if they had to, anything to make a criminal and a conviction. I knew how it worked, and what my chances were, and what it'd cost me in legal fees even if I managed to get off.

So I motored on home, steering carefully over the snow-laden road, singing, as the storm began to slacken, and as hints of a cold dawn began rising to the east:

Oh you better watch out,
You better not cry,
You better not pout I'm tellin' you why:
Santa Claus is coming to town.

At the apartment, at 7:00 A.M., I lifted up the telephone receiver and dialed Montana. From Cicarelli's number came a steady busy signal. I called information, received a cipher for the proper authorities, and dialed again. I told them her address, and explained my earlier call. Said I was just a friend, and gave them my name and number. "Would you please call me back?" Then I remained at the kitchen table, staring at my hands. They were split open, scraped and bleeding, one fingernail was black and blue.

For two hours the phone did not ring. But at long last—of course—it jangled. I answered in a swoon, and listened to a gendarme on the other end detail the sorry facts. Dead as last year's Christmas tree. Overdose of Percodan. Did I know of any friends or family? No, I couldn't recall any pals, but thought she had a family somewhere . . . maybe in Nebraska—?

"Sure," he said, "thanks. Maybe in Nebraska."

Right-o. Maybe in Nebraska.

Well, I opened a beer and clicked on the boob tube. Three perfectly proportioned lithesome beauties, sheathed in shiny spandex skin and mauve warm-up socks, were teaching all us fast-food fatties how to pare down and shape up. Such a ludicrous endeavor if you considered how the rest of the world lives. With starved distended bellies and dilated pupils, elbows swollen to baseball size and jutting ribs, hair rust colored from lack of nutrition, limbs deliberately maimed in order to beg, assholes blistered from amoebic dysentery.

Oh I coveted those energetic happy beauties with their bouncing chests—conjured up Janine Tarr, they did, and I knew I had to have that woman. And I had to have her *now*: no more shilly-shallying. I stroked myself for a while, chasing the malt liquor with enough Jack Daniel's to kill a horse, then I headed for the Chuck Wagon Café.

5

A PERFECT GENTLEMAN

When I opened the tinkling door, the joint was empty. Behind the counter, Janine leaned on her elbows, leafing through a morning newspaper. Hollow eyed, and tragically attractive in a wispy salmon-pink blouse, cheap hoops in her ears, and an emerald ribbon tying back her hair. She exhaled smoke like a haunting, incongruous child-whore, world-weary and succulent, timid and tough, and but two inches shy, in my crusading eyes, of guttural pornography.

I motored unsteadily across the room. As the Vietnamese often regarded us in Nam, her eyes observed me now, helpless and also calculating, unable to flee because in a country at total war, there was no place to hide. I stumbled and almost slipped to my knees while mounting a stool before her. But I righted myself and laid a trembling hand on her paper.

"You stink." She straightened a trifle, lighting another cigarette. "You look awful. You look like two tomcats who spent the night fighting in a garbage can."

She evinced a guarded sympathy for my plight. It was difficult to speak or hold back the tears. My body trembled, and my teeth wanted to chatter—it required an effort to quell them. My eyes fell on her newspaper, the local blat my employer published every Thursday. The headline was upside down, but I could read it easily: "Teen OD Found in Vacant Lot." Of course I knew the story: my photograph graced the front page—of cops and other concerned parties milling around a hump on the ground, covered by a blanket. Little Miss Carolyn Archuleta, aged fifteen; apparently she'd overdosed at a holiday party, then been discarded by her panicked buddies.

I gestured at the article. "You know what gets me, Janine? All this stuff, everybody walks around as if it's normal. Some jerk kidnaps the night clerk at Holiday Inn and holds her hostage for twelve hours, then walks away, and it's all normal as Mom and apple pie. Four teenagers die in a car accident up in the canyon. The son of the newspaper editor is jailed for selling cocaine. Old what's-his-name, the janitor of that ramshackle motel on Route 64, he drives out to the mesa, drenches himself in gasoline, strikes a match and goes to heaven. And everybody struts around like there's nothing wrong, oh dear oh dear, it's just society. These things happen. Here, have another potato chip. God in his infinite wisdom decrees—"

She interrupted. "Did you sleep last night?"

"Sure. Like a baby. Woke up feeling really refreshed." And then I grabbed her hand. "Janine, I need you. I want you. Please quit work. We'll buy a house and build a life together. You can't say no."

Weary, sighing, she pulled her hand away. "Michael, why don't you spare us both the embarrassment?"

"I love you."

"Oh please, gimme a break. I'm tired of men who want to screw me saying 'I love you.' I mean, I guess I can be had, but I ain't that stupid."

"What do you want from me? I'll do anything you say, anything you want."

"Then back off, quit foaming at the mouth, leave me be."

"Anything but that."

"Hey, I like your terms. They seem fair, rational . . . totally insane."

"I *need* you," I protested.

"You need two thousand milligrams of Thorazine," she replied, digging for another cigarette.

"Look at you," I growled. "How long can you smoke like that before cancer lays you in a grave?"

Her eyelids fluttered as she glanced away. "I'm working on quitting."

"I could help you work on it."

"How? By clinging to my skirts and robbing all my freedom with your whimpering self-pity and your rage?"

"I'll treat you like a princess."

"Michael, I don't think you get the drift. I just escaped from untold years of being sick. I don't need any other sick people in my life right now. It's hard enough, taking care of Cathie and myself."

"I'll take care of you both."

"Stop it." She folded up the paper. Another customer had arrived and claimed a table. "We need each other like we need holes in the head."

"Invite me over to dinner tonight."

"Hell no. Go home, Michael, take a bath, shave, stop drinking, go to bed. It'll all look better tomorrow morning."

I trailed her as she headed for the new diner. When she halted to confront me again, I reached out and gripped her shoulders. Obviously pissed, but afraid to cause a scene, she said, "You can't bully people like me around. These aren't caveman times."

Oh no? "If you don't invite me to dinner, I'll go nuts in here, right now. I'll destroy the restaurant. You think that Ku Klux Klan guy was bad? You'll never land another gig in this town."

Fear, weariness, calculation—it was all transcribed in her eyes. If I could not be dissuaded, then a decision had to be made. "All right, Michael. You can come for dinner. *If* you drive home right now, shave that ugly phizzog, take a bath, and put on clean clothes. Nobody enters my house looking like a piece of horse dung covered by flies."

"When?" I asked excitedly.

"I don't know, Maybe around six o'clock."

"I'll be there. Where do you live?"

On a sheet of her order pad she scratched a hasty map, and ripped it off for me.

"Just to refresh your memory," she cautioned, "I've got a gun. And if you are not a perfect gentleman to me and Cathie, I swear to God I'll use it."

"Scout's honor," I promised, lofting the three-fingered sign. "I'll be a perfect gentleman."

Polished, shaved, and showered, in clean clothes and freshly waxed shoes, clutching three long-stemmed roses in his hand, the Perfect Gentleman arrived. The mud-bespattered Chrysler simmered before a ramshackle dirt-roofed adobe hovel, in every window a geranium. I knocked on the lopsided door, dizzy with anticipation. The brat who greeted me wore thick glasses, baggy clothes, and scuffed sneakers made palatable to her by red fluorescent laces and rock stars' names scribbled in bleeding ballpoint ink. Her dirty blond hair was half-assedly spiked, punk style; her pasty sullen features revealed vague intonations of her momma's sexy face. Same height as the old lady, and probably, under the deliberately unrevealing clothes, shaped similar to Janine. She chewed gum and smoked a filtered Camel.

"You must be Cathie," I said.

"Yeah. And you must be the maniac."

"Is that what your mom tells you?"

"I don't need her to tell me, I got eyes." She blew a smoky bubble as she backed up, apparently inviting me in. So I advanced, crossing their threshold, entering their prosaic lives like a beast from a black lagoon. Walked right into their home the way we used to enter villes in Nam, strutting our stuff with the weight of a billion weapons behind us, confident that either we owned the world, or if not, we had the power to blow it off its hinges.

They were poor: the K Mart brand black-and-white TV

showed mostly snow. A few pieces of secondhand junk furnished their three-room hovel. A fifty-dollar stereo occupied a corner— but they only owned six records. Cheap rattan mats instead of rugs covered the main floor. Cathie slept on the living-room couch. Janine's room was neat, spare, and beautiful. A mattress on the floor had a worn patchwork quilt; bucolic country landscapes decorated the walls. A candle sat on her weathered chifforobe, and plants hung in baskets from the ceiling. Cats snoozed unobtrusively on assorted cushions or piles of laundry. The living-room walls featured rock star posters, horses, unicorns, and koala bears.

The small kitchen was dominated by an old wood cooking stove and a dilapidated gas range; leaky faucets, corroded sideboards, and a warped table covered by a yellow oilcloth completed the picture. On the floor, a box of Kitty Litter; cheerful pictures and newspaper clippings were pinned by magnets to the refrigerator door. And more greenery—geraniums, aloe vera plants, wispy trailing ferns.

On the gas stove a simple repast bubbled; rice and steamed broccoli, a stew of chicken gizzards and giblets. "We may eat poor," Janine revealed later over the meal, "but it ain't half bad, I think it's kinda tasty." An operation held together by spit and baling wire, for sure—but it was cheerful, also two-fisted and inherently arrogant; their spirit of making do.

When Janine emerged from the bathroom to greet me, I gasped and instantly overheated. Almost impossible, even in front of Cathie, not to envelop that scrumptious bitch in my arms and rub myself against her belly. The outfit was a cream-colored long-sleeved jersey sweater, and a soft purple skirt that flared below her knees. She approached me on bare feet, saying, "Howdy, soldier, whatcha know good?" And, on tiptoes, imparted a swift Yankee dime, then brushed quickly past me into the kitchen, leaving my startled hands half raised and cupping air, while Cathie across the room glared at me in a defensive rage only partially disguised by her mask of adolescent scorn.

We assembled together, ate hungrily, and made neutral chitchat; but all the while I concentrated on Janine. Lusts for her attacked in droves, rousing fantasies of erotic rape and murder. I might tie them both up and have myself a field day. Janine was perky, funny, a barrel of laughs; Cathie remained sulky, sarcastic, and rudely complaining. And I? I was almost tongue-tied. I smiled and nodded, ate my food, drank a beer, patted my belly, and fought to concentrate on the petty conversation. But I kept glimpsing the helicopter broad at Tom Carp's mercy, and frail women outfitted in diaphanous ao dais waiting to have their throats slit. According to Cathie, every guy in her class was either a dork, a wanglet, a "lunch bag," "a pile of vomit," or an "all-American wimp." She had as obscene a mouth as I'd ever heard on a kid, yet Janine seemed to ignore it. "What a dildo brain!" Cathie exclaimed. "I bet even his dick has pimples." And all the time I surreptitiously ogled her mother, trying to imagine how those ruby lips might look aglisten with my jism.

Did we elevate the small talk to discussions of "J. Alfred Prufrock," Lebanon, or Einstein's theory of relativity? Not on your life, boy. We berated cats and weather, life at the Chuck Wagon Café, and certain TV programs. Pop and soul singers like Diana Ross, Bette Midler, and Stevie Wonder had their day. Then we continued to rehash everything and everybody that Cathie hated. Especially the boys in her school, all those "fuzzbutts" and "assbreaths" and "come bubbles." Already, at sixteen, she loathed men, and made no bones about it.

But suddenly, after refusing to help wash the dishes, Cathie filched a cigarette from her mother's pack, struck a wooden match on her thumbnail, and announced, "I'm going for a walk, I'll be back in awhile. Hope you two parental units don't miss me when I'm gone." And she barged out the door, letting it bang shut loudly—"Adios!"

In almost the same instant I moved behind her mother at the sink, shoved my hands through her armpits, and grabbed those heavy breasts, pressed my groin against her buttocks, and experienced such a powerful surge of excitement that I almost came.

What had I expected from her, I wonder now. Who knows, it's hard to say. Obviously, I had ceased to think things out. She was so small, and I was so big and bad the violent rape would be a piece of cake. But Janine took me completely by surprise. She stiffened, gasped "Oh no!" then instantly exploded. Elbows jammed back hard into my stomach, and she twisted shouting from my grasp, *"You motherfucker!"* One fist bounced off my cheek, stinging sharply, driving me off balance; then her hands rat-a-tatted against my body, raining a dozen incensed blows as I stumbled, grasping her jersey and yanking her off her feet: we toppled grunting to the floor.

But Janine was all over me, battering, cursing a blue streak as I fumbled to ward off blows . . . then finally I popped and started fighting back. Smacked her hard across her apoplectic face, launched a kick between her legs, and punched her tits, slamming her topsy-turvy across the room as I rolled over and staggered to my knees, then lunged to grab an ankle as she scrambled for her feet. Janine snagged a coffee table leg, upending it as I yanked her backward. Then a large glass ashtray was in her hand, banging off my head—it opened a three-inch gash as I grappled her up against me in a tangle of flailing arms and legs. Christ almighty, the blood spurted *every*where as I ripped apart her frail jersey, slugged her a half-dozen times, and clutched her hair between my teeth: but the lunatic woman twisted frantically to break my hold. *"I'll kill you!"* she screamed. *"Let go of me!"* Then her lips burst open against my knuckles and I could feel a tooth give way.

But if killing was to be done, I suddenly realized, the tables had turned. And when I heaved half erect, wrestling that insane floozy in my grasp, I gave an angry yell and slung her hard away. She crashed through a gangly floor lamp and the Tinkertoy stereo and over a toppling armchair, smack-dab against the wall with a noisy thud. A picture frame tipped over, bouncing off her head. I sprang toward her big pink tits bubbling through the rent fabric of her jersey. Yet somehow, before I arrived she had that floor lamp in her hands, swinging it like a futuristic space-age sword, banging it so hard against my neck and shoulder in a bulb-popping explosion of glass and crumpling lampshade, that my charge was deflected: *holy shit!*

I flopped over, absolutely shocked by her fury and her power; she was staggering toward her purse atop the babbling TV: *"Oh no you don't!"* I scrambled up again, catching her ribs with a wild swing, slamming her sideways against the glass front door. Her head thumped against the crossbars, and three little windows shattered, raining jagged tidbits down all over her crumpling body. But when I tackled her, screeching *"I'll kill you!"* her legs punched up, driving hard, and her heel caught my chin. *My God how that little pistol could fight for her life!* I fumbled for wrists and ankles, but she clawed and squirmed out from under me yet again, gasping in great convulsive gulps, and she grabbed my hair, yanking like the devil. I clutched her hair in return and jerked frenziedly, damn near shaking her goggled eyeballs clear of her crimson face.

But she refused to give up, not that ferocious bit of berserk poontang fighting off my angrily striking hands. Coughed, sputtered, and fended off my enraged advances, all of them, gouging fingers into my mouth, almost tearing apart my cheeks. I howled in pain, and she jolted free again, smashing a flowerpot against my shoulder. Then that hellion lunged again for her purse, but she was so disoriented that her spun-around body charged in the wrong direction, pitching pell-mell toward the couch instead. Her feet caught against the overturned coffee table, and she pitched down abruptly, belly flopping on the floor, catching her chin against the couch, snapping back her head with an "Oof" and almost breaking her neck.

I started up, and stopped. My heart banged like a grenade, thumping upward in my throat, and I went dizzy, almost blacking out as I tilted backward into a sitting position, knocking the TV over sideways onto the floor.

Janine rolled over, facing me, caught in a dazed and slumped position, her entire body arched violently, gasping for air; I thought she must be choking to death. Her face was horribly painted by splashes of blood, her shirt was ripped to shreds, her bosom scarlet smeared, her skirt tangled around her waist.

"You bastard!" she sobbed, struggling to wrench up into a sitting position. "You fucking son of a bitch!"

And right there I lost all taste for it. I had certainly met my match. I thought I would die; I wanted to vomit. And my body ached everywhere from that hellcat's defensive blows.

The cunt had saved her life.

"I'm leaving," I croaked. "I'm getting out of here."

"You better." She wiped her mouth, smoothing her messy palms across her brutalized chest. "You better leave here . . . before Cathie returns . . . you sick human being."

I labored to rise, but Lord how I hurt; that little tiger had done such incredible damage. In disbelief, I crouched, bruised over every inch of my body. My heart fibrillated wildly, barely pumping blood into my head, and I wheezed dizzily. But in the end I made it to my feet and teetered there, staring down at that woman who had beat *me* to a pulp.

Her hand automatically sought another weapon; her fingers closed over a small china Buddha used for burning incense sticks. I could tell, though, that she hadn't an ounce of strength in reserve.

"Let go of it," I groaned. "It's over. You win."

"You beast," she blubbered queerly. "You cock-sucking cripple." And she started crying, a flood of tears that drove stinging rivulets through the blood on her face. Her body shook and trembled. "You lousy . . . prick."

"I'm sorry," I whimpered. I managed two steps toward her and actually leaned over, extending a hand to help her up. But she gripped the Buddha tightly and desperately lifted it half above her head to strike me yet another blow.

"I didn't mean," I whispered. "I didn't want—"

"I'll kill you," she sobbed, "if you don't get out of here."

My knees went terribly shaky, and I plopped down abruptly on a wooden bench. My heart refused to quit pounding; I sunk my face into my hands.

Janine stirred into a sitting position, trying to wipe clean her face, her hands against her thighs; she plucked astonished fingers at the torn jersey, ineffectually attempting to cover her breasts.

"You're a pathetic man," she whispered, pushing half erect. "Get out of here right now before Cathie comes back. I want you out of this house."

"I'm sorry," I moaned repeatedly through my hands. "I'm

sorry, I didn't mean to hurt you. I love you, Janine. Why won't you believe me?"

I expected then that she'd go to the purse for her .38 and threaten to blow me away. Wouldn't have tried to stop her, either. In fact, I would have begged her to shoot: the time had come. But instead I heard a door slam shut, and water splashing in the bathroom. Incredibly, she had left me alone. Through the nearby door sounded muffled sobs and spastic coughing noises, and a wet splattering. Then she cut the taps and opened the door, limping to the bedroom. I couldn't move, too stunned to save my ass. In my head no sensible thoughts, only a terrible huge despair that life was over, I couldn't function anymore. Begged my heart to snuff me, end this rotten time on earth.

Yet shortly I began to catch my breath, calming down.

Janine returned, in control now, breathing almost regular, a sweatshirt over the jersey. She halted, saying, "Michael, I'm not kidding, I want you out of here." Her voice was drained of all emotion.

I glanced up, then, pleading like an ugly dog, I suppose, begging for her mercy. She'd put on dungarees and that baggy sweatshirt; washed her face quite clean. One eye was puffed shut, her cheeks had swelled with bruises. Her lips were fat, almost double their normal size.

"Oh Christ," I moaned, "I'm sorry."

"Me too," she said. "You bet. If you want to wash up first, go ahead. Then you must leave my house."

And she turned away from me, limping toward the kitchen, one hand pressed against an aching hip. She actually positioned herself at the sink again, back to me, and resumed washing the dishes. Plates and glasses clattered in her shaking hands.

Well, my heart had slowed to a dull erratic thumping; it was time to get my ass in gear. With utmost care (and fear and trepidation) I arose, made my way to the bathroom, and wearily closed the door behind me.

Healthy plants and cheerfully dripping vines lived here, too; and, scrawled on the mirror in soap was an obviously week-old message: MOM, I LOVE YOU OODLES. The faucet dripped into the discolored tub; the toilet perpetually gurgled. A *Cosmopolitan* was spread-eagled by the crapper, on its cover a tantalizing lacquered bitch whose boobs were half exposed behind teasing strips of Dacron. As I took a leak, I faintly heard Cathie exclaim, "What *happened* to you?" And Janine's frosty answer, "Nothing. How come you didn't offer to help with the dishes?" Then more rattling at the sink and water splashing into soap suds.

I flicked off the last drops, zipped up, and carefully washed my hands. My face was messy, bloody, and as bruised as Janine's; my hair was caked with blood. I tried to cleanse some of it away, but could not bear the sight of myself in the mirror. I should have been wearing a hockey mask and wielding an ax in my left hand. Better yet, big raw stitches should have girdled the top of my cranium and a wooden peg should have been driven through my temples. God, I hated myself; I was so ashamed and wasted. My eyes were red and swollen from crying. Suicide was the only answer. Nervously palming the bar of Dove, I wrote beneath Cathie's message, "I LOVE YOU TOO." And signed it "MICHAEL."

After that I opened the door. Cathie stood on the other side of the jamb, gripping her mother's .38 tightly in both hands, chest-high, aimed directly at me. Around the corner dishes continued clanking; Janine must have been unaware that Cathie had raided her purse. I had no time to react and save myself. Cathie didn't speak, she simply pulled the trigger. I have no recollection of hearing a blast. A force knocked me back against the sink, and I went over sideways, ripping down a thin shelf of doodads, perfume and polish bottles, and two small potted cacti. My chest hit the toilet bowl, tipping me at an angle so that my head struck the tub as my rump bumped the floor. And a darkness shivered sledgehammer nasty across my brain—I never felt hurt at all.

Somehow the wretched, the malevolent, the werewolves, and the golems never die. Justice beleaguers the innocent with eternal incarceration, but allows the guilty free rein to continue plundering at will. Innocent blacks hang from southern trees, and Vietnamese babies resemble deformed circus freaks because of Agent Orange. But our regally talcum-powdered president sits in a luxurious ivory tower plotting the starvation of Latin America. And Michael P. Smith commands the best hospital room, doctors around the clock, and competent precise nurses working desperately to save his life.

So it happens that I woke up hours later swaddled in the whitest, brightest gauze, pleasantly stoned on morphine, and plugged into a dozen machines and respirators and glucose bags determined to keep me breathing. My eyelids fluttered as I sleepily observed the busy scene, listening to the swish of crisp hospital clothes, the bleeping and humming of assorted monitors keeping close tabs on my vital signs, consuming the public's money at the rate of a thousand bucks per day. Worth it, of course, to preserve a tender and compassionate soul like mine.

Then I realized that frightened Janine was seated close by, seriously contemplating my plight. I expected at least one of my arms would be manacled to the bedpost, but no such luck. Nor was a bevy of somber cops lounging about the room to assure I made no dash for freedom. Only that small woman, perched primly in a window chair balancing a *People* magazine on her knees, was in attendance.

I said, "Hello. What brings you to this neck of the woods?"

"You're going to be all right," she said. "You won't be crippled or anything. The bullet missed your heart, it missed your spine, it missed everything."

"Just my luck."

"What do you mean?"

I gave her one of those glances that she had given me after our battle was over. Through still swollen lips she spoke with a lisp; a gap showed where a tooth was missing.

"I'm glad you're alive," she said. "I don't know what I would have done if . . ."

If.

"You could have danced on my grave."

"Yes," she said abstractly, lighting—always lighting—another cigarette. "I suppose I could have done that."

Then she fiddled with her magazine, glanced out the window, exhaled smoke—the mood was very awkward. One bead of gold decorated each ear, and no mauve ribbon brightened her hair. Her outfit—a loose gray sweatshirt, faded dungarees, and old running shoes—was awfully staid: my sex object had turned forlorn waiflet. No pink splashes on her fingernails either, no lipstick or rouge, no eye shadow. Her fatigued face, one eye blackened, bruises yellowing on her cheeks, was quiet and troubled and old looking, like a person who'd given up hope.

"Are you going to file a complaint against my daughter?" she asked, voice trembling, really scared.

"Did you file a complaint against me?"

"Not yet." Her eyes darted, on the verge of tears. And we remained uncomfortable, pretending to focus elsewhere, and fidgeted with things—the bed covers, her magazine. The Twenty-five Most Exciting People in the World: Nancy Reagan, Jeane Kirkpatrick, Farrah Fawcett, Burt Reynolds, Clint Eastwood.

"You're a son of a bitch," she declared quietly as the tears began to fall. "I had a hard enough life without you barging in like this."

"Suppose I don't sign a complaint, what then?"

"Then I guess we got a deal," she said quickly, glancing up with a faint blip of hopefulness. Obviously, she'd do anything to protect her daughter. And what happened, anyway, in this society, to men who knocked around their women?—next to nothing. Plus it had never even gotten close to rape.

"I'm sorry she didn't kill me. Why don't you teach her to aim better next time?"

"I don't want Cathie to grow up to be a killer," she whispered, trembling, determined not to break down sobbing. And then she fixed on me directly, a fierce light in her eyes. "She already hates men. She already hates me. She hates everything. A person like her doesn't stand a chance. *This stinking world.*"

And her face was drenched with salty water.

"I don't know if *any*body has a chance." She snuffled, wiping her cheeks on the sweatshirt sleeve. "Christ almighty," she exclaimed. "What right did you have to come into our lives? Who do you think you are? I was trying to *build* something here. Do you know what that's like, a wrinkled old stupid bitch like me?"

I guess I began to weep myself. Oh Lord, deliver me unto the angels, let them kill me with their unhappy softness. "You're not wrinkled, you're not old, you're not stupid," I protested. And then, "I'm sorry." The world proudly boasts of four and a half billion miserable souls staggering around with cartoon balloons above their heads, filled by the words, "I'm sorry." As they scarf down Big Macs and Finger Lickin' Chicken, and fry children alive, and suffocate from inhaling the smoke of smoldering mattresses set ablaze in prison riots. Wouldn't we all really rather have a Buick?

"'Sorry'?" she snorted disgustedly. "You really make me laugh. Holy fuckin' Toledo. You just casually waltz in and attack my body and ruin my daughter's life, and you're 'sorry.' I don't believe this, I really don't. What in God's name were you thinking about? I really would like to know that. I am honestly curious. What did you hope to accomplish? What have I ever done to you? I don't even *know* you. What is the matter with you anyway?"

I shook my head. How to explain, what to explain? Cicarelli? Those blown-apart gooks we used as human mine detectors? Carp forcing his whores to eat the rubbers, then performing Vietnamese abortions? And that arrogant boy with the stilettoed broad on his arm in the fancy airport, his T-shirt advertising the motive behind the opulence—?

KILL 'EM ALL, LET GOD SORT 'EM OUT.

"What did you tell them?" I finally asked. "About all this?"

"I told them it was an accident. A family quarrel."

"Okay. Then that's what I'll say it was."

"It was no accident," she muttered morosely. "You wanted to rape me. I think you would have killed me if I hadn't kicked your butt."

"You know it wasn't an accident, I know that, but *they* don't know that."

She nodded. Kept nodding, couldn't stop it, dipping and raising her head almost crazily.

144

"So it'll all just blow over," I added.

"Sure." Nod, nod, nod. "Just all blow over. You got a hole in your chest. I got an aching body that you punched to kingdom come. And Cathie's brain is so twisted and angry she won't be able to quit crying and hating for the rest of her life. But sure, it'll all blow over in a minute. Holy fuckin' Toledo."

"I'll make it up to you both," I whispered.

"How?"

"I don't know, but I will."

"Maybe you could attack *her* next time, Michael. It's such a wonderful experience. Just what us cock-teasing women adore."

"I'll try to love you, Janine."

"Oh?" She really arched. "How do you plan to do that? Slit our throats, cut off our lips, jam rocks into our vaginas?"

"I don't know. I'll just try to love you."

"'Love.'" She groaned, pressing her hands to her face. "Boy does that sound vulgar coming from your mouth. Shall we get married? I'll wear a white dress to prove I'm a virgin. Cathie can be the flower girl. Instead of champagne we'll drink human blood. Ought to get us off on the right foot together. You know something—?"

I closed my eyes; I sure didn't want to hear it.

"I can't get the feel of your grubby hands off my tits," she said. "I can't seem to scrub your filthy punches off my body." As I opened my mouth to protest, she cut me off. "And don't you tell me one more time that you're 'sorry.' You do that, and I'll yank out all those tubes, I'll find a razor, I'll slit your throat."

"Big talk from a little woman."

Her head jerked sideways, and she stared infuriated out the window. Things hummed, bleeped, dripped; laugh tracks from re-run sitcoms gabbled down the hallway.

"Why take it out on me?" she pleaded at last. "Am I such a nasty person?"

No response to that. No answers to any of it. I made a hopeless gesture. Rain pelted down while a big hog gobbled human entrails. I kicked and stabbed and trampled a dead VC. Dozens of diminutive gooks on fire zipped around frantically like dying fireflies.

"All right," she said at last. "I think something decent has to happen out of all this. You can't just go your way, and we'll go ours. Neither me or Cathie can continue living in this town, knowing that you are out there. And I aim to live in this town." She stiffened a bit, resolving to be strong again. "I got no place else to make my stand at. I'm too tired to head on."

"I don't think I understand."

"We have to deal with this, you and me and her. For your sake, for my sake. For Cathie's sake. Plus I'll admit, crippled as it seems, I feel downright sorry for you, Michael. Maybe you could use somebody on your side if you'd only let them."

"How do we deal with this?" My forlorn voice could not rise above a whisper. How did you deal with those Vietnamese prisoners suffocating in the Conex boxes? How did you deal with hospital rooms full of gorks and bleeders and crispy critters? And how did you deal with a man who loved to fuck communist skulls?

"I think we have to keep knowing each other." She was hesitant, fearful, uncertain if her plan held water, or merely assured a kind of communal suicide. "We have to develop a relationship, and try to work it up to something decent. Otherwise—"

She halted, uneasy, uncertain, unhappy. So I prompted: "Otherwise, what?"

"Otherwise, it's just like . . . just like a horrible act of God that doesn't make any sense. Otherwise, it's just crazy," she said exhaustedly. "And Cathie won't ever understand. And you'll just find another stupid woman to attack who won't have half the gumption to resist that I did, and you'll wind up in the electric chair."

"What are you suggesting?"

"I'm not sure." But haltingly she attempted to spell it out. "The three of us have to learn about each other. We have to find a way to care about each other. We have to make it turn into something . . . positive."

No doubt, she had not articulated it all that carefully in her head. It was more an instinctive thing, growing out of an obligation to Cathie. Calm down the girl, smooth over the guilt, extend to her a tenable world. So that she wouldn't go off the deep end, committing suicide, or further harden her hatreds and dismays. The idea boggled me, helpless in my woozy state. What incredible depths of forgiveness lie in such weak and vulnerable people that Janine could even *think* of this? Talk about turning the other cheek—

Or was it basically a hard-nosed, profoundly calculated stab at insuring survival?

"How do we make it something positive?" I asked, my fatigue aching to become sleep again.

"When you get out of here, you'll come over for dinner again. We'll begin by talking it over. We can't be afraid of each other. Cathie needs to realize you're really a decent person."

"What happens if I go nuts again?"

She shrugged, all worn out, nearly defenseless. "You already went nuts. And that will keep on being there unless we change it." She leaned forward, raising her voice a tad because she could see I was sinking. "If we don't figure out how to change it, it'll just keep on being horrible forever."

"How about a shrink?" I asked.

"Oh Christ. Shrinks and therapists aren't worth the paper they're printed on. The last two *I* went to wound up making passes at me."

A pause, then a last admonishment from her battered lips: "It's up to just us, Michael. We have to love each other to make it go away."

Guess I smiled at her then; maybe I mumbled, "Sayonara." Then I burbled back down under the mud, where all the leering gremlins, bloody gut butchers, and pearl-handled sadists awaited me with open arms.

When next I unshuttered my bloodshot baby blues, Thomas Carp occupied the fabled chair beneath the window. Pensively, he nursed a cheroot.

No seersucker or flak jacket adorned his flabby torso. Instead, he appeared rather huggable in a baggy charcoal outfit, crewneck sweater, rumpled slacks. When he realized I had returned to the world, he leaned forward and extended a diminutive golden carton toward my bed. First flashes relayed it was a coffin for something pretty small, say the embryo of an Asian child, or perhaps a couple dozen wrinkled ears. But then he reassured me. "I brought you some candy." And sure enough, a Whitman's Sampler landed beside the flowers and Pepsi-Cola cans on the tray table close by.

"What are you doing here?"

"Hey, I heard you caught a round." He settled back, gesturing apologetically. "So what are buddies for? I ran right over soon as I could. News travels fast in this town."

"I'll be okay." But I froze in panic. For I knew beyond the shadow of a doubt he was the devil, all slump-squashed and cozy in his malevolent bigness, contemplating me with a curiously amused expression. The devil, or my own personal golem ready to tackle society whole-hog, wreaking havoc on my behalf. A hired killer and a cute malicious cocksucker come to worship at the violence that seemed to dog my life. Oh that Thomas Carp, what irresponsible orderly had allowed *him* past our phalanx of protective nurses anyway?

"I heard it was the waitress's daughter, works down at the Chuck Wagon." His disarming tone sounded all out of place in my sterile refuge. "Quite a piece of ass that momma, don't you think?"

I studied him, my mouth wide open, one finger on the nurse call button.

"I've had my eye on her myself," he continued pleasantly. "Tits. Christ almighty. I'd love to plow those jugs until they split."

Carp sized me up, assessing his effect. Then he reached and pried open the Whitman's Sampler. His big blunt fingers at the lid functioned with almost the same style prurience they had displayed puttering at Shirley's crotch. Fastidiously, he peeled the silver wrapper off a liquid cherry, and placed it on his tongue.

"Bitch like that could make a guy go crazy." Dreamily, he cast his eyes out the venetianed window. "Tiny cunt, no doubt, but I'll bet she can eat all of it in a single gulp. What do you think, Michael? Is she an intimate friend of yours?"

"I feel weak, Tom. I really can't talk."

Carp hunched forward again, flashing a salacious adolescent grin that seemed to make his big ears suddenly poke out childishly from his head.

"I tried to pick her up a few times, but she always gave me lip. Sassy little thing, ain't she? But you and me, Mike ol' buddy, we could teach her a thing or two. When you're feeling better, how's about we grab the bitch and do her like in Nam? Drive her over to the sagebrush land and work out for a while, know what I mean? Teach her and the kid not to mess with us bloods."

No words could I summon for this lumpy, sniggering man who had me hog-tied in the devil's breathless ozone.

"See, I'm always thinking about you, Michael. We don't break bread often enough. Ought to have a beer together sometime, catch up on life. I miss hanging out with the boys, I get bored, there aren't a lot of jollies in this town, let alone fellow vets. Course, you're a loner, you like to keep quiet company—oh, believe me, that I understand and respect. But this sort of problem . . . well . . . obviously I could help you iron it out."

He resettled complacently, as amiable and conciliatory and as deadly as those dainty, thin green snakes in Nam that could pop you hellward with a single brittle nibble.

"If you're interested, Michael, I'd be glad to tear her legs apart and stuff an ax handle up her ass. I'll hold her down while you shit on her face."

No, no, I began to shake my head, wave a hand, no no no, please go away, become a bad dream again. My mouth opened, my jaws ached as I protested—no no no, please leave, dissolve, desist, don't hound me anymore. But if I uttered a sound at all, it was only an ineffectual gurgle, a squeak of protest feeble as a mouse.

"Well, hey, think it over, bro'. First, let the wounds heal. Nobody's in a hurry. It can wait. Right now, probably you're confused. And believe me, I understand. That's what friends are for."

"With friends like you . . ." I stammered, unable to complete the cliché.

"'Who needs enemies'?" He laughed. "Oh, come on, Mike. You and me go back a ways." He grinned appealingly. Then, in a quick, surprisingly lithe motion for such a big bad boy, he ambled erect and hovered above the bed.

"What happened?" he asked. "You boffed the momma and the daughter didn't like it? Tell me true, which one of them *really* shot you?"

"Why are you asking me these questions?"

Oddly secretive, he reached under his sweater and removed a calling card from the breast pocket of his striped Van Heusen. Almost reverently, he laid it on the table.

"I went to school, Mike. I got a piece of paper says I'm an expert. That's my card." And he smiled so wide his ears literally seemed to flap like buffoonish wings against his head. "I'm an investigator for the DA's office. I'm one of those Mickey Spillane guys who always solves the crime."

Words clotted in my throat. "What about real estate?" I asked stupidly.

"I keep my hand in." He paced over to the bathroom door. "It's all moonlighting, though—under-the-table stuff. Mostly I broker properties for gangsters or famous people who don't want their identities known up front. Moneybags type of dildos. They get things cheaper that way. I pocket all my finder's fees in cash."

I croaked, "I see."

"Well—" He slapped his palms against his thighs. "Think about it, Mike. All of it. That's my card on the table. There's a phone number, feel free to call."

Just when I thought he had left, Carp returned for an encore. That is, he peeked his head around the corner, and smiled in a way I remembered him occasionally smiling in Nam a split second before jerking the trigger.

"I just want to be your friend," he said. "Nobody around here understands what it was like in Nam."

After that, I heard the door close, although no footsteps subsided down the polished hallway. What is it they claim the devil leaves behind, a scent that tarries above the imprint of cloven hooves that leads enticingly toward the inferno? An odor of fire and brimstone, whiff of burning flesh—?

Carp would have none of that sentimental stuff. For after his departure all my nose discerned was a hint of after-shave in the air—Old Spice, perhaps, or maybe English Leather.

You better believe that then I nosedived into shut-eye, gratefully returning to the cradling arms of old Mr. Morpheus.

And there were bodies bodies everywhere, yet nary a drop of love to drink.

Just Barbara Cicarelli and Willie Pacheco, who floated above my head, the only angels left on earth to set the record straight.

6

STARTING OVER

J anine Tarr—exhausted, over-the-hill sex-pot—was determined to save her daughter, and so I was included in the process. Her thinking was never totally clear in my head (nor probably was it in hers), yet after awhile I simply let it pass. I figure human beings act for convoluted emotional reasons even Freud and Jung didn't know shit about. Somehow, sweet Janine, a flat-broke poorly educated floozy, whose only equity in life was her body and a disintegrating gas guzzler, had decided to exorcise the trauma from her daughter by including me back into their lives. The point? I guess to prove that our first ignoble meeting could be mollified by friendship, compassion, and getting to know each other better.

So when I landed on the street again, her invitation awaited me. I had lost twenty pounds, and walked quite gingerly, almost parting the way with my hands as if stroking aside invisible spider-webs. I felt the air itself might bruise me. No more fantasies of rape and subjugation, no sir. I wanted to curl up on a good warm hearth and have a master pat my head, stroke my shoulders, and fill my dish with Alpo twice a day. My chest ached constantly, and

I suffered sudden dizzy spells that always caught me off guard, and occasionally tumbled me to my knees in broad daylight, in the middle of a street.

Better believe it was a chastened Michael Smith who limped into their perky hovel again, adjusted himself cautiously at their poor yet bountiful table, unfolded a paper-towel napkin on his lap, and tentatively sipped from a spoonful of black-bean soup with grated egg across the top. Nobody knew quite what to say for openers. Cathie remained sullen, her frosty eyes lowered; Janine wore an old black jersey with the arms snipped off, and tarnished imitation gold hoop earrings. But her eyes shone with upbeat determination, as if droplets of starlight had been squeezed into them. A single pink candle burned. Background music was provided by a sentimental Julie London record from oh so long ago—before *my* time. Followed by a band that she attributed to Jackie Gleason—Jackie Gleason? Hokey nonsense from the fifties.

We made it through, however. Mostly, Janine kept us going. She was bound to make a positive exchange occur, and after a spell I guess I chuckled. And finally she elicited a muted response from Cathie. Toward the end of our tenterhooks meal, how do you figure this?—she asked me and Cathie to shake hands. As if our indecent little contretemps held no more weight than a playground scuffle . . . and we both regarded her in utter shock and dismay. Yet at her relentless urging, we complied. I stuck out my paw; Cathie ignored the gesture. But Janine insisted. She urged and teased, cajoled and begged, promising we'd all feel better. So finally, biting down hard on her lips, tears falling from her downcast eyes, Cathie placed a mitt in mine. Her body stiffened at the contact, but she managed not to pull away. We held it but half a blink, both trembling. And when it was over, Janine said, "There, now that wasn't so bad, was it?"

Wanting to do right, I smiled and self-consciously allowed as how it had been "No hill for a stepper."

It began as simplistically as that, then. We supped together, shook hands, blew out the candle even before the sun went down, washed and dried the dishes, and then I limped home and slept for twenty hours.

Janine Tarr, sorrowful little vixen, plying her fragile magic. How is it that one so small and ill trained for the job could envision the bright possibilities inherent in such a loaded situation?

But she did. That aging gamine forced it to hold water, applied massive doses of spit, and wound all three of us up tightly in rusted baling wire. I don't know from what reserves of generosity she called forth the forgiveness. It seemed she possessed an odd wisdom that transcended revenge, fear, or paranoia. I understood her theory was to heal Cathie by resurrecting all three of us. Yet once the play had begun, concern focused as much on me as it did on Cathie—else how could the experiment be successful?

Per usual, as winter petered out and spring began to happen, I frequented the café often. But I was a changed, a different person. Overnight my eyes had lost their berserk luster: on my head some hairs were turning gray. Though it was my chest that Cathie's shot had scrambled, my legs ached continually, and I proceeded forward cautiously, terrified of stumbling. A fire had been extinguished, I guess, leaving behind a weary person, always tired, who moved to uncertain lackluster rhythms. I held my job at the paper, though God knows how. Guess my camerawork remained professional; and I could write a decent, prosaic article. But for now I seemed to have bypassed my own generation, losing all interest in the rage that had fueled my dangerous alertness.

Of course, I had a deathly fear of Thomas Carp, and at first I maintained a constant vigil for his distant silhouette across parking lots, or in automobiles headed in the opposite direction. But he had evaporated again, he ran a different maze through our small town, and our patterns never crossed. So the devil makes a proposition, then melts into obscurity, biding his time patiently until the secret hour is come. Carp receded, dimmed out, dissolved, and I grew complacent from lack of contact. Didn't have it in me, anyway, to always be walking point through life, attending his sudden ambush. So finally I adopted a passive attitude toward that big ugly demon crouched at the distant frontiers of my world. If he chose to slit my throat one dark night, then let it happen—I was too weary for resistance. If a danger existed, so be it—I quit being alert, on edge, and discombobulated. Out of sight, out of mind, old buddy. No charges were filed in our case, no investigators poked into our drab lives. They had better things to do. So the essence of Carp dispersed again like tatters of a bad dream, and gradually the aftertaste diminished, leaving me to be lonely on my own enfeebled terms.

I forgot about the big schlub; I had other fish to fry.

Almost catatonic might be a way to describe my condition. Soft and flabby was my paper-thin chest that could even be punctured by small sticks tumbled in early April winds. In the café I read the papers: nothing much had changed out there. Beirut, Somoza, Love Canal; Greenhouse effect, Colombia drug connection, Seven Die in Cleveland Tenement Fire—Arson Suspected. In our own little River City, a twenty-four-year-old beat to death (with a rock) a forty-two-year-old fisherman on a local stream, then tried to drown the victim's girlfriend when she intervened. Apparently, one of them had infringed on the other's fishing terrritory and spooked two trout.

Yet these grisly accounts no longer fueled my passions. They entered my head with a kind of drone, and left no lasting impression. *So what? Who cares? Fuck you!* my tired brain reacted. "Janine, hotten up this coffee, would you, please?"

In quiet times between customers, most often during the predictable midafternoon lull, Janine crashed at my table to smoke a world-weary cigarette. "God," she usually muttered, "my poor old tootsies are killin' me." We might check our horoscopes together, and laugh a bit at the comic platitudes of newspaper astrology. She liked to browse the comic strips, reading them aloud if they seemed funny. Her favorites were "Hägar the Horrible" and "Peanuts" and "Blondie," "Dennis the Menace" and "Dick Tracy."

"Now this stuff is real literature," she teased. "Something a southern gal like me can get her teeth into."

Or she raised a sparkle in her eyes, and, like Lucy in the "Pea-nuts" strip, commanded:

"Okay, Smith—tell me your problems. 'The doctor is *in*.'"

Then our eyes might catch in a hesitant humorous way before they flicked apart; and it seemed as if all the danger was kind of draining off, leaving behind a curiously comfortable sensation.

Inevitably, whenever Janine had a break, the palaver would turn to Cathie. "The bane and torment of my existence," she groaned. "Land sakes that child!" she loved to mimic, a vibrant fire in her tone. "I swear she'll be the death of me."

"So what happened now?" I always asked.

And she loved to roll her melodramatic eyes toward heaven. "What didn't happen now is more like it. Geeze, Louise, I wish one of those damn brilliant scientists out there would invent a retroac-tive abortion!"

Poor Cathie. She had received three tickets for moving traffic violations over the past two years, and so Janine's insurance for that grandiose glob of a Chrysler had been canceled. And you couldn't legally drive a car in New Mexico without liability coverage.

And a twelfth-grade boy accosted Cathie in a hallway between classes; suddenly he grabbed her breasts so hard she screamed, and clobbered him. Startled, he had punched her back, and both of them were suspended for a week.

In a fit of pique over that degrading experience, Cathie had used a can of canary-yellow spray paint to coat the picture tube of their TV. In order to see "M*A*S*H" and "Three's Company" and "Barney Miller," Janine was forced to scrape off the paint with a razor blade.

When Janine insisted one evening that she do the godforsaken dishes, Cathie sauntered over to the sink and deliberately dropped all the plates, one by one, and all the glasses, one by one, onto the floor, where they shattered into a million pieces around her bare feet.

And when the mother embraced her trembling angry daughter, rocking to calm her down, Cathie screamed that she hated this lousy world and wanted to be "etherized" by an atomic bomb. She repeated that phrase a hundred times: "Etherized by an atomic bomb!"

Janine hied them together to a counselor provided gratis by the local welfare system. The young man was serious, portentous, very critical. Cathie folded her arms and dared the son of a bitch to suggest solutions. Until at last the educated shrink cried in exasperation: "You're wasting my precious time, both of you. Please get out of here!"

So where else could Janine turn for aid and absolution, except to a sterling, well-centered, and wisdom-pregnant creep like me?

Hastily, on a peaceful early-summer evening, I wrestled a mattress into the back of my pickup, and filled an apple-juice jar with cool water. Threw in marshmallows, bread and peanut butter, then all three of us drove out to the silent, lonely mesa. We parked in one of my favorite spots, an old sheepherder's campsite near the edge of the wild gorge. Mountains fifteen miles distant were capped by a vibrant layer of new snow. Around us the wide sagebrush plain gave an illusion of infinite tranquillity.

As the sun lowered quietly, we had a picnic on a rock outcropping of the narrow canyon wall, eight hundred feet above the meandering river. Swallows twittered, planing past us full of zest. Two buzzards circled serenely a hundred feet below the outpost, plying invisible thermals with haunting grace and silent dignity. A few bats frittered about as the sagebrush swelled with gleaming. We arranged ourselves on a slab of lichen-covered rock, and devoured peanut-butter sandwiches, sipped the water, marveled at the emptiness of the calm plateau.

Then stars appeared in the immense sky as day turned into gentle night.

Mother and daughter kept lighting cigarettes, smoking them down to the nub. Janine stubbed hers out on the rock, and dropped them into a crevasse. Cathie flicked hers over the edge of the cliff. I said, "You shouldn't do that. It might start a fire."

160

She gave no reply, but the next butt was flicked over the edge, just like all the others. I decided not to comment.

Later, by flashlight beams, we gathered old sage branches for a fire. And after the flames had died away to gleaming coals, we toasted marshmallows, letting them burn like little torches, then peeling off to eat the charred skins. Then we let them burn again.

"Oh I love 'em, I hate 'em." Janine's low voice complemented the mood of our moment. "I'm gonna get a stomachache. Somebody, please stop me before I eat again. I'll gain fifty pounds! My belly will get all swollen. I'll look like the Pillsbury Dough people."

We scarfed an entire bag of fifty, and reclined contentedly, our stomachs aching, farting a lot while the embers gleamed, and far away coyotes unlimbered their raucous cackling voices.

When bedtime arrived, Cathie arranged her sleeping bag and pillow in the Dodge cab, and curled up with the radio softly playing. I should have asked her to turn it off, for fear of killing the battery, but didn't have the heart. Janine and I settled fully clothed beneath a pile of blankets on the mattress in the bed, and quietly perused that delicate foam of nuclear fires—the stars. The Milky Way slanted like a band of fluorescent taffeta across the valley.

"Oh gosh," Janine whispered. "Wouldn't it be great to live out here, like this, forever? I could get a job counting stars. Four-fifty an hour. Time and a half for overtime. Tuesdays, Fridays, and Saturdays off. Wouldn't that be a kick in the head?"

A few minutes later she continued: "My daddy loved the stars. He made a telescope just to look at them. When I was a kid, he stood beside me, pointing things out. I'd squint my eyes, pretending to decipher sparks in the sky, but mostly I couldn't see a thing. Never let on to him, though. He'd say, 'See *that*?' And I'd say, 'Uh-huh, you bet.' I always replied like that when I was a kid, even if I didn't have the foggiest: 'Uh-huh, you bet. Uh-huh, you *bet*!'"

She giggled, remembering.

"He was a sweet man, my daddy. I mean, given the nature of the South, of course. He was racist, but kept it fairly low-key. I think underneath that stuff always made him uncomfortable."

Janine had a brother, one sister; David and Lou Ellen. When they were tykes, her dad assembled them all in a big bed with him and her mom. "He liked to reach out and touch us, make sure we were still breathing. He had a strange phobia that when we went to sleep we might stop breathing. Sometimes I feel that way now about Cathie. She conks out in front of the TV, and I get scared she's gonna die. I always have to check her out, make sure her chest is heaving, or that that big ol' vein in her throat is pumping."

She held silent for a while, until: "You know, I hate the TV, even if I watch it myself. But at least I watch an entire program every time. But the way she watches it—click, click, click, one channel after another. Nothing but bits and pieces. I think that's why nobody has an attention span anymore. We're all emotional cripples because we don't know what real emotions are. God, we change cars like we change TV programs. Don't like this lover?— get another. Job's too difficult?—quit and find a new one. Don't like this town?—move elsewere. Shit on a stick. It's things like TV that teach everybody not to know how to *concentrate*. I hate it."

But of a sudden she waxed apologetic. "Oh dear, listen to me up on a soapbox. What do I know? I barely finished high school. I'm sorry. Even a fish wouldn't get caught if it kept its mouth shut. Hey, look—" she cried, "a shooting star! Make a wish."

It blazed briefly, describing an arc, and dived down into the gorge.

Janine was on a roll. "When we took a journey in the car at night, I always had to sit up front beside my daddy and talk to keep him awake. He put his arm around me. How I loved that, mile after mile in the dark. Trips always excited me, and I never got sleepy, so that was my job. He really needed me. It was important that he needed me, and I could do that for him."

She paused, peeling away the strips of memory, peeping into the corners. I was held spellbound by her voice and the deep, soft obscurity around us.

"Sometimes we were off on a fishing trip. Until I reached puberty, he always took me with him. Then when I got my period, suddenly he wouldn't take me anymore. Women didn't do things like that. You know what they say? If a guy tastes your menstrual blood, he's yours forever. But how that man loved to fish. He couldn't sleep the night before, stayed up going over the gear in his tackle box, sorting hooks, oiling the reels. He got so excited. I remember he had a board he nailed the catfish on afterwards. And he stripped off the skins with a pair of pliers."

She halted and runkled around for a cigarette. Back against the cab, arms hugging her knees, she lit it and puffed away. Inside the cab, Cathie seemed asleep. I could hear the radio faintly playing.

"He was a fine carpenter," she said at length. "Always fixing stuff. That man had a passion for making things right. He cherished his tools and took wonderful care of them. Always sharpening and grinding and oiling them. When he did a job around the house, or made a cabinet or a chair, it was always something that would last forever. I reckon he had no tolerance for weaknesses in things."

She nodded slowly, seriously, and, etched in starlight, I saw her frown.

"We went to drive-in movies together, the whole family. We had an old, black—what was that car? I guess a Dodge. Did they build Dodges way back then? Wow, I'm gettin' old. Momma made picnics, because we were too poor to buy goodies at the concession stands. That was fun. We always had arguments, us kids, giggling and fighting and shoving. And Daddy always told us to hush up, be quiet, *shhh!* He couldn't hear the picture."

She giggled, cute and merry like a little girl. I envisioned her father and his family at the drive-in movies, and experienced a forlorn yearning for Janine, for the way things had been in childhood, long ago.

"Then Momma won a damn TV in a raffle," she said, "and after that we never attended the movies anymore. Daddy stayed home, and we all watched TV. It was a big novelty, and so we watched everything. But the experience was different. Daddy's favorite program was professional wrestling. He sat in front of the

TV nursing an ice-cold lemonade. All those stupid bruising hunks made him laugh."

She paused, then tacked on an epitaph: "But ain't it sad how new things so often obliterate stuff that was precious?"

Carefully, Janine ground out her cigarette against the side of the truck, and dropped the filter into one of the metal wells for a side rack. Then shuffled for another weed. I wanted to say "Stop, wait before you have another." And I experienced a faint pain inside, like the tickle of cancer aborning in *her*.

"Well, then he got sick," she noted quietly. "Emphysema at first. Then of course it became lung cancer. He smoked like a chimney all his life. Always said he had to stop, but never could. Just like me."

She twirled the cigarette adeptly in her stained fingers.

"Finally they admitted him to the hospital for good. Weeks passed before he died. And all the time he suffered I was thinking, boy if *this* don't make me quit smoking, nothing ever will."

The memory shut her up for a minute. But she needed to get out the rest, and started up again.

"So anyway, gee—that was a difficult experience. The man didn't go down easy. He had hallucinations. He would pitch and roll and flail so much that sometimes they tied him down. Once he was thrashing against the side of the bed, hurting himself, so I climbed on top of him and held him down with all my might. The nurses never came around, it seemed. I kept watch over him all the time."

A choke entered her throat, and she cleared it away.

"Toward the end, late one night, he got real lucid. He asked me to climb into bed with him and just hold on tight. So I kicked off my shoes and spent the entire night guarding him in my arms. A big old nurse came and arched her eyebrows, and said I couldn't do that, it was against regulations. But I told her in no uncertain terms to kiss my grits and she went away."

Again came the thickness in her throat, but she swallowed hard, determined to finish.

"Around dawn he woke up. And you know what he said to me?

He said, 'Baby, I'm sorry I never helped you start your junk collection.' He was always collecting things that he thought might be useful one day. So we had piles of junk all around the house. Anyway, he said that to me, and they were his final words. I wonder whatever he could have been thinking? My junk collection. Sometimes I have dreams of that. This big pile of useless crap gleaming in the moonlight outside my hovel. Broken dolls and paper flowers from Mexico, my stinking marriage and my unhappy daughter—Hey, whew, listen to *me*! Whoa, Nellie, git back into that barn! I'm starting to sound crazy as a betsybug."

Suddenly she scooted back under the blankets, plumped up her pillow, and folded her hands over her belly, quiet and pensive. I remained perfectly still, not moving a hair. One part of me was calm, enveloped in the night. Another part was uncomfortable, expecting something strange to happen.

You concentrate long enough on stars and they begin to float around in the sky, changing position, growing brighter or dimmer at will, like fireflies hopping and skipping about, weaving a kind of twinkling web that captures tension from the darkness.

"Thank you for bringing us here tonight," Janine said eventually. "This is very nice. I had hoped an experience like this might happen."

Her fingers searched until they found my hand and clasped it. And we lay pretty far apart, but holding hands, eyes searching the heavens—all that silent, frothy sizzling a billion miles away. That, and the muffled murmur of radio music, the words indistinguishable, old-fashioned melodies.

"Michael—?"

"What?"

"Do you think you could latch on to me without wanting to have sex with me?"

"I could try. Yes. Sure."

"I'd like you to hold me, then. I really need a hug."

So we scrooched self-consciously across the empty space between us and gingerly enveloped ourselves in each other's arms. Janine snuggled her head beneath my chin, settling against me like a cat, flowing into my juts and hollows until she touched me comfortably everywhere. I experienced her wonderful breasts full against my chest, and her thighs pressed to my groin, but what I feared might happen never did. My cock stayed limp and quiet.

A glow spread from holding that woman close. She had one arm bent across her chest, the fist tucked up underneath her chin. Her other hand pressed lightly between my shoulder blades.

"God," she said. "It's been a right long time since anybody held me."

Cool air breathed against my cheeks. Her fuzzy hair tickled my nose, making it itch, but I resisted the urge to scratch. Almost instantly, she drowsed. "I'm so damn tired, Michael." She shifted slightly, getting more comfortable. "I'm sorry."

"You don't have to be sorry."

Her body changed, growing lax and heavy, flushing and settling with sleep. She snored and snorted, gave funny jerky twitches, smacked her lips a little, and, later, sinking deeper, began to grind her teeth. An odor floated off her body, faintly of lipstick and sweat, perhaps deodorant, a residue of shampoo, cigarette smoke, and a tangy scent from the minty fresheners she sucked to kill the halitosis of cigarettes.

Poor child. I didn't move a muscle for the longest spell. Sounds fluttered in Janine's throat. The tiny cab music continued. Otherwise, the mesa had receded so completely we seemed to be drifting through black alabaster space.

Sleepily, Janine opened her eyes, reached into her mouth, and removed a bridge which held three of her side teeth. "I'm sorry," she mumbled, "but I can't sleep with my bridge. My mouth hurts if I leave it in, 'cause I grind my teeth. I know it makes me ugly, my cheek gets puckered, but I'm too pooped to worry about all that rigmarole."

"You're not ugly."

Instantly she was asleep again.

Finally, I could remain immobile no longer. With utmost care, I unpeeled my arms from around her, and considerately nudged her away. She was out cold, and relaxed gratefully exactly as I placed her. Then I unfolded quietly, sat up, and climbed out of the truck. I wanted to douse the radio before my battery died.

But both doors were locked, the windows entirely raised. I peered inside at the illuminated radio dial, at Cathie in her sleeping bag, half-scrunched into a fetal position, asleep. The pulled-out ashtray overflowed cigarette butts. It made me sad to look at her. I wondered somewhat anxiously: Was she still breathing?

I could have banged on the door and asked her to scotch the radio. But she looked too peaceful, so I let it ride, climbed back into the bed, and slipped beneath the blankets.

Janine's hand explored over and laid fingertips against my hip. That's all. Until at last I succumbed to drowsiness, and bid farewell to stars.

Come morning, Janine was curled into me like an embryo, knees drawn up against her boobs, both fists tucked firmly to her eyes. The hot sun beat down painfully, making my eyes raw. When I shifted stiffly, Janine woke up instantly, and for just a flicker she appeared fearful; then animation flooded her eyes, and she began a smile, but caught it. Panicked, she bolted upright and fumbled under the covers and pillows. She spoke in a mumble, lips pressed close together, protecting her clamped mouth.

"Where are they?" she garbled, frantically scrabbling among the blankets.

"Where are what?"

"My stupid teeth," she hissed out the guarded half of her chapped lips. "I ain't talking with you until I find those teeth. Move your ass!"

On her knees, she pitched off covers, shoving me aside. She wore her faded lumberjack shirt, tight dungarees, and had even slept in her moth-eaten sneakers, the little toe (on each foot) protruding: she called them her "Swiss-cheese tennies."

After I scrambled to a neutral corner, she exclaimed "Hah!" and pounced, recapturing her bridge. In an absurdly frenetic motion, she clapped it into her mouth.

"There." She rocked back on her heels, relieved. "Now at least I can talk without looking like an eighty-year-old hag."

"You look nice."

"Bull hockey!" She dived into her purse, capturing a pocket mirror, a powder compact, an eyeliner pencil, her cake cutter, and other assorted female accoutrements.

"You look cute," I said.

"*Cute!*" she exclaimed, totally abashed. "Holy mackerel, when was the last time somebody accused me of *that*! Goddam, Michael." Scanning herself in the mirror, she grimaced. "Dig me, will you? My eyes look like they're full of redeye gravy. I got jowls like a bulldog. And my dang hair is like I just stuck my fingers into a wall socket. I oughtta hire the Marines to repair this damage. Don't stare at me, I hate your chauvinist guts!"

She scrooched around, presenting her back while she labored with cosmetics to repair the ravages of sleep, to camouflage her perception of the ugly tides of time.

"Why don't you relax?" I protested. "There's nothing we can do about getting older."

"Oh yeah? Who says?" Busily, she applied powder, eyes intently gauging the effect in her pocket mirror. "Let me tell you something, Michael. That job I got ain't much of a job, but it's all I got right now, you understand? I *need* that job. And I need every extra little tip I can finagle from every macho asshole patronizes the joint, otherwise Cathie and me don't eat. Who pays our rent—God? And long as I still got my figure, and I wear the right kind of clothes to show it off, and my face looks halfway desirable, we can get by. So don't you tell *me* to start lookin' old."

"Do you dye your hair?"

"I don't 'dye' it, idiot—that's tacky. I enhance it a little. Didn't your momma ever school you in the proper lingo?"

"Why do you enhance it?"

"Because it's a smidgen gray, asshole. Wow, Michael, sometimes your head is a rock."

"It might look sexy, streaks of gray."

"Like a starlet looks enticing with a wart on her nose."

She halted the repair job, glancing back over one shoulder at me.

"Maybe *you* know, and certainly *I* know," she explained carefully, "that snow on the roof don't mean there ain't a fire down below. But that isn't society's vision. So I thank the Lord for Miss Clairol, I really do."

And back to work she galloped.

"How old are you?"

"I'm thirty-nine," she snapped angrily. "Thirty-nine and holding, holding everything I can." And snorted. "Holding everything *back* that I can."

"You're lying. You're older than that."

She quit dabbing mascara on her lashes, letting her arm drop to rest on her thigh. And squinted off into the distance, over the mountains. Shoulders sagged, her spirit took flight, and for just a moment she plumb gave up. Why prolong the inevitable?

"You sure know how to knife a girl, boy. They teach you that in Vietnam?"

"I'm sorry. I was just asking questions."

"Well, you sure ask some pretty dumb questions. Where were you raised, in a barn?"

"I'm only teasing," I said defensively, sorry I had ever brought it up.

"Teasing, my eye."

Then she faced me, kneeling among the bedclothes. Blotches were gone from her cheeks, tiny threads of broken blood vessels had been erased, blackhead pores no longer showed on her nose. She'd even plucked a couple of obstreperous mustache hairs that had sprouted since her last attack of Nair. Her eyelashes jumped out darkly, accenting her small, odd, slanted eyes; they seemed definitely sexier. She contemplated me as she began another cigarette. The sun rose higher, burning through clear, unencumbered air. Horned larks flitted about the sage. The earth was warm and silent.

"Oh hell, you're right, it's all phony," she sighed. "All a great big put-on. Hey, even my tits aren't real." She touched them self-consciously, glancing down wistfully, then away.

"You should see the stretch marks, Michael. Sometimes when a girl bears children, it sure takes a toll on her assets. You know, after Buddy came along, I didn't have much left in the way of jugs. Empty bags against my chest."

"You never mention Buddy much."

"Well, I guess not. Maybe it's too painful."

"Painful, why?"

"Oh, he died when he was just a little boy."

"In an accident?"

"No, he had leukemia."

"I'm sorry."

"Me too. I cherished that kid. It was like everything good you could put into a child, he had it. He was my delight; he was my buffer against Jack, against all the storms. I never wanted another baby with Jack, but when Buddy passed away, well, that's how come I consented to Cathie. I needed another friend in life."

She tossed her head, eyes red rimmed as if about to cry. "But hey, we were talking about tits," she said almost fiercely. "Let's not get off the track."

"What about them?"

"Well, it was Jack who suggested the implants. Said it would make me beautiful again. Promised he'd love me a whole lot more in my old knockers. He craved the way I'd been when we got married. And frankly, I missed it too."

Fleetingly, she touched her bosom again.

"In high school, I had beautiful breasts. They made Momma jealous. She wouldn't let me wear tight sweaters. She bought me too-tight bras to make me flat. But in the girl's room at school I'd always unhitch myself, let 'em romp a bit. I felt ashamed at the boys' wolf whistles and dirty comments, but they made me proud, too. I'm not sure how to explain it."

With the butt of an old weed she lit a new one. Then ragged her hair unmercifully with the 'Fro comb.

"So how did Jack react?"

"How do you think? It didn't make an iota of difference. I hated him anyway. You don't hold a marriage together with big tits. But they made me feel good. Who cares what anybody thought? It was nice to have the old boobs back. Plus now I'm downright grateful for the operation. Like I said, it ain't easy for a girl of limited capacity like myself to turn a decent buck in the cold cruel world."

Gently, I scraped a knuckle across her powdered cheek.

"I think you look marvelous."

"Yeah. Everybody in this country thinks everybody else looks marvelous. Billy Crystal doing Fernando whosit on 'Saturday Night Live.' We all slink around in sexy clothes, wearing Halloween masks, pretending so hard to be what we ain't that we lose track of what we are."

"What are you?"

She cocked her head. "You getting serious, Michael? Is this becoming heartfelt?"

"No. I just asked."

She squinted, considering a flip answer, then decided to take me seriously, and Bic'd another cigarette. I wondered about the score down in her lungs.

"I guess I'm a regular, pretty small person. Not too smart, but maybe with some natural instinct about things. I haven't done so hot by my life, but I reckon I'm a survivor. Ambition doesn't turn me on. I just want to make it from day to day, take care of Cathie, pay the rent, buy the groceries. And I wouldn't mind a bit of fun on the weekends. I like to dance. And I got no hankering to die alone—"

Cathie banged open a door, flopped out angrily, and landed on the ground, trailed by billows of cigarette smoke.

"Jesus Christ, you guys: the radio's broken!"

"It's not broken," I corrected, "the battery's dead. You ran it down last night."

"Well, shit!" She kicked a tire. "What a stupid truck. Do you have any toilet paper?"

"I forgot the toilet paper."

"Jeez, what a brilliant move."

And she wandered off into the sage to pee.

Janine tipped back her head, facing the cruel blue sky. "Oh Lord, gimme the strength to deal with another day." Then she broke into happy, raspy song:

Drop-kick me, Jesus, through the goalposts of life!

Next weekend we camped overnight in the gorge. Natty Bumppo and his two stalwart pathfinders! I carrried a pack loaded with all the necessities of wilderness existence: Spam, corned-beef hash, potatoes, eggs, bacon, beer, blackberry brandy. Heading down on the trail, Janine was bundled in a knitted cap, her brother David's old Army jacket, faded dungarees with purple warm-up socks tugged over them up to the knees, and her Swiss-cheese sneakers. In front of us marched Cathie, an escapee from a low-budget Japanese horror film. Fluorescent red sneakers, ugly baggy khaki trousers, a grungy yellow sweater eight sizes too large, and a torn black raincoat pinched together by safety pins. Another safety pin served as an earring in her left ear. The coup de grace was scraggly hair that seemed to have been chopped by a dull lawn mower. She clicked on her Walkman and diddy-bopped downhill to the shrieks of who knew what outrageous rock-and-rollers: Frank Zappa? Devo? Sid Vicious and the Sex Pistols?

The BLM had built picnic and sleeping cabanas and cement barbecue grills along the river. The wide Rio Grande dashed energetically between numerous boulders clogging the white water. The campsites snuggled among tall ponderosa pines, and thickets of dwarf oak and Apache plume. The camper shelf was about fifty yards wide, bordered on one side by the river, on the other by massive boulder fields rising eight hundred feet to the rim. Arsenic springs burbled past our location. We had the area to ourselves.

Cathie could care less about fishing. "I don't like killing things," she grumbled. "That's all anybody does anymore, is kill things. I think it's gross. Yuck."

I was wearing an argumentative cap. "Well, you eat meat, don't you?" But Janine sidled between us, placed her hands on my shoulders, spun me around, and propelled me toward the river. When we reached the shore, she demanded I rig an extra rod, and said, "Learn me how to fly-fish."

And that was a cuckoo afternoon. Cathie pouted on a rock, sucking on cigarettes and Diet Coke, snapping her fingers to sadomasochistic tapes, while I demonstrated fly techniques to her mom. "Janine was clumsy"?—a bald understatement. Yet that feisty woman ached to do it right: no person ever tried harder than Janine.

"This is the first time I held a rod since Daddy cut me off when I got my monthlies." She smiled. "So you better give me some slack, Smith. And if I catch you smirking, you're dead."

She observed me intently, then tried to imitate my moves, failing every time. Snagged hooks in her leg warmers, her butt, her sweater, her frizzy hair, yet refused to capitulate. Frowned, instead, jutting her lower jaw bulldog fashion, and tried and tried again.

Toward evening, though, she plunked onto a boulder in tears. "God, Michael, this is *hard*!"

"Rome wasn't built in a day."

"I should hope not. This'll take me years!"

"Hey, nobody says you have to. It's not a big thing."

Her face went squinty and mean. "It's a big thing to me, soldier. In fact, it's the most exciting time I've had in twenty years."

And she hauled her aching frame erect, pumped to cast again, and caught the fly high in a pine behind her.

I deserted her, then, cursing me, cursing the rod, cursing the Rio Grande, cursing her uncoordinated, male-chauvinist-inspired inbred female ineptitude. Downstream in the waning light I landed a gourmet supper. The river was low and clear, and in the foamy backwaters and shallow riffles I struck a few big rainbows that jumped and shook off their hooks instantly. But smaller browns I easily played to shore and slipped in my damp burlap sack. We wrapped them in tinfoil, along with potatoes. And ate hearty, guzzling beer, then broke out the sickening marshmallows. Blackberry brandy went down nice and warm as the air chilled. We gossiped about school, rock and roll, the Chuck Wagon scene. Abruptly, Cathie flicked a last butt into the dying fire, and without a word scraped off to bed. Leaving Janine and me alone again, contemplating embers, while wind soughed uneasily in the pines.

Her voice a vessel of weariness, Janine said, "Last week some turkey, one of her so-called 'friends,' offered Cathie fifty bucks to fuck him."

"I'm sorry."

"Me too." She squashed out a cigarette beneath her sneaker. "Frankly, Michael, I've sort of given up on men. After the divorce, I tried to date different guys. You know, couple of drinks, go dancing, have a good time without signing on the line. Just have *fun*. But nobody let me do it. They always wanted my pussy in return. And if you lie down with them just because you're horny, forget it—good-bye American pie. Jealousy, machismo, ownership trips—whee! Finally I couldn't deal anymore and bagged the letches, not worth the trouble."

Janine picked up a twig and flipped it in the fire.

"You should know something about me and Cathie." She chose her words carefully. "Though it might not seem so on the surface, given all her hostility, we love each other dearly. I love her like I love my own life. And it breaks my heart to watch her eating all that mung. Maybe she's difficult, and maybe she insults me a lot. But you know what? Sometimes I truly admire her, all her guts, all the *fighting* she does. I mean she's no dummy, that kid; Cathie's smart. And I happen to feel that mostly she's fighting against all the right things. Can you understand that?"

"Sure."

"Nobody has the courtesy to just let her be," Janine said unhappily. "Nobody likes her. They're always accusing, bitching, mocking the way she dresses. Nobody *listens* to Cathie. I guess her and me, we're pretty kindred. Heck, I sure grew up feeling like a redheaded stepchild. Still feel that way, you want to know the truth."

"What's a 'redheaded stepchild'?"

"Outcast. The kid nobody cottons to."

I fitted another log on the fire, then warmed my hands over the revitalized flames. Janine loved a captive audience, and wallowed in the treat.

"All her life Cathie's been a cantankerous, unpleasant kid. Always challenged authority. If she did something bad, she always stood right up to you and took her licking, never cried. That used to drive Jack bananas. He'd really lay into her with the belt, trying to make her cry. She never did. She bounced right up, and laughed, and said, 'That didn't hurt.' So Jack lit into her twice as hard, trying to break her spirit, but he never could. More times than I care to disremember I wanted to murder that son of a bitch after he had whipped her. Wanted to kill my*self* for being the coward that let it happen."

An owl hooted somewhere, up on the cliffs.

"Cathie and me, Michael, we ain't sissies."

"Nobody said you were."

"We ain't doing all that hot, either. Even before you came along."

"Not many people are."

"Sometimes when I'm comforting her angry body in my arms, I think my heart will break. And I wonder: Oh golly, how will I ever atone for all that crap I let happen to her growing up? How will I ever make amends for sticking to that monster as long as I did? How will I ever do enough penance for being so frightened and helpless that I couldn't stop the outrage?"

Janine clasped her hands under her chin, almost as if in prayer. The mascara she'd lathered on after our fishing expedition had wet streaks through it.

I said, "Atone? How can any of us atone for anything? How can I atone for Nam? How can I atone for hurting you? How can anybody atone for anything? What's done is done. You're beating a dead dog."

We listened to the pines; through swaying branches danced the glitter of stars. Below us, the noisy river rushed toward the Gulf of Mexico, a thousand miles away. Despite more logs on the fire, it was growing colder. She fetched her sleeping bag, and wrapped it around her waist and legs. In the dim glow she resembled a half-pint leprechaun, a sweet bumpkin from some nostalgic fifties netherworld where bad things never happened.

I poked at the embers. In the night sky tatters of moon-etched cloud now obscured half the stars, causing the tall pines to loom broodingly over our campsite. Janine coughed. It seemed almost as if she was choking for a minute. She jammed a fist against her mouth during the spasm. When it finally died and left her gasping, she fumbled in her wrinkled pack for another Kool.

"That's great," I said. "Why don't you have two, they're small."

Calmly, she placed it between her lips. "What do you care? It's my life."

Her tone warned me off in no uncertain terms. She'd had it with people telling her what to do: no more, never again.

A stiffer wind arose and the night became downright chilly.

Standing, Janine stretched and poked a cigarette butt toward the fire. "Well, Michael, me boyo, I reckon it's time to rest these weary bones."

We wriggled into respective sleeping bags side by side near the fire, in a space where our view commanded clear sailing to the stars. And passed the brandy bottle back and forth until it was empty. Janine caught the hiccups, pinched her nose and held her breath, and giggled. I lay still cupping my groin, and I wanted the woman beside me. But the fantasy was different from other dreams I'd had of screwing her. Mostly, I wished to be gentle and considerate, and protective, loving her sweetly and with all my heart, flooding both our bodies with a compassionate release.

I woke up once that night, an echo of Cathie's nightmare screams in my head. Propped up on one elbow, Janine was wide awake, eyes fixed on my face as if they'd been calculating me for quite a while.

176

"It's all right," she said. "This happens a lot. She's okay."

Then she bent over and kissed me. A real kiss. I dared not move, or react. Her soft lips touched mine in a lax surrender, making me almost giddy. Her tongue tip traced the outline of my mouth, just once, before she pulled away.

For the most part, Cathie pretended I didn't exist. Or, to be more exact, she had an odd way of acknowledging my presence, rarely speaking to me directly, but rather addressing me, to my face, through her mother: "Is *he* gonna stay for dinner, Mom?" And: "It's getting late, do you figure Mr. War Hero is ever gonna split so I can get my beauty sleep?" Or: "Would it be too much to ask Godzilla, there, to loan us ten bucks until Friday?"

To that one her mom inevitably replied: "Take money from a *man*, darling? You must think old age and poverty have made me gaga." And she held firm, never asking a nickel from me, refusing alms when I offered. She explained:

"I never met a man yet, starting with Jack, who didn't give a buck but what he thought rights to my pussy or my humiliation were attached."

"Well," Cathie groaned, "I'm sick of cutting open the vacuum bags and pulling out all the gunk, and then taping them up again so we can use them some more!"

Then she might confront me, enraged at her mother, and gripe: "My daddy has a swimming pool! He has a Jacuzzi! We all slept on water beds!"

To which Janine scoffed: "Yeah, he's got the fanciest jail this side of paradise."

But as time passed, Cathie's epithets lost their sting. I guessed she felt more at ease, however obliquely she might show it. For sure it must have been puzzling to watch her mother cautiously take me on. Who knows what clashes they had about me when I was absent. Yet gradually Cathie's apprehension seemed to wane. And the insults became old hat, replaced, apparently, by a genuine curiosity about the process. On occasion I caught her sizing me up with almost womanly calculation—as a prospective lover for her mother? As a new parent for herself?

I succumbed entirely, playing by their rules, awaiting the denouement. Passive and at ease much of the time. Oh, I can't deny that once or twice I felt my maniac stir inside—as if a palpable odor from our initial night together had struck my nostrils—and I'd tense; then we three would be aware of it. Janine might catch her breath, touch her chest, complain of heartburn: and Cathie's eyes would narrow, remembering. Unspoken, but understood between us was if ever a next time happened, Cathie would fire more than once.

We became a distinctive troika, marching about the summer, and then the autumn landscape. Though snow already lay deep on the mountains, the valley still boasted bees and rotting apples, yellow cornstalks, a few late-blossoming hollyhocks, sweet peas, and fields of wild sunflowers. Janine loved to pluck roadside wildflowers as I rifled through her Rocky Mountain guidebook, failing repeatedly to make positive identifications. Cathie usually festered in the car, invisible behind one-way shades and green hair, the Walkman earphones plugged in firmly, complaining that she was bored to death. If I admonished her to "grow up and be human," she nailed me with a patented obscene wisecrack:

"Oh shut up, Michael, or I'll peel your face and shit in your body."

"My daughter," Janine wailed. "Mouth like a sewer."

But we had developed an ease together. Imperceptibly, over the weeks, we had merged into a unit and enjoyed each other's company. Janine was our guide. She orchestrated our tenuous togetherness; it was her work of art. Cathie and I tagged along, grateful for her iron hand on things, though neither of us understood her secret calculations, or her vision of the plot. More than once I thought: We're going to fall in love. Appraising the situation more realistically, I suspected that once Janine believed Cathie had been deprogrammed, she'd push me aside, the mission accomplished. No problem, however—I was grateful for any time together.

178

But just as I came to feel that perhaps the devil had extracted all his pounds of flesh, I felt it stirring inside again, the golem I once had been. Winter was coming on for sure. Out of the blue, one day, I experienced faint clicks of panic deep in my guts, twitches of megadeath and genocide, burning children, and mutilated bodies dangling in naked trees. And I developed a new fear of meeting Tom Carp, or maybe even bumping into Shirley. And I almost tiptoed through town like a nervous cat, ever alert and slightly jumpy, ready to scram at the farthest sighting of those disconcerting space cadets.

Occasionally, while maneuvering a Safeway shopping cart among groaning bins of bananas and pineapples, shopping for Cathie and Janine, I'd catch a blip out the corner of my eye, I'd sight a tortured ghost, or a deformed hobgoblin ducking around the corner or tumbling under a car or zipping into hiding behind a tree trunk. Burnt gamins limping on splintered stumps dived for cover the instant my eyes spotted them. And more than once, among the herbal soaps, perfumes, and organic shampoos at Rexall, I caught a whiff of a different odor, a tiny blast of rot that made me reach to my hip for a gun that wasn't there—

Then abruptly, one dark hour at home alone, I lost it altogether. Downing one Lite beer after another, I watched a detective film on Cinemax. It was typical of the fare that cable channel offered. Rated R, "shown only at night," inappropriate for children under seventeen. A psychopath made amends for his sexual inadequacy by knifing to death a passel of nubile women. On a whim, I taped the more graphic sequences on my VCR. The killer stalked a van in which a gigolo and his sexy blond girlfriend passionately debauched. As the music reached a crescendo, the psychopath yanked open the door and stabbed the man, while the naked wench leaped out and tried to flee. Her plump body joggled provocatively as she ran through the forest. But of course he chased her down. In the end she kneeled at the roots of a big tree, cheeks stained by tears. She pleaded for her life . . . but the killer would have none of it. Approached her coolly, grasped her hair, yanked back her head, and plunged his shiv into her ample belly. She screamed in close-up—then her slumping body went bloody at his feet.

And of course I was aroused.

Later in the film, four women mistakenly allowed the psycho into their apartment. He nailed the first tantalizing kimono-clad career girl—nailed her up against the wall with one quick punch of his blade into her succulent guts. Then marched the length of their apartment to where his next victim, a stacked black beauty, lathered her bouncing chest in the shower. Blatantly, the camera caressed her soapy terror as doom approached. I almost splattered my sick jism when he opened the opaque glass door and sent her wet body drainward in agonized convulsions.

Then he approached a third woman cowering in a corner, and perfunctorily cut her into bloody ribbons.

I rewound the videotape and played those scenes repeatedly, stroking myself, prolonging it into the wee small hours, agonizing at every minute of the sexual tease. Until finally, as the stiletto perforated that damp black bitch with humongous jugs, I let it fly with a savage cry—me and a hundred million other American males for whom such erotic crap was tailored.

Then I lay whimpering on the floor, afraid of myself again, thinking about Janine. Smoke from the fires of Nam circulated around my barren pad. Blood and gore all over the floor, and Dracula, just a little boy who went to war, lies curled in a fetal position, doomed to never escape. In today's newspaper one story told of a drunk on a highway overpass who dropped a cinder block onto a late-model Cadillac passing underneath, shattering the windshield and killing the driver, a chic upper-class woman escorting her daughter to private school. Another tale concerned a Nebraska farmer who refused to leave his bankrupt spread after the financiers foreclosed. Opted instead to open up his AR-15 at a hundred cops. It jammed, and the SWAT team blew him away. Page 3 featured a woman who left her apartment for cigarettes at 9:00 P.M., and woke up hospitalized thirteen days later, bruised, broken, battered, and unable to remember a thing.

180

Then into my wild place came a face, my old buddy Thomas Carp. In my hospital room, all shaggy and disarming smiles, handing me that gilded coffin of chocolate-covered cherries. He offered again to hold her down while I shat on her face, or shoved an ax handle up her rectum. I howled, and he flitted away.

Shortly after a cold and shivering dawn, a real visitor rapped on my apartment door. When I opened up, Janine stood on the threshold, spruced up and eager for work. On her puffy purple jacket snowflakes were melting. She held a potted aloe vera plant in her hands.

"My God, Michael. What happened?"

"I don't know. I guess I had a relapse."

She clacked into the apartment, setting the plant down on the TV. Then opened her arms, moved forward, and embraced me, tucking her head beneath my chin, and squeezing tightly against me her ample body.

"I'm sorry. I brought you a happy."

"What's a 'happy'?"

"Just a gift you give for no particular reason. Because you like someone. Because you feel good. That's what my daddy called them. He gave 'em to me all the time. Stopped at the dime store after work, or detoured by way of the flower shop and bought Mom a single stem of daisies. So I decided this place has been dour long enough. It needs a spot of greenery. And this plant does double duty—if you cut yourself, just break a leaf, rub on the juice, it heals."

"I should *eat* the thing."

She pushed away. "Jeepers, you look rotten, Michael. Didn't you go to sleep?"

"Not really. Not much sleep."

"Well, you need a hot bath, dummy." Janine shed her jacket, and busied herself in the bathroom, drawing hot water.

"It's snowing, did you know that?" she called. "Come on, I

ain't got all day, I'm a working gal, remember? Yuck, what a filthy tub! You could grow cotton in the rings!"

On her hands and knees she bent over the tub, sloshing it clean with a sponge, removing all the crud I never laundered. I slumped on the toilet, baffled by her cheerful energy, wondering: Did she have no *fear*? She made the porcelain sparkle, then flipped the plug knob, all red and breathless, and sat on the edge of the tub, crossed her legs, rustled out a cancer stick and lit it.

"Okay, Michael—off with those filthy rags. And while you're at it, tell me all your troubles."

She obviously felt so good that I wasn't about to let my mood sabotage her high. But I couldn't move fast enough, so she unbuttoned my shirt, squinting against smoke rising from the cigarette dangling at her painted lips. Her provocative cat eyes seemed overemphasized by mascara, her cheeks were too ruddy from rouge. Too much powder and liquid makeup base gave her skin a tawdry, pasty hue. Yet she shined brightly, as if stung into extra aliveness by the falling snow outside. Healthy and incorrigible, the opposite of myself. The shirt fell in wrinkles behind me. Janine set her weed on the sink rim and patted my cheek rather hard, a loving series of slaps that stung.

"Hey, come on, bro'—wake up! Don't be down in the dumps. Life's too perfect. I got the world by the tail, and it's a downhill pull. Stand up, now, and drop those dirty trousers."

I obeyed—what's the term?—putty in her hands. She unbuckled my pants, let them fall, and there I was exposed in my lanky and wasted nakedness to her merrily assessing eyes.

"Whew, look at you, you poor miserable dope." She laughed and pinched my tight stomach. "All skin and bones—don't you ever eat? Jeepers creepers, you're wasting away right before my eyes—you're turning into a skeleton."

And then, incredible as it seemed to me, she went to her knees and took me in her mouth. Only I stayed limp between her lips. It lolled however her tongue chose to wrangle, while steam enveloped us both, filling up the bathroom.

Janine pulled back, licked the tip for good measure, then gave it a sisterly kiss and whirled, cutting off the water just in time. Then she glanced up at me, something of a startled question in her smiling eyes: an apprehensive flush enhanced her cheeks.

"Okay, big boy—hop in." Gingerly, I lowered into the steaming water, and settled back with a sigh as her fingertips traced the hatchet marks of my scars. My left shoulder was compliments of Nam; I owed the hairless patches on my chest to Cathie's violent handiwork.

Without further ado, she started soaping. Splashed water onto my shoulders, then smoothed her sudsy palms around my neck and throat. Gently massaged my chest, surprised by how the scars flared lividly when warm water scraped them. I went limp. She administered as if to a baby, soaping up a washcloth and swabbing my ribs as if each one had been singled out for individual cleansing. Firmly but gently she scrubbed my armpits. When I bowed forward she scoured my back, and wrung hot water from her cloth against my neck: it soothed me into drowsiness. Finally, she dabbed behind my ears.

"Your hair is filthy, Michael. Don't you ever shampoo? It's full of bats and cooties and little wrigglers."

Insistently, she urged me back. I slumped into the water; my knees were raised. Janine set to work on my feet, scrubbing the toes, massaging the ankles. Then my shins and calves and knobby knees. And my thighs. And to my groin at last.

"Raise up a little, baby."

She lathered the penis and pubic hair, and soon I was hard, and her hand grasping me was no longer innocent, just easy and friendly sexual.

"For such a fucked-up human being, Miguel, you sure got a lovely prick."

Then she splashed off the soap and took me into her mouth again, for real.

I reclined in my nakedness, wondering: How could it lead to this bizarre moment? How could this tough and vulnerable little woman, hanging by the skin of her fingernails to survival, knowing all that she did about me, kneel over in such a manner and

183

perform fellatio? "A lovely prick" she had called it?

A foam fleck decorated one of her cheeks like a snowflake. Her breasts, crushed against the tub, swelled up toward her throat, stretching taut the jersey fabric of her dress. A belt gathered the dress in at her waist. She had a run in the left leg of her hose, near the knee. High-heeled slingbacks completed her as every lecher's dream, the sort of pornographic Kewpie doll for whom American onanism was invented.

She pulled off me once, licking it like a lollipop, then gazed at me sleepy lidded and contented, oozing bedroom vibes. "Mmm-mnh, lip-smacking *good!*"

Then she closed her eyes and eagerly gulped me in again. Her tongue rasped delicately as she lowered onto me as far as possible, taking it inch by inch into her throat. She checked a gag; her face flushed from the effort. Just barely she constricted her throat, in patterns of tiny squeezes. Through the slits of my almost-closed eyes I noticed that she had one hand shoved down between her belly and the panty hose, and was rubbing her crotch in a circular motion.

I gripped tightly her kinky hair and lifted her head—she gagged and quit rubbing herself. Inside her eyes the pupils seemed dilated. We confronted each other, amazed, then I pulled her in on top of me. "Ow . . . Michael . . . *don't!*" But she fumbled into the hot water anyway, and we began to kiss each other hard. She squirmed, accepting it after the shock. And this time we were in it together, no questions asked. Water sloshed all over us, drenching her dress entirely. I twisted her arms to the side and down, and with a scooping motion revolved her underneath me. She slipped underwater and came up sputtering, hair swept back against her skull so that she appeared almost bald; her lips sprayed hot drop-lets in my face.

Then her hands grabbed the sides of the tub to hold herself aloft. Wet folds of soaked jersey material molded against and de-fined her lovely contours. I shoved the dress up around her waist, dug a hole in the panty hose crotch, and spread-eagled her feet on either rim of the tub. Then worked myself in slowly between the raspy petals, through the chalky opening, into her body. Defiantly challenging each other, we began to fuck. "Cocksucker," she hissed, surprising me. "Motherfucker," she cried joyfully as water gurgled in waves against her with every pump I gave, with every pelvic thrust she tendered back.

Eventually, I spurred her over onto all fours in the steamy water, yanked back her head, drew down the panty hose, hooked my balls in the band and slingshot myself back inside. One of her hands explored back to rub herself again, and finally she shouted, "Okay, Michael, let it *go*, I'm *coming!*" And I let it go, believe me, like a bullet as she cried: "Oh you devil!" Together, we climaxed— then, incongruously, she burst into happy laughter.

"Shit! *What'll I wear to work?*"

It was then I said, "Hold your breath." And very calmly I pressed her down, until head and shoulders were underwater. She allowed the gesture without a fight. And during the beat I held her at my mercy, I felt an enormous strength enter my arms, and knew that I could drown her in a minute, break her neck if she struggled, or smash her head elliptical. And I held Janine underwater as I shriveled inside her, and all the power of death I had ever possessed laid siege to my heart—but it wasn't strong enough. Long before she needed air, I let loose and she surfaced. Still gripped her soggy hair in my fist while she breathed hard, calming down, dripping into the water.

Janine said, "Holy moly, Andy." And giggled.

I replied, "Some fuck."

"I guess *so*." She swiveled again, onto her back, and embraced me. We kissed gently while volumes of warm water lapped and eddied around us.

"Boy, I hardly expected *that*." She licked a drop off my nose.

"Me either."

"Are you okay? Why are you trembling—?"

"I'm all right. Just scared a little, maybe."

"Well—hey! I'm gonna be late for work," she suddenly exclaimed, grinning as bright as the sun.

"I'm sorry."

"You had better be, Mr. Golem." She laughed, then raised her happy face, filled my mouth with tongue, and squashed her tits against me.

"Oh Michael," she whispered urgently, "let's try real hard not to hurt each other."

And so our love affair began.

7

MAGIC MAKES THE HEART GROW FONDER

Looking back with all the grim advantages of fabled hindsight, it seems like a beautiful hallucination, that loving time I shared with Janine. I still don't understand her magic, nor what she saw in me, nor how she summoned the guts to give it a whirl with such a cripple. Had to know she was playing with fire, and that at any moment I might snap and suddenly end it with a blow as cruel as a gunshot ending a baby's life in Nam.

Perhaps she had an instinct about how things would turn out down the road, and I was the only savior possible. Only a refugee from hell could survive the calamity in store, and so deliberately she cultivated my love against the trauma of that rainy day. Call it ESP or psychic madness, whatever. Some people must have subconscious intimations of darkness, and so they fortify themselves well in advance against the holocaust.

Or maybe it's simply what all the critics, soothsayers, and prophets have always opined: love is blind and accidental, and seeks nurturance in the most unlikely places. "There is no formula to explain the heart." Lovers are drawn together by blood, by smell, by bodies, by primal aches and personalities nobody understands. Killers adore or despise their victims, interchangeably. Calm intellectuals on psychiatrists' couches perfectly rationalize their hang-ups, then howl like crazed apes when their ex-wives take another lover. And inside the rib cages of us all the horrors of war crouch, rattling the bony bars.

Janine Tarr cupped me in her hands and breathed on my naked body, as if to sustain a tiny ember. She never showed an ounce of fear. I responded in no coherent way she could count on, though I was eager to break my chains. We wept and laughed and loved like banshees, and the closer we pushed it to the edge of mayhem, the less threatening it became. Which may sound purple, clichéd, childlike, and haphazard; yet a trust developed between us. All the more startling, I suppose, because that trust evolved from a contact that was overwhelmingly sexual, leading us to the silly barbaric notion that perhaps we could screw our way to immortality. Well, I'm sure that plenty of know-it-alls out there would have mocked us, claiming we deceived ourselves at every turn, and far from building strengths, only exacerbated our deepest weaknesses.

But if it was impossible—too bad. We embraced the possibilities; we accepted our stupefying giddiness, willing to be fools and rowdy dumbbells and ranting jerk-offs. We were determined that as long as it could last, nobody would kill the fun.

Janine favored nitwit epigrams, advertising logos, outrageously hackneyed slogans that defined the mysteries of existence:

"You only go round once in life," was a favorite, "so you gotta grab for all the gusto you can get."

When I scoffed at her simplistic formula, she fired back a salvo of clichés:

"Hey, I want *my* pie in the sky *before* I die! Life is short, neither of us is getting any younger. In twenty years we'll both be hags. Who knows how long this sun will shine, so let's make *hay*, baby, while all the rays are golden!"

Indeed, who could ever know how long that sun would shine? So we embarked wholeheartedly on our adventure, the golem and the tattered floozy. In the flesh, my friends, in Cinemascope and

Panavision and Technicolor, we grabbed for all that gusto. Popped the tops, slurped the foam, threw caution to the tempests—!

Bewildered Cathie didn't know what had hit us. We'd spent weeks being tenuous and polite, cautious and considerate—then all of a sudden, *wham!* We tumbled through their hovel's door like a big pink intertangled snowball rolling downhill, and barely even paused for cursory greetings on our way to Janine's boudoir. "Hey you guys—!" Cathie cried, but the door banged shut, cutting off her protest. "Hotten up a TV dinner!" Janine called back over one shoulder as we scuffled toward her mattress half-undressed already, "we got business to attend to!"

And as we left our feet she already had my cock in her ice-cold hand, and I was ripping open her pink blouse, the buttons popping. By the time we landed on the bed I had her skirt hiked up, her hose yanked down, her legs up over my shoulders, and we crashed, gasping, enveloped in a confusion of sleeves and pant legs, linen, cotton, and nylon: seems like we never had the time or inclination to fully shed our clothes.

"Oh baby," she yawped, "don't move for a minute, let me *feel* you inside!"

We laughed. Then Cathie banged on the door.

"Are you morons all right in there?"

"Yes, we're okay," I said. My voice sounded terribly dazed.

"What about Mom?" she insisted, edgy and worried.

"Mom is in seventh heaven," Janine laughed. "It's okay, baby. We're both alive and happy!"

"So put the gun away," I joked.

"You sounded like a couple of alligators," she grumbled through the door.

"I feel like a lizard on a hot rock," Janine said sleepily.

"Did he hurt you?" Cathie asked, still not entirely convinced.

"Hurt me?" Janine landed a teasing haymaker against my cheek. "This little puppy dog? I had to go easy on him. I want to keep him around awhile, he's *good* to me."

"He's a jerk," she muttered, though without a strong conviction. "You better watch out."

"You better watch your mouth," Janine retorted happily. "Or I'm liable to feed you a knuckle sandwich."

"You and whose army?" we heard her toss backward as she retreated to the TV. "Eat shit, both of you!"

"What'll we do with your clothes?" Janine hollered.

"Use 'em as signal flags to land your boyfriend!" the foul-mouthed child replied.

Janine tossed back her head. "Cathie Lynn Tarr, you know you can't speak to your momma like that!"

"Oh yeah? Try and stop me," echoed from the other room. "Eat come, scum!"

Janine bounced up out of my clutching fingers, hopped to her closet, and stripped off shreds of maimed clothing. Grabbed a pair of red shorts from the laundry pile, hooked her bra together, jerked on a Rolling Stones T-shirt with the neck and sleeves scissored away, and then bent over, throwing her butt at me while runkling further in the topsy-turvy disaster, crying at last "*Ahah!*" She straightened with four boxing gloves cradled in her arms.

I helped her tie on a pair. At the ends of her skinny arms they seemed huge, almost bigger than her head. Then I opened the door, and out she marched, lower jaw jutted. She extended the other two gloves toward Cathie.

"All right, daughter, you asked for it. Let's go a couple rounds."

Gleefully, Cathie accepted the challenge. Proffered her hands so I could lace on the gloves. The two women faced each other, comically pawing the rug, hurling insults.

"I'm gonna punch your tits out backwards," Cathie threatened.

"Not before I slam your nose to the back of your brain."

"At least I *got* a brain," Cathie countered. "I'm not dumb enough to plank a maniac."

"Leave Michael out of this," she snapped quickly, "or I'll punch your teeth to Timbuktu and back."

"Try it, Momma, and I'll make you take a flying douche at a rolling doughnut!"

They pushed back furniture, clearing a space for sparring. "You be the ref, Michael." Janine lunged forward, landing a spastic blow against her daughter's nose. Surprised, Cathie plopped down, but bounced up instantly, green eyes blazing. Her arms flailed and the gloves thudded off Janine, who deflected the flurry by going into a tuck-crouch. She allowed Cathie to pummel at will, the Janine Tarr rope-a-dope maneuver, and it worked. Inside a minute, Cathie had punched Janine all over the room, knocked her down three times, smashed a geranium plant pot, and in the process that energetic kid had exhausted herself.

Soon as Cathie stopped, purple faced and gasping, her momma counterattacked, spinning her daughter for a loop by raining awkward blows, none of which really connected. But Cathie was pooped and laughing so hard she fell down again. They both fell down, pawing each other with overstuffed mitts, hysterically guffawing.

"I'll kick your butt!" croaked Janine—*wham, thwock, pop!*

"I'll knock your face apart, you dildo brain!" her genteel daughter replied.

"Oh yeah? I'll break your kneecaps, you dicknose wanglet!"

Janine straddled Cathie, pounding her with ineffectual body punches, hooting uproariously. "You better say uncle, you dirty lunch bucket, or I'll nail your flabby ass to the ceiling!"

And then they were reduced to groveling weakly in a heap, mother and daughter, laughing and hugging, hiccuping and tearful, kissing each other happily, while I observed from the couch, amazed at the exhibition.

"I need a cigarette," Janine coughed, pushing onto her knees.

"Me too," Cathie blubbered.

They collapsed puffing in the armchair, on the coffee table, clothes and hair askew, sucking on their cancer sticks.

"Who won?" Cathie asked.

"Nobody," I said diplomatically.

"Bullshit," Janine said. "One of us always wins. *I* won."

"*You* won?" Cathie snorted incredulously. "I kicked your butt!"

"It was a draw," I insisted. "You were both magnificent."

Cathie cast a knowing glance at her mom, who tossed a similar expression back her way. And in unison they both rose and advanced toward me, banging together their gloves. For a second I failed to snap. Then, just in the nick of time, I flung up my arms and drew my legs into a protective ball. And as their gloves thudded, I thought: I may never again be so free, nor laugh so crazily, nor feel so buoyed by love for another human being, as at this moment of being bludgeoned into submission by Janine and Cathie Tarr.

Like a flash, winter was almost gone, spring was coming on. And all things seemed possible, new beginnings loomed, relief was just a swallow away.

Janine spoke freely of love and death, hate and ecstasy. No woman's outward appearance had ever fooled me more. She had guts enough for both of us, and strutted among the monsters, a cigarette dangling bawdily at her lips, booting them with stiletto heels. "Wake up, assholes, it's time to get *real!*" She insisted we all do battle, confront emotional hornets' nests, and revel in the scary revelations. "Full steam ahead," she proclaimed. "I only got one direction, forward!"

Of course, the world didn't change—it seethed around us. An American Jack the Ripper in Philadelphia was killing and mutilating (so far) sixteen women. And his or her counterparts—in Fort Worth and Seattle—were strangling prostitutes and runaway teenyboppers right and left. Closer to home, right within the confines of our bucolic River City, a man plugged himself, his better half, and his daughter in an argument about keys to the family car. I covered the story as best I could, tagging after the reporters for candid pics of the ordinary little family gone astray. Stern police officers directed the passing traffic of curious ghouls, all bundled up in bright ski caps and puffy goose-down jackets, seeking a clue or two, perhaps, to their own mortalities.

America, hog butcher to the world, meat market to the universe. Like I said, it was all happening out there, a great fever of maniacs, from Iran and Iraq to Mapleville, running amok as they sowed their relentless seeds of destruction. Yet it seems that I could deal with it better. I had an odd sort of balance, now, an anchor in the raging storm. And if I sat in the Chuck Wagon Café leafing through the daily diet of atrocities, I could never concentrate for long on that catalog of abominations. My eyes were always lifting to observe the antics of my sweet Janine.

She carried out the platters, poured the water, scraped up tips, dropped quarters in the jukebox for lazy customers, and stopped at every table, her coffeepot in hand, bantering with the customers like some nostalgic fifties pinup, trading cheerful innuendos with truckers and construction workers—her heart made of pure unadulterated gold. Then she sauntered over to hotten my coffee, a saucy sparkle in her eye, and asked, "Can I do you for anything, soldier?"

And I always wanted to demand a kiss, or give her breasts a fondle; or order her down on her knees beneath the table to give me a blitzkrieg suck!

I gathered up my odd little crew and drove them onto the sagebrush mesa. Summer rains had transformed the desolate plateau; sage- and rabbitbrush glowed vibrantly; snakeweed and asters bloomed yellow; sunflowers had sprouted from the sand. A lonely stock pond had been filled, and we sat beside the water, astonished by the tenacious life of desert places. Spadefoot toads had laid eggs that spawned a million tadpoles; Cathie hauled out dozens of wriggling critters with each scoop of her cupped-together hands. Other strange creatures had materialized in the pond: fairy shrimps and clam shrimps and ugly tiger salamanders. Above black water beetles and mosquito larvae flew darning needles and dragonflies, gnats, no-see-ums, and robber flies. Killdeer and sandpipers were attracted by the plentiful food supply; avocets and phalaropes landed at the stock pond, avidly hunting their suppers, completely unafraid of us if we rested quietly beside the water. They tripped right past our toes without a glance of consternation.

We collected feathers and tried to identify paw prints and bird tracks in the muck. Rabbit and coyote signs were easy; same with the dainty cloven-hoofed imprint of deer that came to drink. Prairie dogs and kangaroo rats and silky pocket mice were also evident among the claw prints of burrowing owls who came to eat them.

Some evenings ducks—cinnamon teal and mallards, goldeneye and bufflehead—set their wings and splashed down on the tiny evaporating pond while we munched egg-salad sandwiches. Bats hunted insects over the water; bats, and graceful nighthawks who soundlessly crisscrossed the bug-filled air, wide mouths open, scooping in their dinners. The ducks preened after eating, unperturbed by the nearby human "family," holding itself close together, almost always touching for security and reassurance, tickled pink by the wild denizens of that sparse environment.

Sometimes we played basketball on the eroded courts of a weedy downtown park. Cathie was head and shoulders above us both, even though she often exercised with a cigarette between her lips. For that affectation I heaped on ridicule. "Do you play on a team at school?" I asked. "Screw that," she replied, hitting a fadeaway jumper. "Coach says you have to stay in training. And I hate the way the girls play. And they won't let me play with the boys even though I'm better than all of them!"

Janine was hopeless with a basketball. When Cathie fired passes, they hit her in the nose, bounced off her temples, bent her fingers and broke fingernails. "*Ouch*, you bozos—take it *easy!*" If I lobbed the ball considerately, it still cracked off her knuckles, or passed right through her flailing arms and clobbered her in the belly: poor woman. "Growing up nobody ever let me play with balls," Janine wailed, flustered at her ineptitude. "Except stupid men, of course, in bed—the male chauvinist pigs." Yet she was determined to learn the game and build coordination.

And so we cavorted on warm July Saturdays or bright August Sunday mornings, two on one in the deserted park, Cathie the aggressive adolescent versus the klutzy Vietnam vet and the "quadriplegic hooker," as Janine occasionally derided herself. "The decrepits versus the beautiful kid," is how Cathie chose to word it. We played until exhausted. I kept feeding Janine, screaming at her to shoot, refusing to charge the basket myself; and again and again she shot and missed, tossed up airballs, or had it batted away by Cathie, who loved to rub in her momma's clumsiness and win every game going away in a walk.

We laughed a whole lot, and I even learned to take in stride their noisy antics and nonstop epithets: "Gimme that fucking ball!" "Kick him in the nuts if he tries to shoot!" "You're cheating, Michael, that's a foul!" "Shove it down her throat, Michael, make her look pregnant!" "Come on, you asswipe, I was open, *pass it to me!*" "Hey, Mom, you belong in a wheelchair!" And, triumphantly after Cathie made yet another basket: "Suck on *that*, you senile geeks!"

Janine and I embraced to the tune of Cathie's catcalls: "If you two perverts don't come up for air by the time I count to ten, I'm gonna call the vice squad and the search and rescue team!" We flipped her a bird, and exaggerated our passionate kissing. Cathie pried her hands between us. "Break it up! Ding ding! Go back to your separate corners!"

"Shut up," we countered, "we want more, we want better, we want fuller, deeper, harder, we want to diddle ourselves so blind and silly that nothing can sway our joyousness!"

"Fuck hard, come fast, die young!" my rollicking bitch exclaimed.

Dazedly, I drove around town, smelling on my fingers the elixir of Janine. It invaded my nostrils, swam in my brain like a drug of choice. Clung tenaciously to my rumpled clothes. So red and raw was my poor penis it might have been stuck into a cactus, or mailed cross-country in a noncrushproof box, or been stomped on by a hundred midgets wearing cleats. My heart began fibrillating again, so much so that one evening I told Janine, "I think I'm loving myself to death."

"Not me," she laughed back heartily, astraddle my hips on the living-room floor. "This is making me ten years younger. I figure I won't croak for another forty years." She leaned over, rubbing my nose in her perfumed mammaries. "And the way I'm gonna go then will be violent," she bragged. "I aim to be shot to death by a jealous wife at ninety!"

In the dim light my love languished beneath me juicy. Her ringlets splashed over the green pillow, and her eyelids fluttered. Naked, I knelt beside Janine. Brushed back the hair at her ears to view the candlelight gleam off her phony gypsy hoops and buttons of dime-store gold. She let smoke drift out, and lay passively, staring up at me. I ran my finger across her mouth, pushing in the plumpness just a tiny bit. Her tongue tip appeared and disappeared. She wore a filmy orange dress that eddied around her body like salmon smoke. I dandled across wisps of diaphanous material; she didn't move. I stroked the nylon sheen of her inner thighs up near the crotch.

"Do with me what you will," she murmured. "Love me like a shark. Drive your meat into me like a bayonet."

Her smallness scorched my throat. I leaned over her a little, removing the cigarette, stubbing it out in an ashtray by the bed. And contemplated my imperiled love arranged in complete surrender.

"What do you want to do to me, Michael? I'm all yours. I'm everything you ever dreamed about. I am your helpless girl."

Her absolutely fearless eyes floated like dream bullets toward my face. I had her in my power; I was meek beyond belief.

"I think I'll murder you," I said. "Strip off your hose and gag your mouth, tie your hands behind your back. Rip your dress to shreds, and bind your throat. I'm going to butt-fuck you for hours until your guts explode."

"Go ahead and do it. Do anything you want."

"I'm going to hurt you something terrible. You'll be sorry."

"That's okay by me. Don't be afraid."

I was afraid. Afraid that monsters would jump off my teeth

and sink like ice picks into her body. Afraid the theater might fall apart.

"Janine, I love you. I love you."

"Don't let that stop you, baby. Give me all the nastiness you've got."

All right. I gagged her mouth and ripped apart the flimsy dress. The gag strained too tightly at the corners of her mouth, and her lips were peeled back, white teeth exposed like a jeering skull. I rolled her over and tied her wrists together against the spine, rolled her back and wound a strip of dress material around her throat, pulling it almost too tight. Then I flipped her once more, raised her fanny, and said, "Stick a finger in your own ass. Sodomize yourself."

She contorted her bound hands a little, discovered a feasible position, and slipped in one finger, moved it in and out, increasing the tempo. She seemed like a helpless tidbit of erotic foam.

"Stop."

Her finger quit moving. I turned her over and pressed down her legs flanking her torso, making a chubby little frog.

"Open your eyes, Janine."

She obeyed; the tight gag drained blood from her cheeks. But her face seemed to swell with a sensual glow, a sparkle of energized wooziness flooded her eyes—it gave me chills, her puffy erotic gleaming.

"In Nam," I said, "we sometimes killed people just for fun. Just to experience the look on their faces before we pulled the trigger. Or because it was so easy to get revenge. Or because it was sexy to have that power. Or because we hated the whole goddam country. Or because the violence was so perverted it seemed like a natural way to get off, release the tension."

I pinched her nipples hard until her eyes glowered, then I backed off.

"We had the power. You could do anything and get away with it. You could slit a little girl's throat, then piss on her baby brother. You could burn down an entire village because you had indigestion."

I rolled her over again, jacked up her ass, shoved her head and chest flat against the mattress, reentered her with ease. She reached back between her legs and fingered my velvet balls. Each time I bumped her buttocks, flesh shivered forward in a way that drove me wild. I licked my finger and twisted it into her other hole; she stiffened, then relaxed, and squeezed my balls in warning. We held it a horny beat.

"This guy Thomas Carp that I knew. He put rats in a cage, doused them with gasoline, and set them on fire—the rest of us paid to watch. He claimed he had once done the same thing to a gook woman, drenched her hair in gasoline—"

She made a sound of protest, yet one hand continued stroking my balls, the other fiddled with herself. Came time to untie the gag, free her mouth to talk and breathe. "I'm gonna turn you over now and hump your tits, then stuff it down your throat."

"Don't leave me yet, Michael. I want to come like this."

"No no not yet!" I flipped her on her back again—"You bastard, Michael!"—and scrambled onto her chest, flung her arms above her head and pinned her wrists together, caressed and paddled her breasts, played over her ribs and underarms, and lackadaisically tightened strangling fingers around her throat.

"I was wounded in a helicopter when that guy Carp raped a North Vietnamese Army woman before shoving her out the door—"

"Stick it back in, schmuck. Do me while you're talking."

But instead I hunched forward, took myself in hand, and tapped it against her lips. She tried to lick and bite, but I would not let her. Kept her arms pinned above her head and whacked her softly with it like a rubber hose, gently drubbing her entire face. "Put it in my *mouth*," she snapped.

She arched and lunged to no avail. I weighed too much, I was too strong. She kneed my back, but had no leverage, it didn't hurt. Her face reddened from my stinging blows, blood rose from slits in her chapped lips—

"God dammit, you death freak, *stop it!*" Janine ordered. "Michael, you're hurting my wrists."

All right, why not?—I stopped and measured her eyes angrily confronting me.

"Now I want you to eat it," I said. "Eat it slow, eat it good." Her cheeks were flushed, almost bruised looking; veins bulged at her temples, vividly pulsing. Drops of blood looked sexy on her lips. The skin around her eyes had puffed slightly from my truncheon blows.

She licked a droplet off my cock, then swallowed it whole, grooving it against her tongue, cat eyes wide as she sucked. I gripped her hair, adjusting her head this way and that to the rhythm I wanted. Her eyes assumed a lax slurry vacant look, turning inward, sleepy and disconnected. Her spooky eyes grew glazed, erotic, hostile . . . sleazy, and murderous all at once.

God, I loved her groggy like that, heavy lidded and electric drowsy beneath me, cold-bloodedly blow-jobbing me toward ejaculation against a background of hovering gunships, black smoke from napalm rising, and a monkey gibberish of chattering slant-eyed people getting skewered on Yankee knives—

Then she pulled her mouth off—*pop!*—and pursed her lips, taunting me, teasing me, mocking my urgency, it seemed, ridiculing my helplessness.

"Talk to me some more, Michael. Tell me something *really* bad while I suck you off." And she pulled it in again, chewing on it like a baby at the breast, engulfing it in a vacuum of eager pressure that caused a cramp of purple pleasure in my nuts: I let go her wrists, grabbed both her ears, and defiled her face full force . . . until I howled and came.

Oh my, oh my. We both shivered in the chilly afterblasts. Dribbles of semen laid stripes against her cheeks. I lowered my head and kissed her, tasting jism. "Don't hurt me anymore," I begged, utterly exhausted, frightened by her power. "You bastard," I groaned, relieved.

"Bastard yourself, Michael Smith."

We continued kissing as the tension drained.

"Go down on me," she whispered, and all I could do was obey, sliding my lips painfully across her body.

"Lick me easy," she ordered. And then: "Slip in a finger, far as it can go."

I did as I was told, tonguing the pink folds and flaps and nub-
bins of her labia, while my finger probed her twat, pressing hard
against slippery muscles, ridges of slimy flesh. Her hands guided
my head, seeking her own perfection, until a ring of cartilage or
ligament or something inside clamped tightly against my finger,
which she rode up and down so energetically I thought sure my
finger would break. And at last she cried out, stiffened, actually
sobbed and turned blubbery with emotion, orgasm—arched and
rode the torrents with complete abandon . . . then wrenched away
from me, half turning over, and jerked up into a quivering fetal
position, awkwardly emitting noises . . . our killing fuck was over.

We glistened in the aftermath of rage. Lay shattered on the
mattress.

But not for long. A minute later Janine giggled. And said,
"Whew. *That* was a primo lay."

And when I managed to crawl up even with her face, she
touched a finger to my nose. And, grinning like a million-dollar
lottery winner, she crowed, "Not bad for a couple of old fuddy-
duddies, do you think?"

Fists pounding, Cathie laid siege to our door. "Time's up, you
two—the 'Columbo' rerun's about to start!"

Often it seemed that Janine and I were as undisciplined and as
helpless as children, and Cathie was our chaperone, trying to keep
it quasi-sane.

"Hey, you two deserve a break anyway. Christ, Mom, I'm
hungry!"

"Eat a peanut-butter sandwich."

"I eat peanut-butter sandwiches morning, noon, and night. I
want a *real* meal for a change. You're so busy goofing off I'm gonna
starve to death!"

"What?" Janine banged open the door and marched irately to
the kitchen in her tattered robe. "You don't have hands? You can't
light a burner, or read the directions on a can of raviolis?"

Cathie glared at me—but I discerned humor beneath the facade. "You two are nuts," she said. "I hate your putrid guts! I hope you both get paralyzed from overscrewing!"

"Oh God help me!" Janine clapped one hand to her mouth and doubled over, the other hand clasped at her crotch. And, humpbacked, knock-kneed, she clomped half across the living room. "My sex organs are paralyzed from overwork!"

She flopped against Cathie, seated in the old armchair, rolled off her daughter's knees, and landed upside down on the floor. Knees up, hands curled under her chin like a begging pup, eyes closed, she poked her tongue out derisively.

"Very funny, Mom." Cathie practiced her iciest rendition of catatonic boredom. "I think you've reverted to a three-year-old."

Janine scrambled spryly to her feet, flicked a grazing blow off her daughter's forehead, and sashayed back to the kitchen.

"You should be so lucky to reach my age this full of piss and vinegar!"

Scavenging through cupboards, she discovered rigatoni shells and Ragu spaghetti sauce, splashed water in a pot, twisted on burners, then fetched lettuce, avocados, tomatoes, and mushrooms from the fridge, and gaily sliced up a salad.

While her mom rattled in the background, Cathie assaulted me. "How could you like her, anyway? I hate how she always shaves her underarms and legs, paints her fingernails and toes, globs on the mascara, rouge, and lipstick. And wears those fuck-me shoes. It's like she *wants* all the lunch buckets in America to try and jump her bones."

"You don't shave your armpits or legs?"

"Heck no. I'm not gonna be a slave to some kind of male chauvinist fantasy. Paint all that glop on my face? Who needs it? Who wants to be like everybody else?"

"I think your mom is beautiful."

"That's 'cause you're brainwashed to be a dingbat." She opened a book and buried her nose, tossing her head to cut me off.

I tried a different tack. "What's that you're reading?"

"None of your business, Michael. I'm entitled to my privacy."

"Don't be rude to him," Janine interjected from the kitchen.

"I can be rude to anybody I want to, including you." She labored to maintain the scowl. "And especially *him.*"

Me. Michael P. Smith.

"You're just jealous," I said. "You can't stand the fact that your mom and I are having so much fun."

"It's like the wheelchair races at the Special Olympics, watching you two. The Geritol Gymnastics."

"Respect!" Janine hollered. "I don't get no respect, not even from my own daughter!" And her exuberant laughter tinkled about the house.

"That's 'cause you walk around all the time looking like a two-bit hooker in a Chinese whorehouse!"

Cathie then burrowed back sternly into her book, grinding her teeth to keep from smiling.

"Cathie Lynn Tarr," Janine shouted, "you take that back this instant!"

"I hate men!" Cathie clapped shut her book. "I hate the whole crummy dating game. All my friends are incredible douchebags. They just lie around and salivate over guys. Yuck. Gag me with a spoon. I like to read. But you listen to my friends you'd think it's a crime to read books. You're just supposed to be into TV, and guys, and cars. Chevy Corvettes. Trans Ams. *Cars.* Shit, I can't stand cars. All my friends practically fuck their cars. They drop dead, or go on a murder campaign, if their stupid cars get even one tiny scratch. I hate boys, I really do. Especially you, Mr. War Hero, with all your entire dumb brains in your stupid crotch. I think you're an ape-man and my mom is an ape-woman. You two geeks deserve each other."

While these verbal taunts unfolded, Janine crept up behind Cathie and placed her hands on the girl's shoulders. She was used to the outbursts, always handled them calmly.

"What I want to know," Janine said quietly, pinching the knots in Cathie's shoulders, "is what did we ever do to deserve you?"

Cathie slouched, pouted, but somehow didn't wriggle out of her mother's grasp.

"You balled Pop and were too chicken to get an abortion."

204

"That's not true." Janine pantomimed exasperation; she had heard this tune many times before.

"Fucking!" the child spat petulantly. "I've had it up to the gazot with fucking. That's all anybody thinks about nowadays. But it's just a straitjacket. I can't stand all the boy-girl garbage. The jealousy trips. I wish I could just be a tomboy again. Everybody's so nasty. Nobody wants to be gentle. I just want to be gentle."

"If you want gentleness, you have to put out a little from yourself," Janine said.

"I tried that already. It doesn't work. All those dildo noses want are hand jobs and blow-jobs. They want to get into my pants. Feel my big tits. I *hate* my big tits. Everybody thinks because I got big tits I must be the town pump or something. It gives me the creeps. Someday I'm gonna take a bread knife and cut them off. I'm so tired of geeks 'accidentally' bumping into me. You know what I'm gonna do someday? I'm just gonna screw them and make them love me, then drop them like a bad habit and listen to them howl. That's what I think of men."

"It's not all like that," Janine said. "Look at Michael and me."

"What about you?"

"We love each other."

"You love to fuck each other. Not the same thing."

"That's just a wonderful part of it," Janine replied. "Sex doesn't have to be lousy."

"He tried to rape you," Cathie said. "He smells like death to me. I'm glad I shot him."

I closed my eyes, ears ringing, cheeks burning.

"I'm glad you shot him too," Janine said. "Because look at what happened as a result." Evenly, she kneaded her daughter's shoulders.

It was silent in the room. My stomach, tied in knots, began to ache. But then the atmosphere changed again: they understood each other. Cathie's outrageous proclamations always caught me off guard, but not Janine. Her daughter's words lacked shocking power; they were part of a formula of communication.

In a small voice, Cathie said, "I wish I didn't have to grow up. I wish I never got a period. I wish I didn't have tits. It's all too grubby for me. Every time I come home from school I feel unclean. I'm sick of wolf whistles and obscene suggestions. I want to take a bath. I'm tired of fighting off lame assholes and nerds. Adolescence is such an insult."

"I know," Janine said.

"What would you like to do instead?" I asked. "I mean really?"

"Right now?"

"Sure, right now."

"Let's go to the park and shoot baskets under the stars."

"You serious? It's almost midnight."

"I'm *always* serious, Mr. War Hero. You know that."

Cathie and I went to the park; Janine stayed home to cook and clean, setting right her neglected domicile. It was my first time alone with Cathie. The gates were locked, so we parked the truck outside, scaled a fence, and crossed damp lawns to the Tarmac basketball courts. Lackadaisically, we warmed up, lofting the ball toward the basket, dribbling once or twice, nearly blind in dim starlight. Our squeaking sneakers sounded extra noisy.

We exercised for a while, easily adopting a rhythm, happy at the magic and unique cast of the night. Worked up a sweat in no time, and hardly spoke. Faintly, we could see our breathing steam. "Give it here . . . watch this . . . oops . . . your turn . . . try a hook . . ." Casually, we became locked in quiet empathy. No competition, but rather a free-flowing practice session. Sailing off our fingertips, the ball disappeared into a pitch-black background of trees and building outlines. We had to listen for the ball rattling basket chains. At other angles the ball rose against a slightly brighter sky toward the silhouette of backboard and basket. Our reflexes became in tune and kept the rhythm going.

Then she halted, ball balanced against one hip.

"Michael, do you really like my mom? Or are you just gonna get your rocks off, then rub her nose in shit and dump her."

206

"I love her."

"How much do you love her?"

"I don't know yet."

"How much between one and ten?"

"Oh, come on—that's silly."

She switched the ball onto her other hip. "I bet you screw her brains out for a year, then say bye-bye. It happens all the time."

"She is the most special person I've ever known."

"Well, I wish I could train her not to fall in love with bums. All my dad ever did was give her gas. She was so nice to him. All she asked for was a straight deal."

"I'll give her a straight deal."

"Oh yeah?" She shot the ball into the night: it never struck anything . . . and bounced far away, onto grass. "You're a maniac, you're a killer. I should of hit your heart when I shot you in the chest. You're like a monster, aren't you?"

Funny thing is, her voice sounded perfectly normal, curious, matter of fact. As if she had gotten used to my story a long time ago, and now found it rather boring.

"Yes," I said quietly. I felt extraordinarily tired, facing that sloppy ragamuffin with the enormous chip on her shoulder. "I guess I am a monster."

Tilting back my head, I gazed up at the stars, thinking that if ever fatigue could strike a person dead, I was primed for the demonstration.

Instead, Cathie's arms encircled my body. Her spiked hair settled against my neck, and she hugged me almost delicately, perhaps fearing I might break if she squeezed too hard.

"Don't get me wrong, Michael. I'm sorry. I love what you're doing for Mom." Her voice was free of its whiny, bitchy anger. It sounded almost compassionate and womanly.

"I don't think you're a monster," she added. "I'm only kidding."

I couldn't raise my arms to hug in return, afraid she'd spook and run. Cathie gave me a peck on the cheek, then stepped back and reassumed her teenage personality. Flapping her arms in exasperation, she groused:

"Hey, where did that ball go? At least you'd think they'd put up a floodlight or something! We pay taxes, don't we?"

"All the time growing up," said Janine, "all those years in that shit-can marriage, all the terrible put-downs and insults, all the days and decades of feeling trapped and suicidal, all that time I held on to one thing. I held on to the thought that I was special and deserved better, and that one day it would be different."

She paused, dreamily touching my knee with her toe.

"I always believed that I was prettier than other girls, other women," she murmured pensively. "I felt sorry for ugly people, I really did. Deep down in my secret soul I felt superior to them. Like I had been blessed with this lovely face, and a wonderfully sexy body, and I had a spirit that was tuned in to the world in so many positive and magic ways other people didn't even know about. And that gave me a million advantages over most folks on earth, plodding around in their dreary days, being unhappy and miserable all the time."

She smiled at me, licked her lips, spit out a tobacco flake.

"Of course, if you looked at me over all those years, I guess my attitude would have seemed right bizarre. Because from the outside looking in I must have seemed like such a basket case. God, I didn't have *any* of it in my real life. I was like a prisoner in a cage, helpless to break out and make my dreams come true. I was so scared, and I didn't have any of my own money, and I was afraid of losing Cathie. I didn't have any *power*. No power inside myself to change it. And so I wasted all those years."

She halted, thinking, looking sad for a moment.

"But deep inside myself I always knew," she continued. "I always knew that I was special and that one day, come hell or high water, I'd figure it out. For so many years I plotted my escape. Night after night I lay in bed beside a man I hated, and I couldn't sleep. I was traveling all around in this fantasy world that was so different. Jack and I hardly ever made love. I hated it when he approached me. I projected myself into another place when he was thumping at my body. He said I was frigid, but I didn't care. I knew all along I had a wonderful sexuality buried deep in my body, and that someday when I escaped from him I would have a hundred romantic lovers who would appreciate my beautiful passion, and I would experience all kinds of ecstasy."

She laughed, searching for another cigarette.

"I read books all the time, Michael. God, how I devoured books in my lonely cell of a mansion with all the TVs and washer-dryers and microwave ovens and fancy dining-room sets. I read books about Paris and Ceylon and the Costa Brava, and places in Latin America like Machu Picchu and the ruins at Tikal. I traveled all over the world in my head, visiting these places and having unbelievable adventures. I pictured myself as a torch singer during Carnival in Rio de Janeiro. And I rode wild horses across the pampas of Argentina with my handsome gaucho lover. And I sat down on a bench beside a French boy wearing a jaunty beret in the Jeu de Paume in Paris, and we gaped at a roomful of Monet water lilies, holding hands. And I knew it was all possible, see, because underneath I was this special favored person whose spirit could not be broken."

Then she lunged forward and encircled me with her arms, planting a kiss against my cheek.

"And here I am with you," she declared happily. "A living testament to dreams!"

Late that winter we began to discuss putting a life together: pooling our resources to make things easier. Renting a single house—more room for less money: togetherness was a dream we'd forge in practicality. I fantasized on how it might be—the lot of us joined and functioning as a unit. I pictured Cathie all cleaned up and wearing Bermuda shorts, lilac tennis shoes, a charcoal-green sweater, her hair Breck shampooed and silky; oh, I daydreamed in formerly impossible ways. Of a house with room enough for all, a lawn, a rash of hollyhocks, a productive garden. And when I bathed at night, Janine would perch saucily on the toilet lid perusing want ads, gushing about this kitten or that puppy up for adoption in the Pet Parade. Or she'd browse through *Cosmopolitans*, pricing white bikini bathing suits, or jeeringly reading aloud snatches of articles about Career Girl Impotence, Guaranteed New Herpes Diets, bedside astrology, and how to be chic, female, and earn a hundred grand a year.

Funny, how eagerly we demonsterize the world. Spring returns, roses bloom, trees sprout first golden leaves, clear blue skies are atwinkle with magpies and butterflies—all horror recedes. Almost casually, spring eludes the harsh tethers of winter, and children of darkness like ourselves emerge unscathed from the melting drifts. Mountains green up, rivers swell with roaring waters, kites bob and dive high above deserted football fields. Overcoats, mittens, and galoshes land in jumbled heaps at the bottoms of closets, and women's breasts are boldly revealed under the folds of skimpy T-shirts. Friendly weather tap-dances exuberantly across the dusty skin of a pretty valley; irrigation ditches gurgle again; lambs seek equilibrium on rickety legs; and tennis players strut their stuff.

Then explosions of chlorophyll leave everyone agog. And sprinklers unleash their fan-shaped rainbows above the awakening lawns of a secure and vibrant country.

In April, we mentioned getting married, stuck our tongues out at each other, then talked about it some more. Slovenly Cathie had never heard of anything so preposterous. "You klutzes get married," she said, "and you'll wreck it. It'll all fall apart. I'm the only grown-up in this house. And I'm not gonna spend the rest of my life changing your diapers!"

All the same, she often regarded us with amused alarm; never in her life had she witnessed such a breathtaking metamorphosis. And in her few unguarded moments, she openly worried about the heartbreak if it should crash.

"It's not going to crash," Janine said. "I've never felt so certain of anything in my life."

She stood behind me, kneading my shoulders, scooting her fingers lovingly through my long hair.

"All guys are assholes and liars," insolent Cathie taunted. "You just wait and see. He'll Find you, Feel you, Fuck you, and then Forget you ever existed."

It was her patter, her standard plaint, and we came to ignore it. Seemed her words had lost their steam. Probably she really didn't believe them anymore. But it would have destroyed her surly image to give them up.

"I'm not an asshole," I protested smugly, reaching back overhead to pat Janine. "I am God's gift to pulchritude. I am the only angel your mother ever met. I'm so beautiful and perfect I should be hanging in a museum."

"You should be hanging all right," the grumpy daughter said, her brow furrowed in a dark frown that couldn't entirely obliterate the smile struggling through.

"Leave him be," said Janine. "He's my angel. He's my teddy bear." She grazed lasciviously at my ear. "He's my knight in shining armor. He's my prince with a suitcase full of glass slippers. He's my darlin' devil; he's my Man of War—"

Cathie never stopped protesting. "Could you ditch that gushy stuff in front of me, Mom? I'm getting really bummed out by all your grubby kissy face. Do it in private, before you make me blow my lunch."

Janine laughed. "I want you to know how beautiful love can be. It's not all brutes and clodhoppers out there."

"Bullshit." How that kid loved to be *contrary.* "You just wait. Michael will steal your heart, and then he'll just throw it out the window of his car like an empty beer can."

Janine nuzzled the back of my neck, pressed her palms against my chest. "No he won't—will you, Michael? I've got *his* heart in my grubby little fists. He's helpless. He's desperately in love. Aren't you, baby?"

I nodded, and adored her ministrations. Her breath against my ear was coaxing up yet another hard-on.

"He's a prisoner of my love," Janine continued. "And he'll never get away. My body is wrapped around him like unbreakable chains. Isn't that right, Michael?" When I failed to answer right away, she whispered in my ear: "Say 'Yes, Janine.'"

"Yes, Janine."

"That's better. That's the way I like it."

Then she pulled away and went into a bump and grind, paraphrasing an old song:

> *Whatever Janine wants,*
> *Janine gets,*
> *And little man*
> *Little Janine*
> *Wants you!*
> *There's no exception to the rule,*
> *I'm irresistible, you fool—*

"Oh God!" Cathie let her rolling eyes express her distaste for Janine's goofy incantations. "I can't take it anymore. I'm going in town for cigarettes." And, throwing on a soiled Snoopy sweatshirt that said *J'aime New York*, she clattered noisily out the door . . . but was back in thirty seconds, spinning the keys around her index finger, dripping with caustic sarcasm:

"Guess what?—the battery is dead."

"Take my truck." I dug in my pocket for the keys.

"Oh no, Michael. I'm not gonna drive something you have to *shift*. Screw that. Just come on out here and gimme a boost. You got jumper cables, don't you?"

Sure. I always had jumper cables, a towrope, tools in a box under the pickup's seat. So I roused myself and headed for the door. But Janine lassoed me from behind and thrust her lips at my face.

"Oh darling, don't leave me!" she teased. "I can't live a minute without your big hunky body close to me."

"Jesus Christ, Mom, will you *drop* it?" Cathie fluttered impatiently. "I'm all outta cigarettes. It'll only take a minute. You can knock his socks off while I'm gone."

But still she clung to me while I staggered toward the door. "No no, don't leave me, Michael. I'll fall apart if you walk out that door. I'll collapse. I'll turn into a jabbering idiot. I won't be able to breathe—"

Cathie attacked, pushing her away from me, then shoved her

212

giggling across the room. Finally, defiantly, Cathie stood with her legs spread, one hand on her hip, the other hand pointing sternly toward the kitchen.

"Get back in that kitchen where you belong, Mother. Jesus, you're turning into a loony! I'm embarrassed to even be your daughter anymore!"

Janine stuck out her tongue, then pirouetted in a circle, her arms outstretched, a dishcloth dangling from one hand.

"She's gone cuckoo," Cathie said, stomping out the door. "See what you've done, Mr. War Hero? You fucked her right into senility. *Yuck!*"

"Bye-bye," I said to my delirious lover.

Janine unbuttoned her blouse and proffered one breast at me. "Remember me while you're gone!"

I blew her a kiss, then motored into the night, lined my truck up beside the Chrysler, and attached the jumper cables. Cathie flipped the ignition switch, and the car started immediately. I put away the cables, closed the respective hoods, and then when Cathie motioned to me, I headed for her window.

"Listen," she said seriously. "I don't care if it doesn't work out, I really don't. I don't hate you, Michael, I like you a lot. What you're doing for Mom is real special. Even if you're a heel and pull out tomorrow, it doesn't matter. You've given her something she never had before. And it's real beautiful. So even if you turn out to be like my dad, I don't care. I sure thank you for everything. She needed somebody like you. That's real important. She knows what to shoot for, you understand?"

"Yeah, I understand. Thanks." She seemed so terribly serious, her round child's face smeared with wild makeup, her hair so chopped and ugly, her eyes momentarily unguarded and decidedly beautiful.

Cathie kissed the tip of her finger and touched it to the end of my nose.

"Okay, soldier, that's enough of *that* drippy crap. Go back inside and make my momma happy. You need anything at the store? Rubbers? Vaseline? Geritol?"

"No, nothing." I kissed the tip of my own finger, touched it back to her nose. She squinched her face, rubbing it off her nose.

"Yuck." She returned to her old bantering form. "Don't do that to me. Who knows where those lips have been!"

Then she jammed it in reverse and peeled away, spun the wheel, and, with the steering apparatus screeching, she pulled out of the drive onto the dirt road and rattled off into the night.

I waved and watched the car recede a moment, then returned to the house, eager for Janine. And we were still making love two hours later when the telephone rang, and it was for me, the newspaper: there had been a car accident they wanted me to cover. Well, I came into my baby's mouth, kissed her lips and sucked her tongue, then hurriedly dressed and grabbed a can of beer on the way out, jumped into the truck and started it up.

Naked, Janine leaned into the window and kissed me goodbye. "I'll be here, Michael, just waiting for you with my legs wide open."

And we laughed, then I headed off down the road.

8

END OF THE WORLD

I had gone so often to these scenes. Approached them cautiously in Nam, nose wrinkled, sniffing for booby traps, alert to snipers in the trees. Approached with caution and a morbid curiosity in Southeast Asia, always slightly stunned by American firepower. At home—home on this more bucolic range—it had been a different thing now for a spell: traffic accidents and little murders. It had all seemed rather sanitized. Those five kids lined up on the living-room rug before the TV; a single bullet hole in that truck windshield at the trailer park.

I had covered them for my newspaper until they grew routine. Had even lost my sense of smell when it came down to slaughter.

Then the telephone rang, and I spoke into the mouthpiece while Janine happily lapped my dick. And I toodled off into the night, an aftermath of orgasm tingling behind my thighs, hoping enough film remained in my camera bag to satisfactorily record the event.

I parked down the road from the garish blinking lights and crackling car radios, the cluttered grouping of official vehicles, and a streamlined ambulance whose attendants waited around, smoking cigarettes. Casually, I debarked, slung the camera tote bag over one shoulder, and headed toward the activity. And suddenly got hit by the stench—not the normal aroma of car crashes or the almost odorless murders I had witnessed, where one or two small bullets had usually done the job.

No, the minute I descended and approached the glare of twirling lights, I smelled the scent of a deeper corruption, and instantly experienced a chill from Nam. Burnt flesh and explosives technology, melted rubber and flaming hair, and metal scorched by fiery chemicals and boiled blood—trademarks of a killing spree far out of hand.

That I still remained unaware as I neared the grisly scene astounds me now. There was a time when I would have understood instinctively, soon as the phone rang during our act of love. There was a time when I would have known exactly what was up, simply from the jangle of that instrument. Instead, loving Janine had fogged all my perceptions; it had lulled me into a wonderful sense of security. It had captured my heart so thoroughly that I had lost touch with the nightmare world.

Still businesslike, I runkled in my bag for the proper camera, the proper lenses, the proper flash attachment. I even checked my watch, wondering if I could complete the job in ten minutes of cursory shooting, and return to my lover's arms before half an hour had elapsed.

The usual cops and paramedics and tow-truck jockeys mingled about, along with a handful of the curious. The burnt carcass of a big car, windshield shattered, tilted on the shoulder. I halted at the first cop, a burly guy named Mel Apodaca, and asked, "Looks like a mess—what happened?" And I snapped the cover off my lens, prepared to shoot.

"Who the hell knows," he said in a shaken voice that seemed out of character. "It's the work of a real sicko."

Even then I didn't snap. Too busy, absorbed in meter readings. I was self-consciously eager to record the little tragedy for posterity and split, hightailing it home to my real, sexy world.

"Car turned over? Caught on fire?"

"This ain't an accident, Mike. Somebody killed her, him, it—whoever."

I glanced up then, back at the burnt car, the shattered windshield, the gutted interior, the garish streaks where flames had melted paint, the shards of smoking rubber where tires once existed. Then I searched between the legs of milling technicians and law officers until I spotted a lumpy blanket on the ground.

"Killed who?" I said. But by that time, at last, it was beginning to dawn on me.

"Body appears to be female," Mel said, "though frankly it's hard to tell. According to ID in the purse, it's a Cathie Tarr. Registration in the glove compartment wasn't burned. Claims the vehicle belongs to a Janine Tarr."

"That's her mother," I said automatically, and I lost entirely the sensation of clutching a camera in my hands.

"The waitress," a cop named Larry offered by way of identification. "Nice piece of ass." In the shock of the moment, nobody seemed to remember my connection: I was just another functionary at the scene. The callous patter always helped create a distance, keeping it all professional.

My eyes again probed through legs, past hip holsters and walkie-talkies, to that blanket-covered bump. And I began to move forward, Mel at my elbow.

"How do you know it's Cathie Tarr?" I asked.

"We don't. Getting a positive ID on this hunk of meat looks like a job for the boys at dental records."

We stopped at the blanket. Walkie-talkies and CBs crackled, but I could distinguish no words. My eyes had filmed over in a peculiar way, causing an underwater murky effect; the scene was populated by ghosts who loitered about in slow motion, a nightmare languidness come to life. Cottonwoods towered overhead; the Pueblo River gurgled nearby; soft lights shone from adobe dwellings across the water, peaceful and secure—the American Dream. "Hi, honey, I'm home—what's for dinner?" Or maybe she hadn't returned yet from Jazzercise.

"'Hunk of meat'?" I began to feel dizzy.

"Yeah," Mel said. "It ain't a very pretty sight. After it was over they poured gasoline on the body and lit it."

"After what was over?"

"Well, of course, it's hard to tell. We'll have to wait for the judgment of pathology. Ship the body down to the capital. It'll probably take those assholes a month to reach a conclusion."

"Who's 'they'?" I asked. "Who did this thing?"

Larry shrugged. "Your guess is as good as mine. Maybe a gang of sick fuckers. Probably at least more than one. But you never know. I never seen anything like it."

Theodore García—nobody ever called him Ted—an elder spokesman for the state cops, sidled over. "Hello, Mike. Camera all set to take graduation photos? Lempler beat you to it, he was hanging around the office when the call came in. But fire away for your rag, if you want. I haven't had my picture in for a month."

Kevin Longbull, a big, acne-scarred Pueblo cop I had never much liked, said, "Lift the blanket, give him an exclusive."

Larry stooped, reaching for a corner, but I said, "Stop."

"You don't want the picture?"

"They cut off the head before they lit the body," Mel said. "Who would do a thing like that?"

"There's a tire iron stuck up the rectum," Theodore announced, making sure I had all the pertinent details. "At least it appears to be up the rectum," he corrected. "Hard to tell, really. But that makes more sense to me."

"More sense" to him? I queried in a daze: "Makes 'more sense' than what?" But he ignored the question.

Draper, a paramedic, was a long-haired hippie type seriously concerned about humanity. His first name matched mine—Michael. His face was ashen, and he seemed very close to shock. But his voice stayed under control. Important to be a pro in every kind of emergency, always keep it together.

"There's a charred six-pack of soft drinks and the remains of a cigarette carton on the front seat." He was striving to link together details that would give it a shape, a rhyme, a reason. "The victim probably bought the stuff at 7-Eleven. Then maybe picked up a hitchhiker going home."

"Or had a flat tire," Larry said. "Then somebody who was not a particularly nice person stopped to help out."

Mel lit a cigarette, shaking out the match. "After that, things got a little kinky."

"Looks like maybe they shot the victim before they severed the head," another monotone postulated.

"Right between the eyes," Theodore confirmed.

"Somebody really wanted the victim to be dead."

The victim. Not a him, not a her. Just a chunk of charred meat. Sexless, without gender, mutilated beyond recognition. With a tire iron up the rectum.

"I barfed when we got here," Larry admitted, a trifle ashamed: macho cops don't flip their cookies. "I just went over to the river and gave all that burrito pie to the trout."

Theodore sort of sniggered. "Fuckin' creeps, fuckin' weirdos." But he spoke without much feeling. Such commentaries had long been mostly rote with his ilk.

"You okay, Michael?" Draper asked. "You don't look so hot." Concerned, he touched my shoulder.

"I don't understand what happened."

"You want my opinion?" Larry exhaled smoke into the blinking night. "'Course, this ain't official, not for publication. Most you'll be able to write is we suspect foul play."

"You 'suspect,'" I said, "but you're not really certain?"

"I figure the victim is a broad." Larry gestured vaguely at the blanket. "Probably the woman whose ID is in the purse, Cathie Tarr, sixteen years old. She goes to the 7-Eleven, buys a six-pack of Coke, carton of weeds. That big car has a flat, right over there. Another car comes along, sees she's in trouble, stops to lend a helping hand. Had to be more than one guy to do something like this. At least two, maybe more. They decide to have a little fun. No doubt drunk, or high on marijuana or cocaine. She tells them to fuck off, so it gets nasty, a little out of hand. My guess is a gangbang. Then they shoved that iron up her ass. Maybe that killed her before they even shot her or cut off the head. Then they doused the body in gasoline, doused the vehicle, lit them both. It was probably just a spontaneous thing."

He fell silent. Nobody else had anything to add. The last words echoed in my fuzzy brain: *It was probably just a spontaneous thing.*

Draper was the first to tip. He whispered, "You know her mother, don't you, Michael?" I think he used my full name to project compassion.

I nodded, couldn't move, or tear my eyes off the blanket. Repeatedly, Draper's hand brushed my shoulder. I gather he had begun to focus on my personal dismay, and was getting scared for me.

"I better see what's under that blanket," I said.

"It's not pretty."

"I didn't ask if it was pretty."

"Take it easy," Mel said. "None of us likes this at all."

"So lift the fucking blanket."

"Sure." Mel leaned down and raised a corner of the blanket. They were correct, nothing much to identify. A charred hunk, rigid black limbs, familiar stench. Headless. And mighty small. Seared and fused by heat. Could a thing like this be that wounded child who only a few hours ago had kissed her fingertip and touched it to my nose?

They lowered the blanket again.

"What happens now?" I asked, feeling hurried, not wanting to cry in front of these impervious men.

"We're waiting for Bolo Martínez and his investigators, Ernie and Bob. He was at his girlfriend's house, and she doesn't have a phone. So Kiko had to go and fetch him."

"Where is Carp?" I asked.

"Who?"

"Tom Carp. Isn't he an investigator?"

"Oh, that guy. The big son of a bitch. Hell no, we dropped him long ago."

"What about . . . who tells the mother?"

"Well, first we need a positive ID. You know all the rules about next of kin."

"It must be her," I said, starting to lose it. "It must be Cathie Tarr. That's their car." The tremble began in my calves, worked to my knees, started up my thighs, punched the groin and stomach: nausea.

"How do you know?" Theodore García asked. "Every time a crime like this happens, all of a sudden every Tom, Dick, and Harry on the block is an expert."

But I deigned no answer. I had about-faced already and started wandering back through the people at the scene. Time to blow this fantasy before I upchucked. Get away from that blanket and the burned auto, away from their voices and the garish blipping lights, away from the conjectures and the cigarette smoke and the aimless waiting around that makes horror so banal.

Draper followed, hands fluttering in apologetic concern off my shoulders. I hardly even knew the guy. Our acquaintanceship depended on jovial occasions like these. Rarely had spoken. Did our jobs. He had gotten miffed a few times when my picture taking struck him as too blunt and obtrusive on the anguish of survivors. But his anger had always been controlled, understanding, patient. A pro tries to make it as easy as possible for everyone involved.

I arrived at the truck, bellied over the front fender, and cupped my face. I could tell Draper was close by, his weight leaned against the metal somewhere, but he had quit touching me.

"You knew the girl, Michael?"

I didn't nod or anything, but he understood the answer.

"I'm sorry."

Neither of us moved. My nausea receded; the dizziness subsided. But my body had never experienced what remained behind. The soul melts, leaving caverns of emptiness. The golem, without his rage or any other sensation; a dry shell powdered by lingering dust. And the faint taste of Thomas Carp on my lips.

"I guess I should tell her mother before the cops get there."

Draper waited. What you do is let them babble, say anything, get it out. No way to expiate the circumstances. There is no rational explanation. Logical feelings are irrelevant.

"I don't know how to do that," I added.

Came now a weariness impossible to imagine. A fatigue that

said I shall not move from this place, no more, never again. I am becoming stone.

"I don't think I can do it," I said. "But I have to, don't I? Before the cops."

He was there, paralyzed.

"I'm in love with her mom," I explained.

No response. Background noises, crackling radios.

"She'll hate me forever," I said. "How could you love anybody after they bring you this news?"

"She won't hate you," Draper said gently.

"You don't know. I hate myself."

And then he placed an arm around my shoulders. Lightly, and left it for a while. Background noises continued; busywork, waiting, awed and bored. More than anything in my life, I did not want to tell Janine. Nobody could carry out such an impossible task.

"Do you want me to come with you?" he asked.

"No. That would be inappropriate."

I stirred. His arm left my shoulders as I slithered alongside the truck, opened the door, and managed somehow to raise up into the driver's seat. And there I sat, hands clasping the wheel—familiar pose. Draper pushed shut the door for me. Through the windshield I made out gray figures lit by revolving cherry tops: night of the living dead. End of the world. Drab and commonplace.

When I switched on the key the engine exploded. My Novocained hands found the floor-shift lever knob, and finagled into reverse. I backed up and turned around as if I'd never driven a vehicle before. Pointed it in the opposite direction, and cautiously proceeded forward. The steering wheel had little connection to my brain, and the wheels seemed unattached, about to carry me off in all directions, into the ditch or a tree, or through a barbwire fence. Straining to keep it on the road, I crawled at ten miles an hour. For I no longer exercised control over the Dodge . . . or over anything, for that matter.

I tensed every muscle and nerve to guide the clumsy truck along. Hunched forward, head craned, I fought to stay on the road. Sweat poured off my forehead, accumulated beneath my

224

armpits, flooded my thighs and crotch. I feared every leaf and every passing tree limb that nicked the windshield, believing that such a fragile blow could knock my tonnage sideways into the river. I was terrified that every bump or pothole in the rough macadam would flip me over. I flinched a hundred times when shadows danced on the road like frenzied dervishes, or like kids with pulpy skulls for heads and bloody twigs for fingers—they darted across my path.

Bottom line, as the earth cracks open and molten shit suffocates all the magic: We are in this together. The ghastly flourishes intimidate us all.

Crazy. I was crazy as the truck inched on ahead. My knuckles went white on the steering wheel; my accelerator foot could barely press down. Unruly words assembled in neat rows so they could march across infinity to gouge out Janine's eyes, eliciting the broken wail of a widow burned by the fires of hell.

I had no courage for it. Sudden sleepiness creamed my eyes, almost couldn't keep the lids open. With but a mile to go before she wept, I was overcome by a virulent laziness that gripped my body in a drug-deep torpor. I stretched open my eyes, fighting to keep awake.

To off myself first was the only idea that made any sense. Stop the truck, fetch the Magnum from the glove compartment—but it wasn't there anymore. I had lost track of my guns, discarded them in the rubble of a closet floor—"What an imbecile!"

I stopped dead, middle of the road. I would discover their names, their homes, track them down, capture them for Janine. I didn't even know where Carp lived, though, did I? Tie them up with barbwire, and ferry them to Janine. Place a chair on the lawn for her to repose in, the Regal Queen of Vengeance. Then one by one I'd cut out their tongues and break their teeth, gouge out a single eye apiece, smash their kneecaps with a hammer, cut off their balls for her to eat, then present Janine with a can of gas and strike the match—

"Now you're talkin', Michael," Sicko said. "You see, your rap was always bullshit. Nail the motherfuckers up the ass—it's the only language they understand, the only way to seek recourse."

In a white hospital uniform splashed from head to toe by the blood of innocents, she danced across the road.

I started in motion again, only this time, as I let out the clutch, I began to cry. But I made it to her happy hovel, and doused the lights. Hadn't the strength to open a door, nor to rearrange my thoughts in order to say it correctly. How, in the name of all the hellacious garbage on earth, could I speak this thing "correctly"?

If I'd had a gun, when she appeared in that doorway I would have commenced blasting, would have mercifully snuffed us both.

Or rather, just Janine. Myself, first, I would have scoured the brambles for Thomas Carp, and exacted a terrible revenge.

The door opened: another patch of mellow light upon the earth of night, and the long-cast shadow of a woman.

"Is that you, Michael?"

Her cheery voice offered love and expectation. I said, "Yes it is," weird and formal.

"Well, why don't you get on in here, bro'? I fixed a meal fit for a king. Fried green onions and okra, and chicken liver stew, and biscuits and redeye gravy. And for dessert I'm gonna smear tapioca on my tits and make you lick it off."

"Be quiet, Janine."

"What?"

"Don't talk like that, baby. It's not proper."

"Huh?" Sprightly and sexy, she tiptoed out in bare feet. She wore a bra, a pair of shining panties. Awkwardly, she swung her arms to keep balanced, going "Oof!" and "Ouch!" whenever a pebble hurt. At the cab window she leaned in for a kiss, then stopped.

"Uh-oh. Looks like I caught you at the wrong moment. Was it bad? I'm sorry."

So instead she merely bussed my shoulder.

"Come on inside," she cooed, "and I'll love it all away."

"You can't love this one away." My lips were stuck together, all dried out. Terror squeezed my heart.

"Oh come on, you big bozo!" She opened the door. "Whatever Janine wants—"

"Cathie's dead."

"No." It issued instantly from her mouth. Had she suspected all along? Impossible—it caught her by surprise. Yet the moment I spoke, the entire evening's time sequence, Cathie's long absence, must have made total sense.

Janine wavered in her bra and panties, hand on the open door, her plump body highlighted by the cab's dim interior light.

"Yes," I said, "it's true." And I wanted to break down sobbing, anything to create a commotion and deflect me off this hook, avoiding the gory details—but now when I needed all that emotion, I hadn't any. Except that I almost hated Janine for being Cathie's mother, for making me deliver this thing, thus forever clotting me in her eyes.

"I don't understand, Michael. It was a car accident?"

"No. She was murdered."

"'Murdered'?" Janine's hand balanced awkwardly on the door handle. "How could she be murdered?" She let out a snort, half absurd laugh, half pained exclamation—incredulity. "She only went out for cigarettes, Michael. People don't get murdered just for buying a pack of *cigarettes*. Come on, sweetie, I'm stupid but I'm not—"

Then she uttered, "Oh," in a bizarre way, catching herself. And added, "I'm sorry, I didn't mean. Can't we go inside—? Brrr. It's cold out here."

She captured my hand and ushered me off the seat. Then, in a most painful silence, we headed for the house, arm in arm. I progressed slowly while Janine labored over the gravel. "Damn," she exclaimed in a tiny voice, "I should have put on slippers."

Inside, she pulled away and looked at me again. The strangest appraisal ever a human being gave another. Then flipped herself a cigarette, hands shaking, and lit it. I remained immobile, a visitor from another planet . . . an embarrassed Frankenstein . . . one of those stateside henchmen from the Pentagon who wandered the small towns of America during Nam, delivering telegrams to patriotic parents who had fueled the world's graveyards with their milk-fed offspring; they delivered flags at funerals.

"Why don't you sit down, Michael, and tell me about it?"

Then, as if to provide a good example, she settled herself on the edge of the couch, encircled by smoke, waiting for my revelations. Her face looked frozen and grotesque, squeezed oddly out of shape.

I chose a bench across the room, and hunched forward, focusing on her feet. Beside the couch lay tumbled boxing gloves. Johnny Carson prattled on the tube.

"I don't know how, Janine. I can't talk. I can't tell you this news."

She prompted helpfully: "You said Cathie's dead."

"Yes. There's not a positive ID. But it's your car, the Chrysler, they have her purse."

"Positive ID? What does that mean? Either it's Cathie or it isn't Cathie. Did you see her?"

Yes, I saw her all right.

"Well—?"

"The body was . . . hard to tell," I fumfered in exasperation. Why go through any more of this? She had the news.

"I'll leave you if you want," I said. "You don't ever have to see me again."

"*You* didn't do it, did you, Michael?"

"No . . . who knows . . ." I twisted my neck, casting desperately about the room.

"Where is she?" Janine asked. Her face had gone elliptical, rubbery; she strained to understand, keep herself together.

"I shouldn't have let her go in that car," I whimpered. "It was stalling out. I had to give her a boost before she left. I should have made her use the truck."

"Where is she *now*?" Janine asked. Her voice had a creepy, tormented calm.

"I don't know. The ambulance probably took it away."

It, again.

"How did she get killed?"

228

I shook my head: no, no, no. I couldn't tell her that.

"I said, 'How did she get killed?'" Janine leaned forward at a tougher incline. I thought in the next instant her drained pale cheeks might start to melt, like in a horror movie.

"They—I don't know. It wasn't nice," I stammered.

"'They'? Who's 'they'?"

"I don't know. It only happened awhile ago."

"What about my car?"

"They burned the car."

"Wow." Hands shaking, she fought to light a fresh cigarette from the butt of the old one, and blew the smoke out raspingly.

"Well, what am I supposed to do now?" she asked. "What are the procedures?" I couldn't stand her crazy control.

"I don't know. Really."

Her voice picked up a caustic edge. "You've been in this situation a lot. You take pictures. You know all the cops, the ambulance people." Then she halted, sucking smoke in furiously; her cat eyes gave me a numbing once-over. But I still couldn't tell if it was really sinking in.

"Did you take any pictures?"

"No."

"Why not? Isn't that your job?"

Hopelessly, I gazed in her direction: *here it comes. Now it starts to hit. In just a minute she goes berserk.*

"Well—" She stood up abruptly. "Thank God for small favors. I'm going to put something on, then let's go."

"Where?"

"I want to see her. I want to claim the body." She dashed off quickly to the bedroom. I remained in place.

"You can't," I said. "They won't let you. There isn't even a positive identification."

"Then I can *make* a positive identification," she called. Hangers clacked. What does a mother wear to the viewing of her daughter's mutilated corpse?

"No you can't, Janine."

"The hell I can't!" She had chosen a blue-checkered shirtwaist,

belted around the middle, and the black Chinese slippers she wore
for waiting on tables. The old pink sack of a purse wabbled off one
shoulder. "Now come on, Michael, let's get out of here."

I trailed her to the truck, Janine fumbling in her purse for another cigarette; things fell on the ground, but she didn't bother
picking them up. She had trouble lighting the weed as I steered us
toward the center of our little town. And how silently and stiffly we
sat in that dark Dodge, as far from each other as possible. Janine
smoked, leaning against the door, staring straight ahead, biting
her lower lip, gnawing on it nervously. And a great and permanent
loneliness seemed to expand within the cab.

Unusual late-night activity punctuated the scene at the court-
house/jail complex. A half dozen state police cars occupied the lot,
flanked by many town and county cruisers. Janine got out immediately, then waited for me to silence the engine, douse lights, lock
up carefully—prolong, procrastinate, prevaricate as long as possible. We started for the jail entrance. I had to step lively as she
advanced toward a confrontation that I dreaded.

Mel Apodaca was there; also the town cop, Larry, who thought
Janine a nice piece of ass. Theodore García worked the milling
ghouls, accompanied by his state sidekicks, Chuck Harrison and
Lonnie Thompson. Kevin Longbull from the Pueblo lurked about,
his pitted face disguised by smoke. The county sheriff, Eddie
Maestas, glanced up at our arrival. Beside him stood the district
attorney, James Kelter, and another fellow from that office, Henry
Gottlieb. Jack Lempler, the photographer who had "beat me to it,"
insinuated himself unobtrusively, camera clicking, still beating me
to it. And of course Bolo Martínez and his investigators, Ernie and
Bob, held more or less prominent sway.

All the big shots, trying to hatch a plan, when in walks the
cowardly Vietnam vet and his pint-sized compatriot, the outraged
momma of the murdered girl.

Some, but not all, heads turned. A studied casualness defined
the professionals; still just doing their jobs. And besides, who

wanted their eye to be caught first by Janine? Hell hath no fury, they say, like a mother made abruptly childless, with no war to make it viable, no pious official homilies to justify the loss.

Janine veered closer, afraid, she actually took my arm. "Which one do we talk to, Michael?"

"Eddie Maestas, maybe. Or the DA." Arm in arm, we wended through the crowd. Eddie spotted us coming, crouched to flee, then realized there was no escape, and swiveled back, alarm aplenty on his sagging features, bracing for the charge.

I introduced them. "Eddie, this is Janine Tarr. She's the mother."

"Hey, look—" He held up his big hands, callused and strong; one finger wore a class ring from high-school days. "Nobody's made a positive ID yet. We can't assume the identity of the victim."

"Who else can it be?" Janine blurted before I could speak on her behalf. "You got my car. You got my daughter's purse. Show me the body, I could tell by any article of clothing."

Eddie gave me a quizzical, save-me look, then deflected his attention back to Janine. "I don't think you understand, Mrs. uh . . ."

"Tarr. Janine Tarr."

"Mrs. Tarr." And then he collared me again. "Did you tell her the circumstances of, the, uh, deceased?"

"Not everything." Oh how I paled at what came next. In fact, I had revealed next to nothing.

"What circumstances?" Janine's voice rose to a high pitch, growing shrill. "What *happened* to my daughter?"

Eddie appealed to the DA, James Kelter. When bad trouble's afoot, the lackeys always defer to the boss. "Hey, Jimmy—this is Mrs. Tarr. She may be the mother of the alleged deceased."

Janine fired on Kelter immediately, her anger swelling; no more runaround. "Where's my daughter? I want to see the body. You want a positive ID? It seems I could give you that immediately."

"Uh, look—" Jimmy placed one hand on her shoulder, even as his other hand palmed Eddie's waist, including the three of them in a group. "Why don't we go down to my office where we can talk in private, Mrs. Tarr? This is a mess out here."

Janine turned on me. "Michael, what is going on? Why can't I see Cathie—?"

Kelter steered us forward. "Please, Mrs. Tarr. Let's just go down the hall—" This time he scooped her in behind Maestas, who was already on his way.

I asked, "What about me?"

Kelter's role was to be milk and honey, oil on troubled waters, the in-charge guy. "Why don't you remain here, Mike? Eddie and I can handle this."

Janine balked. "He's family. I want him there."

"Well sure, okay, if you wish, Mrs. Tarr. That's fine by me." Responding to his nod, I followed them down the hallway, into the DA's office. It was just another cubicle, fluorescently illuminated. A wide polished wooden desk, green Enduro carpeting, diplomas on the wall.

"Siddown, sit down." Kelter tapped the backs of two aluminum-frame chairs with orange plastic cushions. "Please."

"I don't want to sit down." Janine lodged herself at a gray metal bookcase full of musty legal tomes. The DA settled at his desk. Eddie leaned against a wall behind him. I wished to rest my weakened knees, but on Janine's behalf remained standing. Jimmy Kelter picked up the phone and punched a button, speaking to a person out front:

"Tom?—yeah, James. Listen. Get Nelson over here, okay? I'm going to have a conversation with Mrs. Tarr, and she might need something to calm her down, okay? Yeah, tell him on the double. And you might call Emergency, have 'em be ready just in case."

As he hung up, Janine asked, "Just in case of what?"

"It's merely a precaution, ma'am. Sometimes people go in shock, they lose it. If I'd known you were coming, I'd have had the doctor here already."

"I want to see my daughter." She was beginning to feel hideously trapped.

"I'm afraid that's impossible."

"Why?" Her uncomprehending eyes assailed me, Eddie, Kelter. "Why is that so impossible?"

"For starters, we can't be absolutely sure it's your daughter."

"*Why* can't you be sure it's her? Michael knows what she looks like—he was there. *I* know what she looks like, for God's sake. Just let me see her body."

"Mrs. Tarr, it's not that easy."

"Well you better start telling me *why* it's not that easy, dammit! Michael, do these assholes have a right to torment me like this? Is she dead or isn't she dead? Is it Cathie or isn't it? What happened to my daughter?"

Eddie took offense. "Look, Mrs. Tarr, let's watch the language—"

Jimmy Kelter came half out of his chair. "Eddie, bag it!" Then he composed himself, and addressed Janine again, eager to tranquilize emotions.

"Listen, Mrs. Tarr, it isn't my fault. Not anybody's fault. In a case like this, our hands are tied. Procedures have to be followed. The remains will go down to the capital, where they'll do an autopsy. They'll check out things like dental records, for example— and you can help us there."

Janine said, "What about her clothes? She was wearing that stupid Snoopy T-shirt. Just let me see her. I would know right away by the clothes—"

That created a silence. I inspected my feet, Eddie canvassed the ceiling, Jimmy Kelter observed his fingers spread against a green blotter.

"What *is* it?" Janine's pleading glance hopped from each of us to the other. "What are you people *talking* about? I'm her *mother.* I raised her from a *baby.* I've got a legal right to see the body. You *can't* deny me that."

I snapped, half sobbed, half yelled at her: "You don't *want* to see that body!"

That released it—tears streamed down my lover's cheeks. But just as Jimmy Kelter began to rise, Janine reached into her purse, removed the .38, and aimed it at his head.

"All right, you bastards. Enough shit. You take me to my daughter. You take me right now or I'll shoot all three of you!"

Kelter was young, say thirty-two, thirty-three. He dressed impeccably, with cuff links and a tie, though never a jacket. His shirts were ironed, his pants creased, his hair tastefully feathered at a local salon. He made a conciliatory gesture, then lifted the phone again and punched a button.

"Tom, did Nelson get here yet?"

Janine said, "Not me, I don't want any doctors, no thanks. Show me my daughter. Or show me her body. Or whatever's left of her body. That's my right, you fucking stupid lunch-bucket pigs."

Kelter cradled the phone. "Okay, Mrs. Tarr. You leave me no choice. First put down the gun. You want to see your daughter? Swell. Though let me explain our reticence. Apparently, Mike here didn't fill in all the details. Of course, I can't say that I blame him. Now, first of all, because of what happened to the deceased, we do not yet have a verified identity. The law says until we do we're supposed to keep our mouths shut. It was your car, and your daughter's purse we found with the ID—correct. So all evidence points to the fact that your child is dead. But there's a problem. Whoever assaulted the victim was a pretty ugly person, or persons. They probably raped her . . . or him. We know for certain they shoved an iron tire implement up the rectum. It also appears they shot the victim in the head. Then, and here's the real problem, they poured gasoline over the body and set it on fire. After that, or maybe before that, they chopped off the head. What's left is not nice to look at, without features, and of course there are no clothing tatters that might help. Now listen to me very carefully, please. Put away the pistol, Mrs. Tarr, and take a seat. We'll have a doctor—"

"Tell the doctor to go fuck himself." Janine held the gun in both hands, arms extended, the snout trained on smooth Jimmy Kelter's head. "Get yourself some tranquilizers, Mr. DA, and shove them up your ass. Now, where do they have Cathie? *I want to see that body!*"

234

"For crissakes, quit pointing that damn gun!" Eddie shouted.

"Shut up, Eddie, I'll handle this!" Kelter glared at the underling.

But Eddie had a short fuse. "She pulls a fucking gun on us, she insults an officer of the law, who the hell does she think she is? I'll throw the cunt in a cell to cool off, I don't care what happened to her daughter!"

Kelter yelled, "I'll throw *you* in jail, Eddie, if you don't shut up! Now bag it before you blow this scene!"

Then he lunged up toward Janine . . . but I stepped between them fast. And so Kelter put on the brakes.

"What are you, now, Smith—a hero? Vietnam went to your head, boy? *Step out of my way!*"

"Her daughter just got murdered," I cried. "Did your daughter just get murdered?"

Janine yelled, "I wish your daughter had her throat slit tonight, Mr. DA! I wish that had happened to you!"

"I don't *have* a daughter, Mrs. Tarr."

"Well, you deserve a dead one!"

Then Janine raised the gun over her head, pointed at the ceiling, and struggled to pull the trigger, double-action style. The gun wavered until finally the hammer clicked back, and she fired off a shot. The noise in such a small space had the impact of a grenade: the percussion seemed to blow my eardrums through my brain; and instantly the room was full of white smoke that seared my throat, and I dropped to the floor.

Kelter went down also; as did Eddie. Jimmy toppled over backward, in fact, and for a split second I thought Janine had plugged him. His shoulders hit the desk's front ledge, then the back of his head struck with an audible *clop!* and he slid sideways to the floor, rolled over, and gathered in a crouch.

Eddie dropped behind the desk, and I knew that when he rose up, his own gun would be unholstered and he would shoot to kill her. So in almost the same motion as that which had carried me down, I sprang up again, and as I lunged over the desk I met Eddie rising, pistol in hand. And in one of those weird split-second

235

gestures of salvation, I grabbed at his gun hand and actually got the piece, as perfectly as if I'd plucked a tail feather off a passing swallow.

Momentum carried me over the desk, however, and as I struck the sharp far corner I could feel a rib crack, and the pain clapped into my body like a bullet. I cried out, rolling off the desk, but scrambled quickly into a squat, clutching Eddie's .38 to my chest. When I looked up, Janine held the hot gun barrel to her nose, and her bug eyes stared at Jimmy in his frightened crouch. Eddie's eyes, nose, and fingertips were balanced on the desk edge like a Kilroy Was Here caricature . . . and the impact of Cathie's death on Janine had finally pierced their ivory domes.

"*Mrs. Tarr!*" Jimmy shouted.

"*You fuckers! You unholy fuckers! I shit on your bodies!*" Then she dropped the gun. It landed on her big toe, left foot, and later we discovered it broke the toe. "*You monsters!*" she screamed. "*I want Cathie! You give me my daughter! You give me whatever is left of her, you creeps, you fucking maniacs,* GIVE ME MY DEAD DAUGHTER!"

She collapsed to her knees on the rug, going all loose inside, all her muscles and resolve and courage erupting in a sudden flabbiness of dismay; her body almost disassembled right before our eyes, so much did it change in shape and tension.

"MURDERERS!" she wailed, keening over like a Muslim in a prayer-shaped heap. "MURDERERS!" was driven into the rug. Only the second time she said it, the word was drowned out by the door slamming open, revealing an impromptu SWAT team composed of Theodore García and Larry and Mel Apodaca, reacting to the gunshot.

"WE'RE OKAY!" I shouted.

"DON'T SHOOT!" Jimmy yelled.

But Theodore and Larry were jacked up and scared. I had Eddie's gun, the DA and the sheriff were on the floor, the room was pounding full of noise, smoke, and hysterics, and somehow, in all the confusion, I sensed they might pop a cap at Janine. So I swung up on Theodore, and his instinctive reaction was to defend himself. Hence, incredibly, another gunshot banged off, and it knocked me against the tin radiator, which rattled like hell coming apart at the seams. And I heard Kelter scream "STOP IT!" before, once again—oh bitter and familiar sensation—I blacked out . . . from the impact, from shock and fear, from desperation . . . and all the hope of my flimsy ages gone gushing down the drain again.

"Drop-kick me, Jesus, through the goal posts of life!" The ambulance attendant, my old friend Draper, nervously croaked those familiar words when I came to again—but a few moments later, I reckon. We were moving fast, in a blare of shrilly pumping sirens, official music of the American night. And all the apparatus, all the spaghetti heaps of technological miracles, was at work yet once again to prolong my hapless days, guaranteeing me that God-given right of all White Anglo-Saxon Protestants to a life expectancy of seventy-two years.

"Your heart stopped," Draper said. "Christ, we almost lost you."

"Why did you start it again?" I blubbered. "Whose bright idea—"

"Hush," said the female paramedic at my other elbow. She held a plastic oxygen cup over my nose, determined to prolong my life, whether I wanted it or not. "Don't talk, Michael, we're almost there." Her name, I recalled, was Meg. Meg somebody. Margaret in real life, I suppose. Just plain Meg, however, to those of us attached to the world by dripping IVs and other assorted implements that kept our arteries flowing.

"Janine!" I tried to rise, but was strapped down, hog-tied, and otherwise immobilized. "What about Janine? I want Janine!"

"It's your shoulder," Draper said. He clutched one of my hands. "You're gonna be all right."

"What did they do to Janine?"

"She's okay," Meg said, calm as a cucumber, cool as ivory. "She's already at the hospital. Now hush, don't try to talk."

I dropped back my head, too weary for further fuss, too tired to go berserk. They let you wander across the earth, perforated by slings and arrows, gut shot in your soul, then bind you helpless in your one important moment of rage, immobilized and impotent, powerless to smash your own bones and theirs into the bargain.

"Janine!" I cried, and Janine I needed in my arms. Janine I had failed, had lost through cowardice and indecision; Janine my love and lover; Janine, my sweet happy cunt, so rich in hope!

"Janine! God dammit, what have you done to Janine?"

Does it ever stop? No, it never stops. Visions of reality in the Doom Age: a chorus of moans from Nam. Mutilated corpses dangle from the branches of a million defoliated trees. Among them the charred hunk of a teenage girl whose big tits had launched a mini-Armageddon. I drifted about in a caldron of bloody thoughts, while they raced to save—and once again succeeded, the idiots!—my stupid life.

Details escape me now. Noise, bleeps, human exclamations, motors, doors slamming, orders given, my body jouncing onto a gurney, morphine, Darvon, or some other sopor derivative cooling out the fever of my pain. I went to sleep again, helpless to stem the altruistic ministration of that little band of do-gooders determined to keep me here on earth, whether I gave a damn or not. Technology reigns supreme. Artificial legs, artificial hands and arms, artificial hips, artificial shoulders and faces and teeth—and finally artificial hearts: bionic people. Only what do we *feel* with anymore?

In due course, of course, I regained consciousness, alone in a private room as peaceful and white as an egg. The ceiling comforted me while my shoulder mended. And by then of course it was too late. My lady had learned all the gory details, been bludgeoned half senseless by the Fourth Estate, and in no way could I lessen the blows.

Janine paid a visit shortly after my eyes opened. She leaned against the opposite wall like no creature I had ever loved. Pale and disheveled, eyes listless and red rimmed, no makeup, and clothes that hung shapeless on a body that seemed to have lost all its proud bearing, had caved into a permanent slump.

She fidgeted with her purse. Finally, my mouth so dry I could scarcely enunciate, I explained, "I thought they were going to shoot you."

"I know. They didn't. Not with bullets."

Then we waited, numb, burnt out, helpless. Eventually, she essayed a further remark:

"Thank you, Michael. I do appreciate the gesture."

"Are you okay?" Talk about banal and preposterous questions. Yet she nodded faintly.

"Oh sure, I'm okay."

I hesitated. Wanted a smile, a bit of tease, or something, but couldn't sort out stuff in my brain to make it happen.

"You look great."

Drably, she replied, "I don't much care how I look right now."

Stupidly, I nodded. "I can imagine."

"Do you need anything, Michael?"

No, nothing—what did she have in mind? An Almond Joy candy bar? Razor blades? *People* magazine with which to while away the hours? A Big Mac and a side order of fries, or perhaps a nine-piece box of Chicken McNuggets? All the necessities of life, eats without vitamins to make me fat and undernourished as well. *All our food is toxic.*

"Did they hurt you?" Apparently I had a knack for asking stilted questions.

Deadpan and weary, she said, "Only when I laughed."

Rote, monosyllabic questions and answers. The listless sounds we make when all meaning has been sucked from life.

"Did you find out about Cathie?"

"Yes." Her lips were bloodless. "They did it through dental records. Finally got their positive ID. I had it cremated. That seemed appropriate."

It, again.

I told her, "I don't know what to say. Any more words just seem grotesque."

"Then stay quiet. What's to say?"

All her sexiness was gone, all the flamboyance departed, all the energy dissolved. Flaccid, drab, and doleful, as animated as a potato. Like the stupefied survivor of a nuclear bomb.

"When I get out of here," I said, "maybe we can go to the mesa, scatter the ashes, do a little ceremony."

"Yes."

But that ended our conversation for a while. Seems I could not even lift my hand and gesture her forward, attempting solace in each other's arms. For solace seemed irrelevant when absolutely nothing could be done.

"What day is this?" I asked.

"It's tomorrow." The answer made little sense, yet I was not compelled to demand a more precise definition.

I said, "I love you, Janine."

Her expression didn't change. "Love," she murmured absent-mindedly. Nothing else. Silence bloomed in the room, enough silence to drown us both.

"Did they make an arrest?" I finally managed to croak.

Her wounded head moved slightly from side to side. "No. Nothing."

Beasts materialize, tap-dance their little holocausts, cackle once, and evaporate. Good grief, good God . . . good copy for the local blats. Underground the corpses stir a little, at My Lai and Wounded Knee. History fluffs its breast feathers, licks the wound, takes a dump, winks at the battalions of assassins sneaking by.

With great effort I phrased my next question: "Do you want to come over here and hold me for a minute?"

"Okay."

Janine, a lackluster, dry-eyed robot, moved across the room; my zombie little valentine. At my bedside she stopped. Her hand touched my good hand, fingertips atop the knuckles. Her dull eyes observed me without much feeling, just exhaustion.

"I want to hug you, baby."

Obediently, she leaned over, limbs without sensation. Cautiously, I slipped my one good arm around her shoulders, drawing her closer until her heart beat against my chest. She was almost inessential: pliant, unresponsive. But she did nestle her head beneath my chin.

"We'll figure it out," I said at length. "I'll move into your house. I'll take care of you."

As I spoke, a flood of feeling began to gather in my chest. And from my own dead zone a rabble of confused tears materialized; or anyway, an instinct to tears raised its ugly head. Though it stopped far short of my eyes. Janine's weight against me was indifferent. I knew she'd given up.

I slipped fingers into her matted, kinky hair. In the best of times it required a lot of brushing. But she had not attacked it in days.

"Did you hear me?"

Her palm pressed against my shoulder.

"I love you," I said again. It engendered no reaction.

I held her to my wounded body. She shifted her weight a little, that is all. Nothing mattered. In such times the heart retires; passions trickle into the sands of emotional deserts, disappear.

"Do you want to talk?" I asked.

"What about?"

"About . . . Cathie. Us. What happened."

"No. What's the point?" The deepest grave on earth can never contain the violent death of a single decent soul.

"Maybe it would help."

She was quick to respond: "Perhaps someday. But not now."

Suddenly she sat up and teetered on the edge of the bed.

"Don't go, Janine."

"I have to work later on."

"You can't go to work. You're crazy—"

"I have to pay the rent."

"But—"

I closed my mouth. Better for her to sit at home, sifting through mementos, striving to imagine her daughter's last minutes on earth?

Her hands lay passively in her lap, one atop the other: she inspected them drearily.

"I'm driving your truck, Michael. Is that all right?"

"Yes. Of course."

"Okay. Then I guess I'll be leaving now."

But she tarrried awhile yet. I touched her hip. Many things went on in my mind. I wanted to hold her, asking for succor, crush her in my arms. And even cry, but that felt hideously selfish. How could I make demands of Janine? The second time I said *I love you*, it had sounded pornographic, an imposition, a selfish plea, the grotesque whining of a pitiful man. Yet I needed her to say, "I love you, too." What a monstrous demand. If I begged Janine's forgiveness, would she absolve me of all the blame? I wanted her to admit that our romance had not ended, assure me that her impish sexuality would rise again from the ashes and taunt me with erotic shenanigans. I relived that moment in the driveway when I gave Cathie a boost, and received a kiss on the tip of my nose. Just a word, just a different move might have spared her life.

I'm so sorry, Janine, for attacking you, for all my sad assaults upon your tiny body. If only I could rescind the travesties on earth, stick flowers in her ass, smear honey on her breasts, then lunch on her good meat while she laughed at how it tickled. I must design a plan for saving both our souls. I'd promise to don my guns and hunt for Cathie's killers. But oh what scared me most was that maybe she'd withdrawn forever: our time was over. Never again to tie on boxing gloves and bash each other silly.

"Are you sure you don't want to talk?" I said.

She glanced up, pallid, uncurious. "No, not now. Maybe later." Everything was vague, remote, impossible. Her essence had flown the coop.

A living testament to dreams.

Night abandoned me to that wasteland born of Nam. Born of Carp, the man who plugged 'em up the ass and tumbled them into the ozone. Born of a whore on the floor, eating come-filled rubbers. And born of whatever demons had chosen to incinerate Cathie Tarr.

That field again, covered by mangled bodies. All those dismembered torsos, beautiful limbs, and cool ceramic fingers. And me again with my motley barrow, poking about the carnage, seeking to make amends, turn back the clock, retrieve some lives from the account books of devastation. I pushed my wheelbarrow, gathering a soft blue harvest devoid of souls, a jumble of human parts that never added up to even a single human being. Until over on the edge of things, I spied another lonesome hunter, my pal Janine, performing a similar task, a lobotomized floozy pausing here, pausing there, bending over to peer thoughtfully at the detritus, searching for her daughter.

In the end I blindly performed my rote task. Earnestly reassembled limbs and heads and knee joints, shoving the parts together until I had grotesque concoctions all around my feet. But nothing worked: not the Vietnamese kids who somehow turned out backward; not Willie Pacheco and his daughter, Mariangela, whose blue tongues refused to fill up with real blood; not Cicarelli, whose body looked almost perfect, except it lacked an arm I couldn't find; not Cathie Tarr, whose luscious teenage torso ended in the stump legs of a dwarf.

Janine arrived with a gas can and splashed the bitter liquid on my corrupt handiwork. We stood among the feeble writhing brutes as they burned, fluttering our hands stupidly at the end of broken wrists. And greasy smoke evaporated into opposite corners of hell.

Hot and cold sweats greeted me when I pawed my way into wakefulness. And bloody shoulder or not, all patched up with nylon twine and steel rods, I wanted out of there. Yanked all the tubes in one swift motion, then fumbled in a closet for my clothes. And chose the window for an exit, so that no medical factotum could accost me in a polished corridor. And I fled on foot, heading for Janine.

Panic made me run.

Each step cost a dozen howls.

Blood gathered down my arm.

I could smell the gasoline from far away. I could smell it from across the field near her darkened home as I staggered through weedy grasses damp from recent rain: grasses soaked and slapping against my thighs as I raced to save Janine. The air was moist and heavy, and should have smelled exclusively of dust and sage, but instead fumes of gasoline stung my cheeks, burned streaks across my eyes. I ran, stumbled, fell down sobbing; slippery earth made me skid time and time again; weeds clutched at my ankles. Pell-mell I fled to reach that darkened house where my truck was parked at a weird angle outside her door. Her open door, exuding volatile vapors as I arrived, all staggering and gasping huge raw billows of breath out of my seared lungs. I balanced for a second in the doorway, recapturing my bearings as I peered into the blackness of her home—

"Janine!"

No answer from the stillness, only the reek of gasoline.

"Janine, are you here?"

Again I received no answer.

So I stepped inside, fumbling for a light switch on the wall. But when I located it, my fingers wouldn't act. I didn't want to blind the room in a glare, and learn the secret of that bitter stench which filled the house, ready to explode. As if just the heat from an illuminated light bulb could ignite that fuel, setting off an explosion that would kill us both.

I hesitated; once again, Michael P. Smith arrives too late to save a drowning soul. Janine and Willie Pacheco and Cicarelli, an entire country of Asiatic kids—

But of course I had to flip it on. The room went white with light, garish and merciless, electricity without pity.

She sat cross-legged in the middle of the living-room floor, drenched by the stuff. Hair plastered against her skull like a bedraggled kitten. The one-gallon red-and-yellow can was tipped over at her knees. Her face was already burned by the poisonous liquid. She seemed to have been idlized like that for hours, contemplating death, awaiting a faint signal that said, "Okay. Bye-bye. The time has come."

When the light blasted, she didn't flinch. Her permanently opened eyes stared into nowhere. She was fixated on a point beyond me, out the open door, where the night sky opulent with stars offered taunting whispers from eternity.

I guessed that she had already departed the world, gone crazy (the doctors would surmise), gone south where the sun is always shining through the pelting rain—

Crossing the room, I knelt in front of her, and carefully removed the matchbox from her lap. A tiny murmur passed her lips, not of protest or of comment on the situation. Call it rather a small acknowledgment that I had arrived. No anger; no embarrassment either. Suicides often rant against the misguided wretches who save them, but not Janine. She remained indifferent in her spreading puddle of doom.

"Oh no," I said, "you can't."

"I really don't care, Michael."

"I won't let you." I unbuttoned her blouse, peeled the soggy lapels around her shoulders, skinned off the sleeves, and laid the garment to rest. Her breasts burned from the gasoline; the aureoles around her nipples had turned a fiery crimson.

I bent, lifting Janine up in my arms. She had become a weightless person. I carried her into the bathroom, propped her up against the wall, and gently tugged down her panty hose, exposing the raw and knobby knees, the spindly lower legs, slim ribbons of calf. I arranged her on the toilet lid, where she huddled without resistance, my hand on her chest to keep her balanced, while with my other hand I fitted the stopper, and turned hot water into the tub. When it was half full, I maneuvered her listless frame over the porcelain side, and lowered her into the steam.

She had cakes of soap and bath bubbles and beads, bottles of shampoo and cream rinse—all sorts of lotions that lathered. With as much care as I could summon I scoured her shoulders, breasts, and armpits, swished washcloths against her nipples, then worked up fluffy piles of suds in her hair, massaged the sting out of her scalp.

Janine remained wide eyed, never made a peep. Her limbs stayed limp, acquiescing to however I chose to pose them. Whether I salvaged her body or not may have been immaterial: perhaps she had not struck that match because the immolation was unnecessary.

Desperately, I soaped and polished, ruined a brand-new loofah. In my head thoughts stampeded. Would I be lashed forever to a hollow woman, spoon-feeding her pabulum three times daily, queasily loving her floppy body in hopes of resurrecting a passion she no longer recalled?

Softly, I rubbed her throat, cleaned fluid from behind her ears. Janine's skin pulsed rawly beneath the foam. I propped her up to keep her from sloshing under. Frothy dabs clung to her eyebrows, lips, the tip of her nose—I swiped them off. Soothing water lulled against her belly. I maneuvered her in my wet arms, cleansing with utmost gentleness. Finally, I scooped up water and splashed her hair, rinsing it thoroughly. My eyes burned and my nostrils hurt. Eventually, I lifted her slippery body from the water, composed her on the toilet seat again, and drained the noxious residues. Then sprinkled Ajax in the tub and labored to sponge out grease and gas. Janine slumped passively, barely able to hold herself erect. I drew another bath, tapping in droves of herbal beads, and scrubbed her all over again.

Her head lolled almost as if severed. After our second go-round, I drained the tub again. Then stepped beneath the shower fully clothed and embraced her to me under the sputtering stream. When that was done, I arranged her on the toilet once more, stripped off my clothes and dried myself, then found fresh towels in a cabinet and patted her dry. Though it must have pained, she gave no sign. I kissed her without response. Then carried her into the bedroom, and laid her down on green sheets, head arranged on a pillow. And abided beside her, admiring the body I loved. Smoothed my palm over her skin, then noticed goose bumps, a shiver, and drew the blankets up underneath her chin. No thanks from Janine; no anger at the intrusion; no reaction whatsoever.

"Are you hungry? Do you want some tea and honey?"

She stared at me, disconnected. The house still reeked of gas.

"I love you, Janine. I'm not going to let you disappear."

Motionless, her eyes remained open.

"It's not the end of the world," I said. "It's never the end of the world, no matter what."

246

If she heard, or cared, I could not tell. I kissed my fingertip, and touched it to her nose.

"I'll take care of you," I promised.

Then she raised one arm and touched my shoulder. Her fingers came away painted in blood: I had forgotten all about my wounds. Her touch released an excruciating pain. No matter. She held that painted hand aloft; I leaned forward and licked her fingers clean.

9

LITTLE DETAILS

All around the mulberry bush skipped death and devastation. Trees sprinkling leaves gilded the earth; hummingbirds sucked dry the purple hollyhocks. Fields of sprightly yellow sunflowers raised their chipper blossoms, and the dust of passing automobiles created a golden haze across the valley. Summertime in the Rockies. Irrigation veins off many rivers fanned water out to make green fields of corn and beans and alfalfa. Birth; regeneration; ripe tomatoes on garden vines. Puffy sheep meandered across deep pastures. But none of that for the macho man from Nam and his festering moll: we had different fish to fry in the gray gloom that typified our shell-shocked days.

The ashes arrived by mail in a cylindrical carton not much larger than a can of corn. Janine fixated on this package from the underworld with heavy, unlustered eyes, her body, grown slack and dismal from grief, wreathed in cigarette smoke. Her lips were dry, cracked, crusted. Makeup never touched her skin; she'd lost all interest in a theater of seduction. When I proposed we take the ashes to the mesa and memorialize her daughter, she coughed and protested feebly: "What's the point? Who cares? Who wants to remember how she died?"

"How she lived is the point. Who she was."

"Who she was never lived. She had a shit-can life. I dragged her through mud on my stupid coattails. Asshole father, fucked-up childhood, moronic mom, dingbat boyfriends like you. Let her be free, Michael. Our show would only insult her more."

But I prevailed. If I was not bold now, everything would collapse. So I cajoled her into the truck, drove to the mesa, parked near our sentimental overhang, and led her through sagebrush, flowering snakeweed, and stunted yucca to a jumble of basalt rocks covered by colorful lichens at the edge of towering yellow cliffs. A merry confusion of swallows darted; a canyon wren was calling; blue sky arched unblemished. Across the plain peaceful mountains, harboring last splashes of winter snow, extended northward along the horizon. The stones exuded warmth, almost soft beneath our feet.

I cut the seal with my pocketknife and pried open the canister, exposing a gray and grainy fluff containing knobby chips and sharp splinters of bone that hadn't been vaporized by fire. Dipped in my fingers and removed a palmful of bony powder. Extended it to Janine, but she deferred.

"You do it, Michael. I don't care to touch that stuff."

"You should. It will mean something later on."

"What will it mean? You're so wise all of a sudden. Tell me."

"This ritual is important."

"How do you know? It's something they taught you in Vietnam?"

"I just know that one day when you wake up again, you'll care about this moment."

"Oh? When do you plan for me to wake up again?"

She wore a gray sweatshirt, baggy and shapeless; the sleeves half obscured her hands. And faded dungarees decorated by bleached driblets of white and lavender paint. On her feet the tattered Swiss-cheese sneakers. No lipstick, no mascara since that awful night. Otherwise, she puttered around the house in her terry-cloth bathrobe and tattered slippers, disinterested in the physical image she presented. Her hair was combed, the snags cake-cuttered out, only because I insisted on doing it myself. I had moved in, lock, stock, and barrel: before the Chuck Wagon fired Janine, I forced her to take a leave of absence.

Well, no guts, no blue chips, they always say. So I took each arm, and turned her hands palm up together, and I jiggled in a heap of bone and ash. She followed the procedure wooden eyed. Then glanced bizarrely up at me, disturbed by the puffy weight of Cathie in her hands.

"Now what, Michael? What do I do with this?"

"Sprinkle them here, among the rocks, however you feel like doing it."

"I don't feel like doing anything. This is creepy."

I touched her cold fingers. In response, she allowed the fingers to spread a little; ashes and bone chips sifted between the spaces, bounced against her sneakers, skittered over lichen-covered stones, and disappeared into small crevasses.

Janine said, "That's it? That's Cathie?"

"Put out your hands again."

She obeyed; I filled her palms. "Walk around, scatter them among the stones."

"*You* scatter them among the stones. This isn't my daughter." She let the gray dust puff to earth again around her tattered sneakers.

Why fight? Not now, not over this. I wandered among the rocks, balancing from stone to stone, scooping Cathie's ashes from the canister, sowing them among the boulders. Silence, except for twittering swallows. Blue sky serenely enveloped the wide plain. It seemed as if nowhere on earth could there be human beings at war. Janine remained in her position, dumbly watching me perform a ritual I deemed important. She watched, and lit one cigarette after another.

I finished the job, tapping free last pellicles of human dust. Then returned to Janine, and hugged her. She neither resisted nor responded. I suppressed tears; perhaps my grief would accuse her coldness. In her all vitality seemed to have been sealed up forever. I listened to the swallows; the zigzag ruffling dance of their wings sliced up the oxygen around us. I heard the distant whisper of the Rio Grande far below our perch. A notion crossed my mind: to wrench us both outward over the parapet's edge, ending our story in a short dive through space onto the boulder field below. But the urge passed quickly, and I hugged her even more tightly. Smoke lightly stung my cheeks. A raven gave a single croak before it flapped stolidly into the quiet immensity. Then I pushed back and looked down at her; she considered me.

"Tears." Janine spoke in a dead voice, inhaling a final drag. "Why are you indulging in this sentimental shit?"

Then she gestured at the idyllic spot. "What do we erect for a gravestone, Michael? A big stone dick, wrapped in an American flag? And Cathie's name engraved across the balls?"

In my frantic head, I knew I had to make a plan. But I was befuddled, at a loss for words, incapable of sorting out logical answers or a rational mode of attack. For the last decade of my life, it seems, my natural instinct had been to push things toward collapse. Now, of a sudden, I latched on to the crazy idea that it was my role to hold the world together. But I had no schooling in the strengths required for such a role. All my education was weighted on the side of lunatic experience: blow a fuse, go bananas, let insanity flower.

But not now, not this time, I admonished myself. Let's grow up at last, fly right, try being unselfish and unself-possessed for a change. And salvage some small decency from the horrors that trammel earth.

During that heady loving time with Janine, I told myself, I had learned that joy is possible. And the gift seemed so precious that it was absurd, now, to simply let it fall upon the ash heap. That even a small part of our former ecstasy could be salvaged from the nightmare now defining our days seemed like an absurd presumption, and yet I chose to make it. Don't ask me why. I just could not stand, nor accept, the magnitude of such a loss. Given the plight of the world's night, the loss made perfect sense. But I mentioned once that Janine had cupped my broken body in her hands, blowing on my life as if to keep alive a fragile ember. And it seemed imperative, now, that I return the favor.

Good idea, Mike. But how to begin in such a stark and miserable time? I had saved Janine from immolation—big deal. But the question I asked myself repeatedly as the days extended wearily and nothing in her myopic state changed was: *What* had I rescued? The lady had shut down, withdrawn, curled up inside herself, and lost all interest in trying to dig clear of the gloom. Never had I intimately witnessed anything like it. Her energy had vanished. Left behind was a shell of meat, trapped in total enervation, responding to nothing.

Meanwhile, in my head all manner of related subjects danced. Foremost, of course, was a plague of suppositions about the way that Cathie had died. And the suspicion that Tom Carp must have participated in the crime. I was torn about how to deal with that. Especially as it had no concrete basis in fact.

I thought first, of course, to spill beans to Janine, at least admitting the bastard lived in town—I had never told her. And several times I almost let that cat out of the bag. It might give her a focus, something to cling to, hope for retribution. For it must have haunted her at every level, the lack of clues to Cathie's murder. Certainly fantasies of revenge were a constant fire in my guts, so they must also have entered her mind sometimes.

God, how I yearned to discover that madman's lair, and burst into his sick pad with all my guns ablazing, sending him off to hell in a violent pyre of sparks and roaring flames!

Trading an eye for a villain's eye that any golem, even Carp himself, would admire and understand.

Except that I was terrified of the consequences. Should I locate Carp, and exercise my terrible revenge, then I'd simply join him as just another killer. If I was apprehended, and there existed no proof that he'd offed Cathie, my own doom would be sealed. And if I'd included Janine in the play, I'd take her with me. No matter how you justified it, revenge would destroy our lives. Arrest, jail, trials, newspaper publicity, long-term incarceration. No way not to make things worse. And Cathie's blood, instead of being cleansed by our retaliatory savagery, would become forever tainted by the blood of Thomas Carp.

I wrestled with the problem and came up utterly frustrated, devoid of rational answers.

My hope, of course, was that the authorities, by themselves, would stumble on Carp, or the other assassins. But as the days dragged by, that seemed an increasingly unlikely proposition. They were stymied, had no leads, nothing and nobody at which/at whom to point a finger. I stopped in often at the DA's office during the weeks immediately following the murder, but James Kelter had nothing concrete to impart. They had followed all the usual channels of investigation and come up empty-handed. No witnesses, not a tattered shred of evidence at the crime scene beyond Cathie's mutilated body. They had grilled Janine extensively while I vegetated at the hospital, but in her dulled and hostile state she had nothing valuable to reveal. No bitter feuding, no personal connections that might link Cathie to a killer, or suggest a possible motive. And besides, they were all convinced that it had to be a random atrocity, an unfortunate happenstance: the perpetrators could not have known Cathie, nor have plotted beforehand her brutal massacre.

They grilled me also, half a dozen times, and frankly I had nothing pertinent to add. Kelter dared suggest even I might have a motive—hadn't Cathie shot me way back when? Before I could properly flare at that, he backed off . . . they knew I had an alibi. But still, they'd tracked it down behind my back; and he just wanted me to know. They had covered all the angles.

Oh admittedly, more than once I wanted to finger Carp. But an odd caution stayed my hand. First off, the man had been out of my sights so long, I guess I wasn't absolutely certain if he still lived in our town. But if he did, then what could I truly add to link him to such a random deed? I understood a bit about the rules of evidence, and the slim chances of fabricating a guilty label on totally vague and circumstantial hunches. Hating and fearing a man were not enough in anyone's book to seal a watertight conviction. Instinctive, emotional postulations were no reason at all, in the eyes of the law, to drag a man before the grand jury, seeking an indictment.

So in the confusion of that traumatic time, I decided to keep mum. Though perhaps a muddled decision, it made sense to me. I chose to push all thoughts of Thomas Carp into the background; I concentrated wholly on Janine.

And after the initial stories were published in our weekly paper, I refused to have any further truck with the case. I even buttonholed my boss, the editor, demanding that reporters leave us alone. And in such a small town they were cooperative. Stories about Cathie's murder died right quickly after the initial flurry that made it news. Naturally, reporters checked in regularly at the DA's office, but gleaned nothing new from those bozos.

And so the matter settled beneath the surface, awaiting further developments. And Janine and I were allowed to deal with the torment on our own.

For weeks she lay in bed among rumpled sheets, scarcely stirring except to light cigarettes. In a kind of wide-eyed stupor she smoked the cancer sticks, blowing smoke at the ceiling. Her fingers browned from nicotine, she seldom washed her hands. Ashes stained the sheets, she never brushed them off. A sepulcher, that bed; a remote world I could not fathom. Her pall made me jittery and fatigued. I placed records on her cheesy stereo, country-and-western tunes she had once adored, the nasal laments of redneck blues and sawdust barrooms, lost love and aching heartbreak that had always made her laugh. And quiet, classical recordings—Casals, Menuhin, Rubinstein—but nothing moved her. If she had thoughts I could not tell, for she never opened her mouth. When I brought her tea and a piece of cinnamon toast, her "thank you's" held no fire I could decipher. When I asked about the music, she replied, "Play whatever you like, Michael, I don't care." I sat for hours by her side; what to do? What to say? What words could break her torpor? Nothing worked; I couldn't prick her bubble of dismay.

I was at a total loss. Just being there, I reasoned, might keep her living until the terrible season passed and she opted for aliveness again. But after awhile I let the music lapse; and we dwelled together in a total absence of vitality. Distant noises connoted a world at play out there: car horns soporifically beeping, police sirens wailing in another universe, the shout of a galloping child. But to contemplate her face in the shadowy bedroom revealed nothing. Was she even conscious of my presence? Janine had withdrawn into regions I could not fathom.

Hours crawled by in dimness and lack of motion. She coughed a lot; the rattle seemed to have tendrils attached to festering polyps deep inside her chest. But always when the fit was done, she lit another cigarette. At first, I often stroked Janine, toying seductively with her large nipples that never grew erect. But she remained so placid I soon despaired of arousing an erotic response. Then, when I laid my palm against her, it was only to assert my presence, indicate I cared, I had affection and compassion for her plight.

Many days passed uneventfully. I cooked suppers of rice and vegetables—she hardly ate at all. I maintained the place neat and tidy, did laundry, washed windows, made sure dishes were put away, emptied ashtrays, concocted a zip juice of Diet Coke and orange juice, and made the bed around her, sheets all crisp and clean. I drew baths and washed her body. I chatted with her continually, ineffective conversations about weather, childhood days. Read the sports pages aloud, and spoke to her of teams and batting averages, towns like Minneapolis and San Diego. I noted films that came and went at the local theaters. Even recited the horoscopes aloud, also silly comics. And described horses in nearby fields, nursing spindle-legged colts. A magnificent blueness of summer skies hovered outside our windows; we never activated the TV.

Perhaps Janine listened; perhaps I made no impression whatsoever. Sometimes, in her terry-cloth robe and furry slippers, she paced slowly around the house. Occasionally, she alighted at the windows and for long spells observed magpies and grackles disporting in wild plum thickets along the backyard fence. It frightened me to leave her alone and go to work, but somebody had to earn the rent. I called often from the newspaper, or from phone booths about the town. Sometimes she answered, sometimes not. I asked, "Are you okay?" She always answered "Yes."

But she was dying before my eyes, losing weight head over heels. Her skull blossomed through taut facial skin. Her eyes were bruised from lack of sleep, yet she drowsed all the time. In the evening I made drinks, Kahlua over ice, lightly spiced with half-and-half. She sipped them slowly, one after another. They had no impact— it would have been a blessing to get her drunk. But she was trapped in a reverence for decay, becalmed on oceans of expanding insanity.

Cathie's residue in the house she never altered: the posters of rock stars on the walls. A basketball lay in one corner; schoolbooks were stacked neatly in a pile. Pictures of Cathie hung on our bedroom walls, occupied a silver frame atop the chifforobe. At first I wanted to remove them; then supposed the empty places might attract her attention and somehow seem obscene. So I let Cathie's photographs remain. Janine seemed not to notice them at all. Her eyes might have grown blind. Switched off, gone fishin', hung a shingle on the door: BACK IN TWENTY YEARS, perhaps . . . OUT TO LUNCH . . . MOVED TO ANOTHER PLANET. She spoke without nuance or inflection, inert, almost inaudible.

"Janine," I said a hundred times, "we have to talk."

"I have nothing to say."

"Well, I can't stand what's happening to you."

"You don't have to," she replied.

"Don't have to what?"

"Don't have to stand it if you don't want. You're free to leave."

"Then what happens to you? Are you crazy? You have no *right* to give up!"

She cocked her head, then shrugged and lit another Kool. Headed for the bathroom next, and lowered onto the toilet seat without closing the door, disinterested in privacy—time to take a shit.

When I raged, it made no impression. Tenderness dribbled off her shoulders like water off the proverbial duck.

"This is a real dumb way to commit suicide," I badgered.

"Suicide? Please, Michael—don't be so melodramatic."

"Oh Barbara Cicarelli," I cried. "What do I do now? How do I handle this situation?"

She lit a cigarette, coughed, eyed me thoughtfully.

"Try it the way I did with Eleanor," she said. "Talk, say anything, maybe you can bring her back to life."

"And if that fails?"

"Hey, what do I look like, a noodge with all the answers?"

"You saved their lives," I whimpered. "You were like Florence Nightingale."

"Florence Nightingale eats babies for breakfast, Michael—don't give me that sentimental crap."

"But all you ever did was *save* people," I moaned.

"All I ever did was stick my stupid finger in a dike holding back tidal waves of blood. It never worked. I should have let them die."

"Don't say that! I don't believe it. You of all people—"

Wearily, she ran bony fingers through her blotchy hair. "Michael, my well-intentioned sweetheart, don't let it get you down. The earth belches a million cadavers every minute. There ain't much we can do."

"Then why bother? How come you never quit?"

Absently, Sicko unbuttoned her soiled tunic, exposing a ravaged torso, ribs poking through, the chest of a scrawny little boy, nipples almost black from being blue.

"Human life is sacred, Michael. Can't you tell? Ain't my body beautiful?"

Then in a puff of acrid smoke that made her instantly a web of dissipating vapor, she waved good-bye—ta-ta—and took a powder.

260

One night I awoke startled, reaching for a gun that wasn't there—back to soldier days. Instantly, I realized she was not beside me. I heard a scuffling noise in the corner. Cautiously, I reached for the bedside lamp, then stayed my hand. Skin scraped against old wooden floorboards, cloth rustled—her nightgown. But my eyes refused to focus in the dark. I held stone-still, apprehensive, trying to understand. I could hear Janine breathing, that phlegmy rattle from her throat. She moved slowly, patting the floor from time to time. A diminutive fluttery whimper passed her lips. It was a terrifying moment because I couldn't find the rhyme or reason, or even locate her shape across the room. I had awakened to one of those insane moments in my own nightmares. And I blinked a couple of times, testing if it was real.

Eventually, I had to speak. But given the eerie mood, I thought surely my voice would shatter something, or unleash an ungodly scream. I sucked in air and strained to comprehend what she was doing. Gorgons, dragons, little monsters from the dead world, gremlins with bloody teeth, fat rats snooping for putrid tidbits, trolls with Cheshire grins and monster cocks dragging between their legs, broken-backed rattlesnakes twisting in flip-flops on the floor—

"Janine?"

The scuffling ceased.

"Janine, is that you?"

No sign of life now from the vacuum-black corner.

"Baby, what are you doing?"

Zilch, absolute silence, zero noise. Beast or being crouched a dozen feet away, attending my next move. The air hummed with a sense of danger or delirium: one false step and the gun goes off, the mine explodes, the snake strikes forward. I tried a final time:

"Janine, for crissakes, speak up."

It didn't work. The darkness remained cocked above a hair trigger. So I finally hit the lamp.

Her eyes stayed perfectly wide open, totally disoriented. She hunched in the corner, one hand cupped over her ear, the other balancing against the floor. Her nightie was rumpled up around her crotch. In the glare Janine resembled a kind of albino misfit, a twisted little ghost hardly bigger than a rabbit.

"I don't understand," I said. "Are you okay?"

"I'm looking for something," she said evasively.

"What?"

"Her head. I thought it rolled into this corner."

Before I thought to catch myself, I'd asked: "Whose head?"

Her voice had steel in it that I hadn't heard for weeks. "The pope's. The president's. Mick Jagger's."

"I'm sorry. I didn't mean to ask that question."

"Turn off the light, Michael. I can find it in the dark."

"You're having a nightmare," I explained, hair prickling behind my neck. No moment in my life had ever been more weird. She had gone totally bonkers in the night. A gust of horror danced coldly up my spine. And a scream without echo or reverberation was poised to rend the room.

"Turn off the fucking light, Michael."

I switched it off. The scream remained, like the non-noise sound a wounded soldier makes, back arched, lips wide apart, throat torn open and minus its vocal cords, chest full of air that can't escape until that moment when life bolts.

"That's better. Thank you."

The scuffling and patting resumed.

I had no experience with such things. What to do now?—call a shrink, a medic, the men in white, lace her into a canvas contraption, cart her off to the loony bin and shoot her full of Thorazine? I listened to the searching a moment longer, then slipped out of bed, knelt beside her, and placed my hand on her rump. Again, she quit her activity.

"Come back to bed with me, Janine."

"I can't right now, I'm busy."

"There's nothing here. You had a lousy dream."

"It wasn't a dream, Michael. It actually happened. They cut off her head. I know it must be around here somewhere. I *want* that head."

It surprised me, the ease with which I could lift her up and convey her back to bed. Light as a feather, so they say, my floundering Janine. Weightless as the bony kids in Nam—napalm blistered and punctured from crown to callused toe by bits of butterfly pellets—that we offered to the bereft mamasans. Our frankincense and myrrh.

I laid her down, smoothed the nightie across her listless thighs, arranged the blankets, slipped carefully in beside her. Together, we reposed there, listening to the dark. I took her hand in mine. In due course her other hand ruffled for a cigarette on the bedside table, fitted it in her mouth, and scrabbled for a disposable lighter.

She smoked, her drawn features illuminated each time the tip flared in response to her inhale.

"I'm sorry you had that dream."

Ponderous silence greets the compassionate schmuck, all thumbs in this territory of madness. Tippet embers flared, died down, flared again, lighting up her passive face. Eventually, she stubbed it out. The darkness was stirred by electric eddies rising from my brain, her brain, the devil's broom at work, sweeping sanity under the rug.

All at once Janine began speaking. "It *was* her head. The face looked like somebody had dug into it with a shovel. One of those little shovels that fold up and you take camping or on a picnic. Big holes all over it, the face, bits of teeth, gristle, lots of blood, sticky like molasses, matted in her hair."

She paused.

"Molasses. Daddy had an expression when he was impatient: 'Move it, lovebug, you're slow as molasses in January.'"

She reflected on that, then returned to her original tack. "I was licking her face, eating on it, chewing pieces of flesh, trying to clean up the holes. It tasted like horehound candy. Momma always made us that at Easter and at Christmas. Yummy."

After that, she quit talking. I squeezed her hand and waited in vain for a like response. The darkness stooped and diddled prurient fingers against us. Blackness like crude tunnels under the jungle hiding people soon to taste our white phosphorus grenades.

Tension strained at all my muscles; what now, Dr. Spock? Treat it like measles or appendicitis?

"Roll over, sweetness." I hunched above her body. "I want to give you a back rub." It was a way to let her feel my warmth, my concerned human connection.

At my prodding she scrooched over onto her stomach. Straddling her waist, I worked the sinews of her neck and shoulders. My fingers sank into her lax flesh without resistance. Lightly, I plied her shoulders and her arms. Pinched and rolled her biceps; even probed her knobby elbows. I fondled the shape of her bones and elastic joints, the most insignificant ligament or muscle. Counted every vertebra in her spine, carefully and adoringly. Smoothed my palms in a sweeping circular motion around her ribs. Then kneaded her tiny buttocks that had almost wasted away.

"Are you awake, Janine?"

"Yes I am."

"Feel better?"

"Better than what?"

"Better than a little while ago."

"Just for your information," she said abruptly, "I never stop thinking about it. Not once, not even for a minute, ever since it happened."

That came as a shock. I had imagined her daze impersonal, dumb, unthinking. And once again I chose the articulate response—a bewildered silence. My thoughts tripped all over themselves, scrambling to locate a safe verbal shelter.

"I keep picturing her on fire," Janine said. "I can smell her flesh all day in this house. I can smell it burning at night. It smells like cracklin's and human shit in an outhouse. They take an ax and chop off her head. I don't know if that happened when she was on fire, or before they torched her. Or later . . . you know . . . as an afterthought."

She spoke clearly, precisely, leadenly.

"But I am puzzled about several things, Michael. Do you think they kept fucking her after they cut off the head? Do you think they screwed her while she was on fire? Suppose one of them had his cock in her mouth, holding onto her hair, when the other one cut off her head, and then the first one kept fucking her mouth until he came? Walking around with the head, pressing her mouth over his cock until he was finished? I think probably they kept fucking her on fire, but neither one got burned. I'm certain they kept fucking her after she was dead. But I can't really line up the details. I mean, the time sequence of how things happened, and what they did to her. I wish I could figure out the little details. Do you think one of them shit in her mouth *after* the head was severed? Or maybe they both pissed on her body to put the fire out, so it wouldn't raise attention? The coroner's report isn't very clear on the little details. It doesn't even know if they stuck that iron thing, the tire iron, up her ass when she was still alive, or after she was dead. That makes a big difference to me. I keep hoping it was *after* they cut off her head, but I can't be certain. I keep trying to tune into the scene with my brain waves, and make certain of the order in which things happened. But I always get a fuzzy picture. I've been meaning to ask you for days if you have any insight into the matter. Maybe some of those creeps in the sheriff's department told you details they kept from me? If they did, I really wish you'd reveal them now. That might help me sort out the order of things. I really have trouble figuring out the sequence of events . . ."

My fingers continued massaging her buttocks, digging through pliant flesh to rub against wide, jarring bones.

"Every *day*?" I said miserably. "Ever since it happened?"

"I don't want to lay anything heavy on you, Michael. That's why I didn't bring it up."

Another kind and insightful suggestion came from her caretaker, masseur, kitchen boy: "You shouldn't think about it."

"What else is there to think about?"

"It'll drive you crazy."

"Well," she droned, "I keep thinking that if I could only understand the order of events, everything will fall into place, and then I can ditch it. I know they must have butt-fucked her, but I don't know if they did that first, or if they fucked her pussy first before they tackled her ass. And some other little things, stuff that probably most folks wouldn't notice, comes to my mind and seems kinda pertinent. Like was there shit in her ass, down near the anus, and did they get covered with it, and make her all messy too? That would have upset her a lot. Even in the middle of being raped and killed, that would be an embarrassing indignity. So I hope that at least she was clean down there. And if I knew that for *sure*, it would make a difference. It might set my mind at ease a little, you know? A woman cares about that sort of thing."

"Please stop talking, Janine. You don't want to speak like that."

A force squeezed the room, absorbing half the air.

"It makes you nervous? I'm sorry. I don't want to hurt you, Michael. Of course I'll stop. I won't mention it again."

I continued the massage. Tickled her back, wispily stroked it, caressed and lightly prodded. A nearby windowpane picked up a delicate spurt of light like the flare of a match struck a dozen miles away, then went blank again.

"That feels good," Janine said.

Time to get up, get out, get real. No more self-indulgent lollygagging in the throes of despair. Alley-oop, up and at 'em, lazybones, rise and shine. "Get dressed, Janine, we're going for a ride. I'll make a picnic."

"I don't want to leave this house."

"I don't care. You need fresh air."

I forced her to dress, tug on rumpled jeans that had once been tight, don her floppy sweatshirt. Then sat her at the kitchen table with a makeup kit and plastic mirror that plugged into the wall, and asked her to paint her fingernails, do her face. She peered into the illuminated mirror, ignoring my command. Smoke drained from her idly pursed lips.

"Come on." I slopped mayonnaise and garlic salt on slices of Bunny bread. "I want you to look pretty again."

"Why? What's the point? I look like a hag."

I drew up a chair beside her, opened a compact, removed the puff and pressed it to one cheek. "You're a beautiful woman," I said. "I love you with all my heart. I can't let you trickle down the drain. You have to start making an effort."

I dabbed powder on her cheeks, chin, forehead, and patted the tip of her nose, hoping to elicit a smile. Her haunted eyes assessed herself in the mirror.

"Seduce me," I pleaded gently. "We haven't made love in ages."

"Is that what you call it?" She never took eyes off her sunken image in the mirror. "'Making love'?"

I poised an eyeliner pencil at one lid, and carefully began applying color, making her more seductive.

"All the times we had," I insisted. "All that joy we shared. We can't just let this stuff destroy us. We are too valuable for that."

In my heart a despair as overwhelming as the war in Nam expanded. But I suppressed it, forcing a twinkle in each eye. I labored mightily to avoid a tremble in my voice.

Janine remained quiet during her conversion. I applied makeup, accented eyebrows, brushed mascara on lashes, dabbed a dot of rouge on either cheek and smudged it in. Then opened a lipgloss tube and to her parched lips added a rashly glistening color calling Sizzling Ochre. While I assessed my handiwork, she continued dully confronting her self in the mirror.

"Hey, not bad for a beginner," I said. "Tilt your head a little."

She obeyed, but her eyes remained on the mirror.

"What do you think?"

"I think 'making love' is a funny way to describe it."

"Doesn't it feel nice to be dolled up a little?" Two lunatics adrift in purgatory converse about inanities. But I would attempt anything to break the spell.

"They killed her," Janine answered quietly, "because of me. Because I dressed sexy with my big tits hanging out all over the place. If I hadn't had my breast implants, they wouldn't have killed her. She was ashamed of her breasts. She always wore floppy clothes to hide her embarrassment. She hated the way I dressed."

"I loved the way you dressed, Janine. You know that. It made me happy. You saved my life."

"You attacked me, Michael. You would have raped and killed me if I hadn't fought back."

"I loved our sex," I said, panicked. "It felt so wonderful, funky, bawdy, happy—"

"You keep using that word, Michael."

"What word?"

"'Love.' 'Love' this, 'love' that. It's such a funny word."

"I love *you*," I said.

On she droned, never for a moment deflecting her gaze off the mirror. "You 'love' to fuck me in the ass, Michael. And talk about stabbing me in the stomach when you come. You 'love' to fuck me in the mouth and talk about cutting the tits off dead Viet Cong ladies. You 'love' to fuck my pussy half apart and pretend there's a piano wire around my neck, slowly choking me to death."

"That was all theater, all pretend. That was erotic make-believe."

Dustily, she mouthed the words: "'Erotic make-believe.' Is what they did to Cathie 'Erotic Make-Believe'?"

"Oh for Christ's sake!" I stormed back to the counter and finished up the sandwiches. And whirled angrily on her, shouting: "You can't dwell on that forever! You can't just let the world end! Our loving was different and you know it! It was powerful! You know it was sweet and crazy and incredible! You said so a million times!"

"When they killed Cathie," she said, atonal, still regarding her painted visage in the mirror, "it was like all your dreams come true, wasn't it, Michael?"

Stymied, checkmate—how to answer that? Leap forward and knock her down? Pummel her helpless body gone so quickly to wrack and ruin? Knock sense into her fixated brain, wake her up, smash her back to aliveness?

"You don't know what you're talking about."

At last she activated her head, glancing up at me—and for the first time in ages smiled. The job I had done on her features recalled messy Halloweens. And that smile, the faint parting of her incongruously auburn lips, shot toward me like a splinter of glass.

"If you want to chop off my head," she said, "I wouldn't mind a bit."

Holy Moses!—we got out of there.

I almost had to drag her to the truck. Popped open two beers and handed her one, and headed for the hills with a bag of sandwiches between us. Peaceful summer reclined across the valley in a lazy daze. Sheep and cattle, sleepy horses, a noontime indolence characterized all things, all landscape. I drove us up a picturesque dirt road beside the Rio Chiquito. Through narrow meadows and stands of spruce the river meandered, its banks lined by russet willows and alder trees drooping with seed catkins. Hummingbirds buzzed at roadside veins of scarlet gilia and penstemon; butterflies busily worked over flowering rose hip thickets. When I parked and took her hand, guiding us down a steep embankment toward a grassy patch beside a bend in the cold clear creek, we could smell the tangy odor of crisp mint. Raspberries were turning red, and after I spread our blanket, I picked a handful of berries and fitted them between her lips.

Outdoors, she resembled a ghost from the grave, a living cadaver, a painted skull. A gross mistake, the makeup: now it was difficult to face her. Janine seemed not to notice. I unwrapped a sandwich, she ate it; delivered another beer, she drank it. Steller's jays croaked in the pines; magpies flounced raucously among towering cottonwood branches. I thought: Never a day waned more beautiful. The earth generates a million gifts for anybody willing to accept them. I had an almost wild expectation that all at once Janine would blossom, burst forth radiantly like the miracle of a Mexican virgin, fling her arms around my neck and commence sobbing out the poisons.

But no such luck; her monotonous demeanor never altered. Sunshine baked us. Removing my shirt, I lay back in the grass. Solar heat probed through the ache of my mending shoulder. But Janine remained seated in a slump, beer can in hand, incessantly smoking bitter cigarettes, staring off at the tiny river. When she spoke, it was only to reiterate the same old theme.

"How long do you think it took, Michael?"

"How long did what take?" A chickadee chirped in nearby evergreen branches, an odd harbinger of winter for such a swooning summer afternoon.

"How long did it take for them to kill her? I mean, from the very beginning to the very end?"

"Janine, look at the sky." I roused myself and kneeled beside her. "Lie down, baby." Carefully, I pushed her back onto the grass, positioned her limp arms outward above her head, palms facing upward. Then crumpled up her sweatshirt, exposing pasty white belly flesh to the sun.

"That's better now. Doesn't the sun feel warm? Isn't it soothing to your skin? You should absorb it like the breath of life itself."

Eternal smoke, rising out of her throat, circled in plumes toward the sky.

"Five minutes? Ten minutes?" she asked. "I mean, do you think it's something she said that made them angry? That kid had such a mouth."

I dribbled tufts of grass onto her sternum and lax belly. That chickadee again cast its busy note across our picnic ground, minuscule bleat from a colder clime.

"I don't know, Janine. It happened, that's all. Thinking about it now, rehashing all the details, can't change a thing. We can only deal with it if we heal ourselves. Life belongs to the living, you always told me that."

Janine contemplated the utter blueness of the moment. A blueness as clean and unfettered by cloud imperfections as a porcelain glaze on an ancient bowl. Blue and blue, insistent blue, blue everywhere and absolutely beautiful, blue without noise or wind, blue without emotion, blue enveloping the earth with lucid disinterest, blue demented in its totally false and peaceful entirety.

"I'm pretty sure she was a virgin," Janine said quietly. "So it would have been the first time she got laid. Does that strike you as ironic?"

"Please don't talk anymore about it. Not now." Leaning over, I settled my mouth lightly against her unresponsive lips. "You're just making yourself crazy with stuff that can't be explained."

"When they cut off her head," Janine continued, soon as my shadow lifted off her face, "was it with an ax? I assumed it was an ax at first, but now I'm not so certain. Nobody at the DA's office seemed to know for sure. The coroner's report mentioned the severed head, but don't you think it odd there's no conjecture on the kind of implement used? So maybe it wasn't an ax. Maybe they used a machete. Maybe it was just a big knife, like those pigstickers you guys used in Vietnam you're always telling me about—what are they called? Those K-2 knives from the Navy. My brother brought one home. He said it had cut off nineteen ears."

"K-bar," I muttered hopelessly, dismayed by the relentless pall of our conversation. How could I shift the focus here?

"K-bar," she repeated listlessly. "Thank you. Maybe it was one of them."

Stretched out beside Janine on the grass, I nudged against her body, remembering that human contact is sometimes all it takes for reassurance. Yet how to deal with the horror? A child is casually butchered by fiends in the night, and forever after a pig probes the open wounds of each survivor. In Nam we left behind a nation of babbling idiots, clutching their shriveled privates, a host of befuddled peasants wandering the devastated countryside in the aftermath of a flippant genocide that destroyed the very earth.

I placed her hand on my groin; she removed it quickly, and said: "Maybe all they had was a saw. Some old rusty saw that was lying in the back of the pickup among hay bales giving it weight so it wouldn't get stuck in the mud. Maybe that's what did the job, Michael. Maybe they were lumberjacks."

Now a thing happened in the sky. A hatch of bugs, perhaps— who knows? The triggering mechanism was invisible to my eyes. But all of a sudden a million swallows began twittering above our heads, filling the immensity with fluttering, hungry bodies. A vast commotion of little birds voraciously crisscrossed the ether, snapping up their noonday meals. They battered the airwaves with a kind of joyous insanity for fifteen minutes, then, as abruptly as they had appeared, evaporated into the all-encompassing blueness: swallowed by the sky. Life in all its virulent apoplexy, leaving invisible scars across the universe. Moments later, a single hawk, a redtail, cruised by. After that a flight of ravens, the outermost tips of their wings steering through rising thermals, drifted across the cerulean space.

My wistful concubine had no comment on the active canvas. But shortly thereafter her muddled brain came up with another creepy line of thought to make my scrotum prickle.

"You always fucked me, Michael, talking about kids chopped to bits in haystacks, whores gang-banged in mud, naked enemy bodies dropping from the sky, rats shrieking on fire. Do you think the guys who did it pretended Cathie was a gook?"

"I don't know, sweetie, I wasn't there."

"You weren't?"

"What?" A Steller's jay glided from one tree to another, flapping its wings but twice.

"You weren't there?"

"What do you mean?"

"Well," she said, in that voice which never connected to viable emotions inside, "sometimes, when I add up all the logical evidence, I think it must have been you, Michael, who killed her. It makes perfect sense, excuse me for saying so. It sounds like your kind of fuck."

Lord knows, I wanted back my happy-go-lucky woman. But it came to be an incredible relief whenever I left our house. Relief, yes, and a fear hounding me every minute of the day that on my return I'd find her crumpled in the tub, wrists slit, body drained of blood.

Co-workers at the paper never brought it up. In my perilous state I gladly accepted their outwardly uncurious stance. With casual ingenuity I was assigned to the less volatile stories of small-town life. The crowning of a Fiesta Queen, the Jaycees' annual chili cook-off, the local Junior Miss Pageant, the Little League play-offs. And ceremonies to open the massive new K Mart store. I photographed the proud dignitaries, the triumphant children, the grinning Eagle Scouts chain-mailed in merit badges, the plump housewives beside a winning floral arrangement, the local artist in her studio one day after the Guggenheim came through.

And the softball leagues were in full swing, so I covered their rousing antics.

One morning the strangest thing went down. Our town experienced a summer snowstorm; it sneaked in overnight. When I stepped outside to go to work, the verdant landscape was stilled by a magic mantle. Steam radiated off puzzled white-capped flowers, alfalfa fields, and outraged vegetable gardens. I raced back inside, crying, "Janine, Janine, look what happened!" I roused her from bed, stubbed out the cigarette, and dressed her in a fever of excitement, then propelled us out the door. "Jesus," I said, "have you ever seen anything like it? It's a miracle!"

I drove us around the white valley on steaming roads, pointing out snowladen apple trees and perplexed sheep and cattle knee-high in whitened grasses, waiting for the sun to declare it summer again. Janine absorbed it without a flicker of comprehension; landscape revolved slowly past us, tantalizing in its incongruity.

At length, she asked, "Is it winter already, Michael?"

Winter already? I could have smashed a fist through the windshield, and spun the steering wheel, overturning us in a ditch! I could have braked the truck and shoved her angrily onto the glazed roadway! How could I arouse this stubborn bitch who felt compelled to dwell in a stupefying bereavement? What right did she have to ignore my desperate concern? How could I dislodge the brutal ongoing momentum of Cathie's murder? She was mocking me for spite with her tenacious despair, her bloated grief, her ecstasy of puddled numbness. I wanted at least one drop of recognition, just one small grateful sign that I was standing fast and toiling for her soul!

Even as we traveled, sunshine burned through the mist, and in an instant all the snow melted: it had soaked the spongy fields by noon. Long before then I had driven my catatonic partner home and left her there in her private holocaust while I peeled off to bring home the bacon. In a few green yards where children had obviously roused themselves early and set to work, lumpy, shapeless snowmen rapidly collapsed as temperatures climbed into the eighties: they all reminded me of Janine.

My lady never stirred when I slipped in bed beside her late that night. I settled uncomfortably into the lumpy mattress and released a careful sigh. Mind a blank, I invited sleep to knit the raveled sleeves. In the morning, with renewed determination, I would again assault her soul. My dedication would go down in history; a gold star on my forehead; The Patience of a Saint.

"I think there's something that might interest you, Michael."

The shock of her wide-awake voice lurched my heart, it caught me completely by surprise. I stiffened, and immediately regretted my entire life.

"You're awake," I said.

"No, I'm fast asleep. This is a recording."

"I'm sorry if I woke you up."

"You didn't wake me up. I never sleep anymore."

Okay. "What do you think might interest me?" Our tones were almost normal: eye-of-the-hurricane patter, the calm pronouncements of maniacs before a brawl.

"Somebody telephones the house when you're not here," she said. "He talks to me about ugly things. I listen. There's a real creep out there."

"What does he talk about?"

"Well, of course the major topic is Cathie."

Of course. I waited. Seems I was always expecting another shoe to fall. In Nam a context had existed in which all horrors made a kind of bloody sense. But how to deal with peacetime blurps of insanity, here among the pretty haystacks and gaudy shopping centers of Hi Ho Spaghettio, Smalltown USA?

"He talks about her murder." Janine fumbled for a fresh cigarette. "He describes it in all the nasty details. He tells me she got what she deserved, and that I'm next. He talks about her big bazooms, and informs me she was a whore. He says I'm a sleazebag, a rotten mother, and a slut. He asks me how would I like an ax handle up my rectum? He's gonna ream me like Cathie got reamed. He talks about cutting off my head and mailing it to you at the post office box. He tells me that while he's talking he's jerking off—'pulling my pud' is the way he describes it. He's been calling sometimes two, three times a day, while you're at work."

"Why don't you hang up?" I whispered.

"I'm interested in his opinions. Curious, I guess. I listen to his voice and I think: Maybe this *is* the murderer speaking to me. Maybe this is the guy who killed her. I'm trying to memorize his voice so that if ever we meet in person, I'll know."

"Why didn't you tell me?"

"You would have said 'Hang up the phone.' You would have called the cops. You would have unlisted our number."

"Tomorrow I'll have the number changed and unlisted."

"I'd really rather you didn't."

"Janine, you can't listen to that crap. I can't believe you didn't tell me. I can't—"

"He talks about you too, Michael. He says you're fucking three different women who work on the newspaper. He says you walk around showing naked pictures of me to all your friends. He says you've given six women herpes, and fathered a dozen illegitimate children. He says you murdered Cathie. He says I'll open my eyes one morning, and my head will be in our toilet bowl, and you'll be sitting on the lid above it."

She ran out of steam. That silent scream again defined the dark. I decided to never move again, or leave the bed, or deal with the world. It wasn't worth the effort.

"So how do you like them apples?" she concluded.

Emitting a groan I rolled over and gathered her in my arms. She lolled unresistant in my desperately tight embrace. I heard telephones jangling, and envisioned her picking up the receiver, listening expressionless, smoking cigarettes. And hanging up afterward, remaining there, letting the conversation filter through her brain.

"It's all right," she said. "I don't mind. Reckon it just comes with the territory."

I hugged her close, kissed the top of her head. And in my breast at long last stirred revenge. It dawned on me again, without equivocation, that Thomas Carp was to blame—no other beast abroad could initiate such actions. It was almost as if the series of atrocities that began in Nam had led inevitably to Cathie's annihilation. Who else out there could have killed her, then employed a telephone afterward to bombard Janine? It all fit clearly now: Tom Carp and his AR-15 at the Tree Star Barn; Tom Carp's fingers puttering between Shirley's thighs; Tom Carp in my hospital room offering to shove an ax handle up her ass. No other hoodlum on earth could have been responsible. It was time to face that fact, and deal.

I said, "It must be Tom Carp."

"Who?"

"Tom Carp, that guy I told you about. Who shot the Pig Boy, dumped the heads on my bed, set the rats afire. He lives in this town, I never mentioned that. His invitation first brought me here. I've always been afraid and avoided him like the plague. But over the years he keeps turning up, making obscene propositions, pretending we were good buddies in the Nam. He's a psychopath."

"Describe him to me," she said quietly, though her voice had picked up an edge, an abrupt inflection of keenness and self-interest.

I described the man: big, crew haircut, stomach paunchy. And the Denny Dimwit ears which made him seem incongruously childlike for his size.

Janine sat up in bed, tight and quivering, and lit another cancer stick. Her eyes were in gear for once, penetrating and intelligent, all guises of passivity discarded.

"I know that guy. He used to eat at the café. He liked to make off-color jokes, and he asked me out a couple of times. I brushed him off with a laugh. Just another trucker, full of Doan's pills and NoDoz, feeling lonely. Definitely not my type. So that's your friend, Thomas Carp, Mr. Flaming Rats himself? How come you never told me?"

"I didn't want him in any way in our lives. We didn't cross paths that often. I made it clear I had no desire to be friends, hash over the old days, or get sentimental about the war."

She actually lowered the cigarette, irritated, and extinguished it as if the smoke hindered her concentration.

"Tell me everything you know about him, Michael. Everything that happened between you two."

The litany I repeated; she clung to every word. Details of Vietnam massacres, the Tree Star Barn, the afternoon Willie Pacheco died, Shirley, and that apparition in a hospital chair beside my bed, offering to dismember Janine.

It was dawn by the time I finished. Purged of the poisons yet again, I wanted to curl up and beg for sleep. But Janine was wide eyed and bushy tailed.

"How could you not have told me?"

"I thought you had enough problems."

"It has to be him," she said.

"We can't know for sure."

"Who else can it be?"

True enough, I guess; certainly, I hadn't a different answer.

"Did you talk with the DA?"

"On what grounds? What kind of evidence?"

She toyed with that, narrow eyed, honing in. "I suppose you're right. Lack of evidence. That makes sense."

Sure it made sense. Like cigarettes make sense, and the bombing of Cambodia. And the final touch, of severing Cathie's head—from what macabre instinct had evolved that profane gesture? Motives galore?—don't make us laugh. Motives die in babbles of emotional anarchy.

"Explain to me again, Michael, why you never brought him up."

I explained it again to her.

"And if we hunt him down and kill him?"

"We're no better than him ourselves. We become criminals. If we're caught, we go to jail. I'd kill myself first. If they don't apprehend us, we worry about it the rest of our lives. If they do catch us, you and I never make love again. The only way to survive Tom Carp, it seems to me, is to ignore him. Let others do the job if they can ever get their act together."

Never had I seen her as ferociously contemplative. Her mind churned a mile a minute. She lit cigarettes, batted smoke from her eyes, crushed the weeds out immediately. She paced the floor, antsy, agitated, adding up the score. Then came back to bed, swung her leg over my hips, and kissed me, her lips and tongue alive again: I couldn't believe the transformation. Her hand fiddled with my dick until it was erect, then she slid me in. It was not an erotic, teasing, or tantalizing fuck: it was as hard as a professional hooker working over an embarrassed john. She did not feel *there* to me at all. Sexy and evil might be a better way to describe it, Janine the budding killer experimenting with her new skills.

She fucked me; I wanted to make love back. But she wasn't interested. Janine came screaming, pounding her fists against my chest, jerking as if wires attached to her excited body were being yanked. Then she folded over, gasping, lips cruising my chest and throat, my chin and mouth. I knew what to expect long before she spoke: no surprises at last on this voyage of the damned.

"I want us to kill that man."

I had wrapped them carefully in plastic, in Cannon towels, in sheepskin cases, and stashed them underneath the house. The .357 Magnum, the army .45, the Weatherby 270, that Browning automatic. All carefully oiled and rustproofed, laid to rest by me when I had believed the Nam was over. Buried them in crawl space dust that only plumbers had ever disturbed on their callused knees, down among the albino crickets and black widows, insects that perambulated brainlessly in breathless worlds under human habitations.

A trapdoor beneath the kitchen rug gave access. Janine

hovered above me, naked, while I twisted into the darkness. One by one I extended the guns up to her grasping hands. She laid them in a row in front of the TV. I brushed off cobwebs and slumped onto the couch, dumbly observing her unwrap each gleaming implement. And when she had completed the unveiling, Janine said:

"This ought to do the job."

The job of killing Carp. How many bullets could his big body absorb before it keeled over? One, ten, twenty, a thousand? How totally must we snuff him to even up the score?

Janine kneeled before the guns and raptly fantasized her catharsis.

"We have to think it out carefully, Michael. We can't simply track him down and put a bullet in his head. That would let him off the hook too easily. I want him to know what's happening. He needs to think about it before he dies." She roused herself, searching for another cigarette, then returned to the elegant display on our living-room floor.

"A nice touch would be if at first we did nothing rash. Get a bead on him, of course, but then maybe chat for a while. I want him to realize Cathie was a human being. I want to recount anecdotes about her life, convey her sense of humor. He should understand *who* he murdered, not just *what*. She wasn't just another disembodied gook."

She traced the graceful lines on the Weatherby's stock; perhaps this baby was the specialist to tap for the final job?

"Then I think it would be interesting to torment him a little. You know, poke the gun barrel in his mouth, tell him to suck on it, give it a blow-job, see if he can make it come bullets into his mouth. Don't you think that'd be kind of funny? Give it a blow-job, suck it off, do fellatio on a Magnum. Only of course if he's successful, if he actually gets it off, that's it—*bang*. An American abortion."

It wasn't funny, but Janine smiled.

I was appalled, but she continued on her roll. Wide awake and enthusiastic, finally: her fantasy, her revenge. Me?—I was the hired hand.

"I bet he begs for his life," she said. "On his hands and knees, dripping sweat. 'Course at first I think we should let him believe there's room for negotiation. If only he performs a few simple tricks we'll let him off the hook."

She smoked, regarding the guns.

"One thing that comes to mind: we ought to take a broomstick to his house, in case he doesn't have one himself. I want him skewered on a broomstick before we kill him. And don't forget, we need at least a gallon of gas. I want him on fire, still alive, before we shoot him. In fact, it might be apropos not to shoot him until after he's dead. Bullets are too quick, too merciful."

Too quick, indeed. Obviously, my brain-damaged wench had done some postulating while I had her crossed off as catatonic.

She asked, "Do people die if you cut off their balls?"

"I don't know."

"Would he pass out?"

"I don't know. Really."

"Suppose we cut off his balls and made him eat them. Like that pig in Vietnam. We could promise not to kill him if he'd just do that. We'll bring along some of those capsules you mentioned once, that wake up fainting people—ammonium nitrate?"

"Amyl nitrite."

"Yeah." She handled the Magnum, set it down. "So if he faints we can revive him. If he refuses to eat his own balls, we'll douse him in gasoline and start the party."

"And if he obliges?"

"We'll drench him in gasoline and light it." She actually giggled.

"A problem is he'll know from the start how it's going to end."

"Good. I hope so. But nevertheless, he'll beg us not to kill him, I bet. He'll be frantic to change our minds."

"Janine, I can't go through all that. It's too sick."

"I want to go through it, baby. He deserves it."

"But we don't."

"Michael, I'm sick of you being fainthearted. I'll find him myself and take care of business. I *owe* this man a thing or two."

"And afterwards?"

280

"Afterwards," she said icily, "you and me live happily ever after."

"You know that's a lie."

"I know he's waiting for us, that's all. He wants us to do it. He needs us to come and kill him like this."

Well, I guess it was settled then. Thomas Carp, on your mark; ready or not, here we come.

10

REVENGE

More as a matter of form than anything else, I suppose, I checked in again at the DA's office. Jimmy Kelter had fled to Mexico on vacation, so Henry Gottlieb ushered me into his office and closed the door.

"Siddown, Mike, make yourself at home." He gestured at a chair; I took it; then he dashed my hopes for good.

"No, nothing new in the case, Mike. I'm sorry. If we'd had some leads, then at least maybe I could list for you a couple of intriguing dead ends. But that kid's death is like a random lightning bolt that smashed her from the sky. Semen, hair samples, blood types? You saw the condition of the body. Tire prints?—they, him, it, whoever must have parked on the macadam. Footprints?—there was just a shuffle in the dust. Maybe one of them could have been kind enough to drop an engraved lighter, or his wallet? Dream on, Macduff. Witnesses?—nobody, nothing, not a single schmuck. We talked to the mother about enemies—none, no dice. Mrs. Tarr hadn't the faintest idea. And she wasn't all that cooperative, anyway, if you must know the truth. Obviously, I understand—she's under a lot of stress. Did you come forward with helpful insights, Mike?—no, you did not. You were like all of us, stunned and horrified. What kind of maniac did a thing like that? In New York City or South Chicago, maybe—but in *our* town? God forbid. So what are we supposed to do? Nobody in the 7-Eleven remembers a shtarker hanging around, giving the kid the eye. In fact, nobody was in the store when she purchased her soda pop and the cigarettes. Least not that the cashier remembers. Every friend, acquaintance, classmate she had at school we've grilled a dozen times to no avail. She didn't seem to be a well-liked person, but you can't fabricate a case from vague, teenage prejudices. So the prevailing attitude around here is that her death was accidental—wrong place at the wrong time when a transient, probably from out of state, also a monster, just happened along. An unfortunate coincidence, which makes it damn hard to dig up something relevant."

"That's it?"

"Believe me, I'm sorry I don't have more to report."

Gottlieb leaned back, evidently satisfied by his personal dissatisfaction. "We put it out on the wires, all over the country, to every law enforcement agency has a computer. They do profiles of serial killings, similar modus operandi, and they're always on the alert for crimes that fall into a particular pattern or category. So there's an avenue that might eventually pay dividends. Cathie's killer, or killers, hack apart some other babe in exactly the same fashion. Only he/they slip up this time, drop a handkerchief, lose a shoe, forget their machetes—and they nab 'em. Then run a make, a profile, and start calling in unsolved chits around the nation. It works a lot, Mike, it's not as much of a needle in the haystack as it seems. There's a whole bunch of weirdos running around out there."

In the end, I held my tongue. Thanked Henry Gottlieb for the audience, stood up, circled the chair.

"By the way, how's she doing?" he asked. "Mrs. Tarr."

"How would you expect? Not too good."

"That's a shame, a real shame," he said sincerely. "I never see her around anymore. I liked her a lot. She was always pretty cheerful at the café."

"Well," I said, embarrassed, "I guess she'll recover after awhile."

"That's a great thing about humanity." He nodded emphatically. "It always does."

Little did he know.

Our search for Thomas Carp began at a number in the phone book: 759-2360. No addresses were listed in our town. Still, easy pickings if he answered: "Hey, hello, old buddy—long time no see! How the hell they hangin'?" Residence revealed, demise sealed. It could be over in a matter of hours. But when I dialed the number, and geared for his familiar voice to answer, the phone rang once, then crackled, and a recorded female informed me the number had been disconnected. Twice I allowed polite electronic tones to impart the information. Janine loomed close at hand, dressed up for once, hair brushed out, makeup carefully applied, murderously eager—pen in hand—to record the information. I hung up slowly, relieved, and transmitted the news: "It's disconnected."

"How can that be? The bastard calls me on the telephone. I know he's still around."

"Maybe, but this number's disconnected."

"Dial again. Maybe you hit a wrong number."

I obliged, and activated the same recording. Passed the receiver to her ear, so she could hear it for herself. Janine cradled the phone, rechecked the directory, peered at the number. With her pen she began to underline it; I said, "Stop, don't do that."

"Why?"

"Even an underlined number could be incriminating evidence if they started putting two and two together."

Janine glanced at me, back at the number, then back at me; and smiled appreciatively. "Well, I'll be darned, soldier—you're right. You ain't as dumb as you look."

She dialed the number herself, carefully and deliberately, almost counting the ratchet of clicks spelling out each digit. Then listened, totally expectant, as bells rang . . . and the recording came on again. She hung up thoughtfully, exhaling smoke, and her shoulders sagged a bit.

"Son of a bitch," she exclaimed softly. "How could he do that to us? When do you think he did it?"

"I don't know."

But Janine was motoring now, all keyed up and focused on Carp, determined to track his ass.

"Okay," she said. "No problem. I know a woman who works for the phone company. She must have access to all their records. I'll go and ask her to look it up."

"Look what up?"

"The date he asked for the disconnect. I'll bet it was right after Cathie's murder. If he's still around, maybe he just changed the number, or had it unlisted."

That gave her an inspiration: she dialed information. And in her most seductively casual voice addressed the operator. "Howdy, I need a number for Thomas Carp—C-A-R-P—it's probably a new listing." She listened spellbound, ballpoint poised above an envelope, but never wrote a thing. The light changed in her eyes a hundred times. A smug triumphant look transfigured her face by the time she hung up.

"He's still around." She could not control her excitement. "It's unlisted now, and they won't give out the information. I was right. We've *got* the motherfucker."

"How do we have him?" My brain had ceased working; Janine's was at the controls.

"I'll go to my friend today. Tell her to look it up for us. Ask for dates and times the change occurred. That should nail him in spades."

"How do you explain to her our reasons? It's against the law to give out that information. So she'll become implicated in whatever happens to Carp. Accessory to a crime. We can't jeopardize her like that."

Janine cast a scornful glance, then walked around the room, high heels clicking loudly whenever they left the rug, thinking, thinking, thinking: how to convince her spineless man? Hate made

288

her beautiful; the contemplation of revenge had rouged her cheeks to an electric hue.

"I don't have to give her a reason, baby. I'll tell her to do it and keep her mouth shut. I want that unlisted phone number and the date of disconnection. She needn't write anything down. Thirty seconds at a computer screen, pass on the information, then forget about it. It's as simple as ABC."

Oh, she had changed overnight into such a hard little moll, eager to mow 'em down. Her sweetness I once loved had flown the coop. In but days her flab had disappeared; behind remained a taut and electrified body, by revenge possessed. Eerie and disconcerting, the transformation; scary as all get out. No way could I deter her now. I'm certain she regarded me without feeling or compassion—a trained robot functionary at her disposal, an unpaid assassin at her beck and call.

I gave in. Her rage made sense to me; I knew the feeling well myself. So I let her go, all primped and spicy, out into the world again. Was her friend Noelle Johnson? I never asked; I didn't want to know. And in half an hour she was back, grinning from ear to ear. Her friend had accepted the request with a simple nod— "Okay"—and never questioned why. We had his unlisted number: and the disconnect date coincided neatly with the time of Cathie's murder.

Janine regarded me all jittery while I dialed. The phone rang and rang, jangled and jangled, I was terrified Carp would answer. But ten rings passed, then twelve, and fourteen, blaring in an empty house; thank Christ!—I hung up.

"He's not home."

"How many times did you let it ring?"

"I think I counted fifteen."

"That's not enough. Suppose he's outside in the garden? Maybe he's taking a shower. Maybe he has a girl in bed and doesn't want to be disturbed. Try again."

I licked my chapped lips nervously while it rang fifteen, eighteen, twenty times. When I gave up her eyes bored in like icicles. "Well—?"

"He's not there."

"Oh for Pete's sake, Michael!" Janine snatched the receiver and dialed the number herself. She let it ring forever; ring and ring and ring. The strident bells of hades bugled in his silent home, waiting for him to wake up, finish screwing, get out of his car, fumble for keys, open the front door, and race to pick it up. I do believe Janine would have let it sound ten thousand times, until at last he returned and answered. She would have let it blare all the rest of that afternoon, nonstop, and far into the summer night, until at last that bastard heard and picked it up.

"Janine, he isn't there. Hang up. We'll try again later."

Reluctantly, she slammed down the phone. "I *want* him, Michael. I want him now. I want him tonight. I want to get this over with."

"Maybe he went away, took a vacation until this whole thing blows over."

"'Blows over'?" She eyed me, incredulously askance. "How does something like this 'blow over'? Like it 'blew over' in Vietnam? When the Americans left town?"

"I'm sorry. I didn't mean—"

"Where's his house?" Nervously, she prowled again. "Where does he live? It's not a big town. We should find it easily enough. You never visited his house?"

"No. He invited me once or twice."

"Well why in Sam Hill didn't you take him up on one of those invitations?" she snapped. "What were you thinking about?"

"It was before Cathie's murder!" I shouted back. "Fuck him and his grubby world!"

"Well, you stupid boob!" she hollered back. "You *are* a part of his world! You two assholes are like twins! Every time you balled me this last year, Michael, I felt like I was getting it from Thomas Carp!"

"Oh Christ!" I headed for the door.

"Wait a minute. Where do you think you're going?"

"Out. I'm leaving. Kill him yourself, however you want. I'd only get in the way."

"You can't walk out on me, Michael. You owe me his life, you traitor!"

I stopped, my hand dramatically on the door handle; she quivered in rage, a human hand grenade ready to explode. I'm surprised a photographer from *National Enquirer* didn't appear in a puff of smoke.

"You aren't here anymore," I said. "You're not anybody I ever knew. You're crazy."

Janine melted, summoned a supreme effort, and walked over, lacing arms around my neck, lips against my throat.

"Wait a minute, baby. I'm sorry. I stand corrected. This whole thing's destroying me. Come on, come back inside." She tugged persuasively. "Don't go away like this. Where would you go to anyway? We need each other, Michael, we really do. We're in this together. You know it's crazy. If we do this thing, both of us will be freed forever. I promise, don't you understand? I know you understand. Now, gimme a Yankee dime."

Fingers through my hair, lips against my lips, body pressed seductively into me. Yes indeed, I owed her his extinction. If there had been no Michael Smith in Cathie Tarr's life, there would have been no Thomas Carp. Results?—a long and happy existence. You really had to admire Nam for how the melody lingered on. The glory and the agony of the young.

"Let's make love." Janine tugged me toward the bedroom.

"'Love'?" I thought, mimicking the stupored complaints of my once saucy diminutive brat. "'Love'?" I groaned as she unbuttoned, unzipped, and accepted me in her mouth. "'Love'?" I cried silently as she bandied my stiff tool.

Up along my torso she swished, burbled the semen across my lips to taste, drowning in small puddles of salty waste. "Eat it, Michael," she said, pushing it in roughly with her tongue. "Eat it all up."

Abruptly, she rolled off the bed, scampered to the telephone, dialed his number and waited, the receiver cradled against her shoulder: ten times, twenty times, thirty times. Sooner or later, a hand would pick it up. And then us Lurps, us Seals, us Green

Berets would swing into action. Charcoal our faces black, don camouflage fatigues, buckle on our K-bar knives, and set forth to greet the enemy on his own turf.

But Carp never answered the phone. Perhaps he realized agents were on his scent. Two ragged hounds, yelping through the woods, determined to track him down. Time passed, and the Sunday after Labor Day crowned our bountiful valley; a change of seasons quickened the atmosphere. I sallied out for newspapers, and, drained as ever a human being felt, I had difficulty maneuvering through a normal world of neighbors and acquaintances performing their jolly mundane tasks. I piloted my spaceship across unfamiliar territory, obeying the little rules: stoplight here, No Left Turn there. Scared stiff that one false move would get me pinched by a groggy cop bitter at having to toil Sundays. And during the process of my citation, I'd break down, start blubbering, beg to be arrested and stashed safely in the local hoosegow. I'd collapse, fall asunder, let our cat out of its greasy bag—squeal on my lady. Then a phalanx of well-armed flatfoots would converge on Janine, who'd meet them with my guns ablazing, daring all comers to take her alive.

I fumbled for coins at the vending boxes in front of Safeway, extricated the newspapers, blearily scanned the headlines. Front page hysteria; out-of-register news photographs. Big uproar in our Capital City, sixty miles down south; a young woman, a visitor from the East, was strangled to death on the outskirts of town. She had parked her car at midday, set up an easel, started to paint scenic cottonwoods along the creek. Two hours later she was dead. No tracks, no evidence, no motive. Confounded cries of pain from friends and family members. Gloomy promises of vigorous sleuthing by the fuddled police department.

I sat in the Dodge, in the middle of a vast parking lot, newspapers spread across my lap. And eyed the busy surroundings with desolate disinterest. Perhaps an unsuspecting Carp would trot into the Safeway food emporium for a carton of Pall Malls, or a can of paint thinner. Casual happenstance had thrust us together in the past, so why not now? Wish for a thing intently enough, the wise pundits are always telling us, and just the power of our directed psychic energy can make it happen.

Self-fulfilling prophecy and all that jazz. Come on, Thomas, *please*, why delay the inevitable?

I must have waited for hours, watching people come and go, maneuver shopping carts, spank their children, chain bicycles to parking meters, scoop Sunday papers from vending boxes. Clearly, I had no lust for returning to Janine. She showered and shaved herself these days, powdered her crotch and stabbed her hair into frowsy repute with a plastic cake cutter, applied makeup in all the expert ways that rejuvenated her mask, fixed a sexy slur on her pouting lips and made deliciously devious her tightly lidded eyes, and dressed herself in suggestive clothing that had always stirred my lust. But none of it worked as it had before. The facade failed to hide the burning vision underneath, the one-track concentration on our numbing job at hand. The more normal she made herself, the more frightening her lust. Bonnie, of Bonnie and Clyde, never achieved the sullen rapture of my Janine, the absolute focus on a single depraved act, or the stupefying courage of her convictions.

So for hours I canvassed the crowds for my prey. At one point I actually was convinced I could will Tom Carp to appear. But, of course, no deal, Lucille. A plump fussy child tantrummed in a perambulator. An old man dropped a sack of oranges that split open on the pavement. A teenage girl hawked a box of free kittens: no takers.

In gear, I began an aimless drift about our village. Turned up back streets, cruised down Main: I actually parked a few times and entered restaurants, assessing Sunday diners, hoping to hit a bingo. Along dozens of residential streets I meandered, searching for his telltale yellow Volvo. Names on mailboxes popped into view; I braked, backed up, leaned forward and squinted intently to make sure. Johnson, Martínez, Archuleta, García, Thurston, Anglada—no Carp, never any Carp.

At intervals, I telephoned Janine. Her breathless voice answered; it wilted when she recognized me. Anything to report from either bunker? Nope, nothing to report. Every ten, fifteen minutes she dialed his home, let it ring a hundred rings; he never answered. I could hear the TV behind her, an unusual prattle long denied our home. She was back in the world again, accumulating a cloak of normalcy, honing her ordinary talents so that when we performed the dirty deed, nobody would suspect.

"Tomorrow I'm gonna ask for my job back, Michael. I know they'll take me on. I double their business by being sexy. It's a fact."

"You're in no shape to wait on tables," I protested.

"You don't know the shape I'm in. And anyway, I have to be out there. That man used to come on to me: I'll be a bait he can't resist. I'll listen to people talking. Sooner or later something will happen. Curiosity will lure him to the trap. I'll tickle his chin, and if he winks or makes a proposition, I'll take him up on it, go home like his little whore, and kill the bastard."

Come the new week, a Monday morning in the last autumn of our last year on earth, Janine applied for her old job and won it. Never even returned home to change clothes—she slung on an apron and went to work. They were glad to have her on the line again. Business had already picked up by noon. I dropped by for my usual cup of joe, and to read the daily blats, making sure she was okay. Same as before, she seemed, a lady purified by the transition. Chipper sexpot, all smiles and casual tête-à-tête, joking with the boys and scooping up platters as if nothing in the interim had gone down dirty.

I was appalled by her aplomb. Though I must admit that for a minute I myself was seduced by the transformation. Then I saw Janine pluck a quarter from her purse and accost the pay telephone in an alcove by the door. The number she dialed could be none other than that cipher tattooed in vitriolic permanence across her thoughts. But as she listened to it ring, luxuriously exhaling smoke, she actually winked at me across the room. Her face dive-bombed when nobody answered, but she recovered immediately, rubbed her earlobes to make sure the earrings sat correctly, and returned to servitude camouflaged in her old peppy demeanor. She chanced by my table, said, "It's great to be back," pecked my forehead judiciously, then proceeded with her tasks.

All shaken up, I fiddled in the newspaper darkroom, I faddled at the typewriter. Our football team looked like an even bet in Triple A, if only Joe García the quarterback could conquer mononucleosis, and Harvey Leyba could muster a dozen more of those "bone-crushing" tackles. The Forest Service auction of wild burros might save those crafty mesa animals from a fate worse than death. Coincidentally, three nobodies had perished in traffic accidents last week, two drunks and a teenage pedestrian. And one middle-aged woman had been raped—but those weren't my stories anymore. I could thank my lucky stars the editor was sensitive to my dilemma.

Thank my lucky stars indeed.

No matter when we dialed, Carp never answered the phone. I lost heart early in this aspect of the operation. But Janine bent to the task each morning, indefatigably purposeful. Out of bed at the alarm clock's chime, and straight for Ma Bell's instrument of coercion. Dialed and listened while she slapped a coffeepot on the stove, lit a cigarette, mixed Diet Coke with orange juice and used it to chugalug a half-dozen vitamin pills. Sometimes she doubled over nude, eyes squeezed shut, one fist balled up, straining to make him answer. "Come on," she admonished, out of her mind with need. "Come on, you son of a bitch. Just pick it up. Just *once*."

And more than once she cast her eyes at the ceiling in supplication. "Come on, God, please, quit messing around—make him answer that phone."

Where had her daughter gone to in her head? Blood lust for Carp seemed to have erased Cathie from Janine's mind. In that sense, perhaps our quest was healthy. Trade one disaster for another: at least she was no longer passive. Where there's life there's Bud, they say. I mean, Where there's life there's hope.

Not much hope did I entertain, however. Though perhaps if Carp stayed invisible long enough, Janine's fire would sink to embers and wink out. People do sometimes tire of nurturing hate, I thought. Time deals dust; radicals mellow; old soldiers put away their guns. Memories of Maginot Lines and Khe Sanh grow palsied after awhile, the heart forgets—horror becomes sentimental.

Things weren't destined to transpire that way, however. Yet how I wished.

How I wished in vain.

And I was a sad veteran as the autumn cooled; yet on I hunted, despising the situation. Only one thing was clear, as our search approached a climax: sooner or later we'd locate our man and make a move. One way or another. Janine never doubted for a second that he lived somewhere close at hand.

My nightmares rekindled; I labored through that boring field of broken bodies. Me with my wheelbarrow, my pot of glue. The bodies were more garish now, twisted at excruciating angles, stiffer than I remembered. Their faces were largely familiar: Janine, Cicarelli, Mariangela Pacheco, an old man in Vietnam. I stooped, peering inquisitively into their dead eyes. In earlier dreams I had spent hours piecing together a single body. But now I performed less courteous rituals. Sizzled a cigarette against Sicko's wounded lips; shoved stones between the teeth of Thomas Carp; pissed into my own mother's gaping mouth.

Cathie's head and Janine's face coexisted near the farthest corner of the field. I rolled the heads closer and stuck them together, kissing.

We made love now, often, but I have difficulty describing the passion. Janine's small body was tough and rigid from the all-consuming purpose of her fixation. She dressed in tight, elastic ted-dies that molded her breasts and belly into perfectly erotic contours, catering to my groin. She donned high-cut Brazilian panties and sharpened heels and crawled over me in bed like some plump electrified insect slowly eating me alive. Her aggressive behavior was a turn-on that chilled me to the bone. As we grappled against each other, our tongues became soft daggers, and a keening moan of anguish ebbed constantly through the peculiarly avid seductions. Once I had brutalized her body, spewing horror stories from my mouth and cock, until she had made me docile in exquisitely prurient ways that bound us tightly, each to each. But now it was a different game. Janine tackled me bluntly, disinterestedly, as if honing the butcher in her heart. All her wiry supplications evolved from a killer's concentration. She had a strength in her that could have broken me in half, had she so desired. Her physical power startled me no end. Make no doubt about it, the lady screwed me royally, efficient as a machine. But I never felt us joined together during such rough copulations. Curiously dilated, her eyes bored into my skull, lacking all humor, romance, tenderness. I never pounced or flung her skinny arms akimbo, or joked about our sticky game. Instead, she worked me over with a kind of professional disdain. My once-playful sprite had retreated into fucking as a war zone.

She sank teeth into my shoulders, chewed my throat until a ring of bruises girdled my neck, bit my lips until they bled, and raked her vicious heels across my buttocks, leaving scars.

"Does it hurt enough?" she whispered eagerly. When I nodded yes, she said, "Good, I'm glad." Her cold fingers caressed my brow. "You're a good boy, Michael. Come on, lemme hear you howl."

And I howled, yes I did as the pain split wide my hips and ripped a hook up my spine.

We never climaxed together. Her intention, in fact, was to keep all that apart. Janine would brook nothing that reeked of weakness or connection. She gauged herself with blinded eyes and blinded body, reveling in the hurt. And I always feared that in the middle of her self-contained eruptions, a long-bladed knife would sud-

297

denly appear in her fist, slashing across my throat. In me, for her, must have dwelled the sins of Carp. How else to describe her bitter aloofness, except to believe that balling me was a necessary prelude to his murder?

All sexed up, she licked maggots from my open sores like an erotic raptor mesmerized by the pornography of coming attractions.

"Oh baby, you're so beautiful," she crooned. "I love you like eagles love air . . ."

And snakes love little rabbits; and cats have an affinity for trembling birds; and pigs desire the glossy hearts of wounded Asian boys.

Finally, I began to pray for Carp. Come on, you big lummox, show your face, let's get it over with. Can't you hear the siren call?

Twenty thousand souls inhabited our town, but only three of them actually mattered anymore. All the rest were simply backdrops and decorations, like the flowers in surrounding fields growing crisp and pretty as autumn deepened. It was a ghost town, really, crisscrossed by dusty veins and arteries where nobody who counted traveled. Houses were empty boxes unlived in by anyone germane. Their blind windows faced the world neutrally, totally disinterested in the plight of three tormented human beings. All life, all action, all plot, all *feeling* resided uniquely in our three bodies headed toward catharsis. The rest of the ville and its petty characters had receded out of sight, out of mind; had become a vague chorus of locomotion as our tragedy gathered heat, building toward its violent conclusion.

Silent mountains girdling the deserted village grew whiter by the hour. Passels of geese flapped by overhead, their lonely gurgles falling against a deserted valley: deaf ears, blind eyes hailed their passage: only myself, Janine, and Thomas Carp paid attention to their beauty. All the rest of humanity was trapped in a kind of time-warp amber that had halted its irrelevant escapades. Janine and me and our potential victim alone could move, walk, drive cars. And it was this trick of utter isolation from the rest of the herd that would no doubt expose Tom Carp at last. Three such determined cancer cells, afloat in the vacuum created by our passion, just had to bump into each other.

And bump into each other, at last, we finally did—I spotted Carp.

Spotted his car, that is—the yellow Volvo—idling along the main drag at the end of a working day. It pulled out into traffic from a sporting-goods establishment, and headed north, in no particular hurry, totally unaware of the bleary-eyed sleuth behind. The sun was setting on a bluebird autumn evening. Veins of dust churned up by people going home spread a veil of mist across the valley. Piñon-wood smoke trickled out of stovepipes as wives and teenage kids stoked up fires to cut the evening chill.

Carp had the window rolled down, his elbow poking out. His lax hand held a cigarette that he puffed on in an easy, relaxed manner.

And when I spied him, my heart did not lurch. No spurt of cold sweat shivered in my body. I nodded in mild surprise and said aloud, "Oh, there he is." And fell nonchalantly into pursuit, aware that I'd follow him home. My breath did not quicken. Catching him at last seemed dull and faintly boring. I couldn't rouse the rage, or any small ecstasy of fear and excitement. The discovery simply did not jolt me. I guess it clarified the muddle, sweeping other thoughts from my mind, and gave me a mundane purpose in life. Now that I had him in my sights, all that remained was to trail him to his lair. After that, Janine and I had all the time in the world to figure out next steps.

I remained behind the yellow Volvo at a respectful distance and didn't blow my cool. Rarely had I been so calm and quiet inside. He traveled up through the heart of town, past the plaza, and turned right at a traffic light, heading east. Past tourist shops, a few art galleries, the dry cleaner's, and the gingerbread bookstore, then down a hill and past a gas station, a small adobe Baptist church, and two mediocre motels into a more residential neighborhood.

About a mile east of town, his blinker signaled, and he hung a left onto a narrow street flanked by enormous old cottonwoods flooding the speed-bumped pavement with wide golden leaves: DRIVE SLOWLY—CHILDREN. I remained a goodly distance to the rear, obviously uneager to tip my hand. I had prowled this neighborhood a dozen times and never suspected, never seen the car.

Carp slowed down shortly, steered into a driveway, and braked. His car must have held one of those remote-control gadgets that open things, for in a second the door on a tin, prefab garage clattered smoothly up and Carp drove inside, the door came clattering down. I parked in the leafy gutter and turned off the ignition, awaiting some further sign. A light went on in his nondescript frame house. I wasn't close enough to see in the window; but there was no hurry anyhow. Darkness came, devouring many of the details. The lawn surrounding his home was small but neatly mowed; no mailbox cast a shadow on the sidewalk. From an old basketball hoop riveted above the garage door a shredded net hung limply.

In other homes similar yellow lights burned comfortably. From a few windows issued the metallic glare of TV sets. Peaceful and mundane the evening atmosphere. Some cars, two pickups, cruised along the street, turned into driveways. Mothers, fathers, and kids got out, a few with briefcases, school books, groceries. Quiet murmur of their cheerful voices; a bit of laughter; a radio playing somewhere featured the top forty pop tunes on the current charts.

Three dogs trotted along the west sidewalk, happily bumping against each other. One, part Lab, perhaps, but mostly mutt, stopped to pee against a tree: then all three trotted on. Two young boys wheeled down the street on BMX bicycles, performed tricks for a minute on the leafy macadam, then said good-bye. They walked their bikes to separate houses, dumped them trustingly on the front grass, and went inside. Three doors down from Carp a lawn freak had left his sprinkler system on, trying to prolong the summer green, no doubt, postpone a little longer the fearful ides of winter.

The street settled down completely. Suppers cooked behind peaceful windows. America at its best and most seductive, at rest after an honest day's work.

I grew a bit drowsy. Hard to imagine that our drama lay at the end of such an ordinary street. Hard to feel passionate in such a banal and comfortable setting. Our security breeds contempt and conflagration throughout the world, yet it was easy to love it at this moment. So what if we purchased these safe streets by pulverizing Guatemalas and Vietnams? Why did we fight across the seas?—so that lazy Tom Carp, in a yellow Volvo, could click open a garage door with his magic gizmo.

A porch light went on; a Persian kitty scampered across the street; a shiny Toyota Tercel stopped about a dozen doors down, and a college cutie with flouncing Breck hair hopped out, followed by her little sister, laughing—with a lisp? No doubt braces were making her teeth perfect.

GUNS, GUTS, AND GLORY, I reminisced, ARE WHAT MADE AMERICA GREAT. On the Datsun truck in front of me a bumper sticker read: HONK, IF YOU LOVE JESUS. The slogans that we tote around on our careless paths; reminding me of that T-shirted creep in the airport during my first moments back in the world: KILL 'EM ALL, LET GOD SORT 'EM OUT.

Breezes rustled in top-heavy treetops, and scatterings of big, tickling leaves floated down, settling on the hood of my truck, on lawns and sidewalks, up and down the pretty street. Perhaps if I waited long enough, I could hatch a plan. But for the longest time my brain refused to function. I was there; I absorbed it all quietly; I had no desire to act. Could not arouse an antagonism toward Carp. In a war zone I might have caught a glint off the metal of my hatred for him. But in a Norman Rockwell setting like this, no grand brutalities entered my mind.

Leave the poor bum alone, Michael; none of it really matters. Why shatter the pleasant neighborhood with my petty complaints? Rest in peace, all you gullible nudnicks cooking potatoes in your microwaves, giggling at "Three's Company." Tonight was Monday night? Oh jeepers, I was missing Don and Frank and Howard—or was that now Don, and OJ, and Joe?—on the Monday night football game. Who was playing—Dallas and New York, the Bears and the Falcons, the Saints and the 49ers? Somehow I'd lost track of those crucially important facts.

Wearily, I started up the truck and proceeded down the street, mesmerized by the everyday calm oozing from the everyday houses. Turned around and idled back, peering in to catch a glimpse of Carp through his uncurtained windows; but I was past the dwelling before anything registered. I pulled over opposite where I'd parked before and turned off the engine again. Then got out and strolled over to where he lived, hands in my pockets, nonchalantly whistling Dixie. I stopped in front of his digs and looked inside. Couldn't see the man from where I stood, only the edge of a TV set, and that aluminum glare—diffused by an ordinary light— playing off the ceiling.

Time for a closer look, Michael. Still unruffled as you please, I circled the lawn and padded quickly up beside a low coyote fence to shadows cast by a leafy bush at the corner of the house. There I stationed myself at the edge of a darkened bedroom window, and peeped inside. The bedroom door was ajar, allowing a view of half the lighted living room and of the Melmac kitchen area beyond. A glimpse at last into the private life of Thomas Carp, the Meanest Man on Earth.

What did I expect, I wonder now? Arcane gadgets of torture decorating the walls? Framed photographs of My Lai in place of a needlepoint HOME SWEET HOME? Automatic weapons stacked inside glass display cabinets, just waiting to be fired on hapless peasants, deranged Nam vets, quirky hippies, and obstreperous Chicanos? Skulls and mummified black-pajamaed skeletons displayed openly on the rugs? And great spiderweb tangles dripping off the lamps, like Dracula's condo in Transylvania? Interspersed by obscene X-rated posters and glossy eight-by-tens of garish hookers twisted into contorted poses by burly, hooded, horrendously hung executioners? Plus slimy leeches and other black bugs wriggling in his beer?

Maybe that would have surprised me less than what I actually viewed. And then turned away from after a moment of quiet gawking, and walked—tiptoed surreptitiously—back along the coyote fence and up the sidewalk to my vehicle, feeling dizzy and dismayed.

Quietly, I opened the door, slipped behind the wheel, draped my hands wearily over the steering apparatus, and rested my head against the knuckles. And finally allowed myself to release a long long breath, absolutely mystified by the horrors of this world we live in.

So many scenarios I had envisioned, but never this. Slowly, I began to weep; tears stung the corners of my eyes, they drenched my hands. An unusual pain in my chest swelled between the ribs, and almost crushed my heart against the sternum. How is it that on this fateful night, of all nights, I had been allowed to find Tom Carp? How is it that on this peaceful autumn evening, of all the evenings when I could have accidentally spied his car, we had at last come together?

How long I remained in that posture crying, I couldn't say. The moon rose from behind the mountains, casting fractured patterns of pale light onto the leafy street. If I'd raised my head to peer intently through overhanging cottonwood boughs, I suppose I would have glimpsed a twinkle or two cast by the innocent stars. Life continued in all its klutzy haphazard ways up and down the street. The sprinkler went off, some lights winked on, others winked off, curtains were drawn. Those same three cocky dogs came trotting along the sidewalk, heading in the opposite direction. Cars appeared and parked; other garage doors, activated by remote-control mechanisms, rattled up, rattled down. Smoke issued from some chimneys, and, in the windless air, it seeped mistily up through the overhead foliage. Blurps of energetic music—top forty, country and western, peppy Spanish ranchera tunes—faded in, faded out, marking these gentle lives.

"The old masters were never wrong," I thought, remembering a poem which had made a lasting impression from my boyhood days. Never, in the final analysis, never wrong at all.

And to me, as I gathered my forces to split, came a quiet whirlwind of scenes that for too long had plagued my withering aliveness. Willie Pacheco's truck, so mutely engulfed in the hard November sunshine. And a thousand floppy little gooks sailing out Huey gunship doors, trailing red ribbons of blood up at the clouds as they fell toward unbroken green jungle canopies where their ancestors awaited with open arms—

So many memories to clog the arteries of hope. How could a single human being experience these gruesome things, yet still survive to raise high the champagne glass, toasting the miracles of existence?

I didn't know, and I didn't care to delve into any of it any longer. Janine would be waiting, my eager basket case, for the glad tidings I now bore. Teeth filed, body supine, hands reaching to pluck me against her hardened breast. No point in delaying any longer. I had news for my cutie that would boggle her brain, and no doubt snuff some fires, start others, launch a crystal tirade against the fates.

First time, every time, the truck engine kicked into its powerful growl when I flipped the ignition key and pumped the accelerator pedal. I backed up, swinging into the street, turned around, and headed for my domicile, my lady, and my future. Eyes swollen, chest aching, lips parched and hot and peeling, ears burning, hair disheveled.

Answers?—don't make me laugh.

Answers are for morons, zombies, paraplegics; answers are for high-school teachers, generals, and presidents.

All the rest of us simply muddle through.

11

END OF THE TRAIL

"**D**ead? What do you mean 'he's dead,' Michael? You fucking illiterate soldier, you've gone crazy, you don't know what you're saying! He *can't* be dead! You're nuts! You're like all the rest of them! You're a liar, a cheat, a Neanderthal! A mental case to end all mental cases!"

Her eyes were so wide I thought they'd burst her face. Her mouth was so incensed I feared it would tear apart her cheeks, sever her ears, and set her hair on fire.

"*Dead?*" she gasped, struggling to breathe, control her outrage, resist the impulse to slug me, start crying, go berserk. "You liar, you fucking liar! I hate you, I hate your guts—you *want* me to fall apart!"

"I saw it with my own eyes," I whimpered pathetically, the words all tinny as I spoke them. In a world so irrevocably depraved, I actually felt like the guilty bearer of bad news in olden times, who was usually beheaded for his revelations.

"'Your own eyes'? Michael, your own eyes don't mean shit! Your own eyes are so crippled I wouldn't bet my last dollar on their truthfulness! You're protecting him, you son of a bitch! You're protecting your pal, your buddy, your sick comrade in crime! The two of you deserve to be dumped into a garbage truck and squashed into pulps! You evil fucking soldier! I hate your stupid violent guts! I hate you, I really do!"

"Janine," I begged.

"Don't you 'Janine' me!" she hollered. "Michael, you got no right to pull this shit on me! *I want that fat cocksucker to pay!*"

"He's paid!" I shouted, knocking dust off the rafters. "He's paid for everything! It's over!"

"Over? *'Over'?*" she yelled incredulously. "'Over'? Michael, what the hell does that mean? 'Over'? you fucking homo dipshit, you have the guts to tell me *that*? It isn't 'over' till I *say* it's over, not before! You lie to me! You lie through your stinking teeth! You lie, you bastard! I hate you with all my heart!"

Round and round she tore, ripping blankets off the bed, swirling them in the air. She grabbed whatever hit her hands and pitched it against the wall—a bedside lamp, photographs of Cathie, perfume bottles and nail polish samples, hairbrushes, the cake cutters, an aloe vera plant—she smashed it all against the walls, and battered her fists against me when I tried to intervene, when I fumbled to pin her arms down, when I clasped her wretched body to my own—she wrenched free, kicking at my shins, spitting at my face.

"*It can't happen like this!*" She tripped and stumbled to the floor, kicking at my groin when I bent to help her up. She rolled away so fast I lost my balance and hit the carpet as she bolted upright and continued destroying things, clawing down curtains and pitching splintered rods through the windows, firing trinkets and geegaws that bounced off my head and flapping hands. "It can't possibly happen like this, Michael; it isn't fair!"

"Fair!" I sputtered in a daze. "'Fair,' you stupid cunt! What are you talking about, *'fair'*?"

Oh and then I screamed at her apoplectic face: "*Who the fuck ever promised you a rose garden?*"

"You sick son of a bitch," she uttered stupidly, "whoever promised me *anything*? MY DAUGHTER GOT DISMEMBERED! Have you forgotten that?"

"Yeah, I forgot it," I sobbed. "I forgot all about that." I rolled onto my stomach and held my head. "Who gives a shit anyway about just another punk rocker who got greased? Dime a dozen, baby. She got what she had coming."

Janine kicked me, kicked once, kicked twice, kicked half a dozen times—her shoes popped off and banged against the wainscoting. Then my moll gone mad had a gun in her hand, fully loaded as were they all, and she began to fire it in a dismay of outrage that nobody would ever understand: *Blam! Blam! Blam! Blam!* Bullets splintered the floorboards, punched into walls, shattered mirrors as I scrambled squeaking among cascades of glass convinced that yet another slug with my name on it would scatter my dipshit brains against eternity, open my fool's head up like Mount St. Helens, concluding for once and for all this baroque and mind-boggling scene—*three times lucky, Michael!* But I never caught a round. Even in her insanity she refused to kill me. So all that happened is I was clobbered by the noise of the explosions, bouncing me herky-jerky hither and yon, humping and thumping and screeching in terror until the cylinder was emptied and there came the shock of a lull.

"*You pervert!*" she screamed, and flung the weapon at my head, missing by a country mile. "*God, I hate you Michael!*" Then she heaved herself bereftly onto the bed.

Holy shit, still alive. I maneuvered half upright and dragged myself to the bed, grappled up the tangled blankets and sheets, and crawled over to her sobbing form.

"Janine, I didn't do it. I didn't know. It doesn't make any sense."

"Sense," she sobbed deliriously. "Sense," she spat like a delirious hag. "Sense," she blurted into sheets and ripped-apart pillows, feathers puffing off in all directions at every exclamation. "*Sense!,*" she wailed in frustration and abject disappointment. "*Who are you talking about sense to, Michael?* Where were you brought up, in a barn?"

I held on to her shivering body, held it tight. Held on for dear life, for dear death, for all the murdered children whose souls blinked down at us like stars. I squeezed her mortal frame against me, while both of us shuddered out the tears of anticlimax in a world estranged from sensible solutions. Held on to her with all my clichéd might and fragile clichéd main. Held on to her while the mountains trembled, and tidal waves of frustration inundated our home. I held on to her in brazen fury while my words sank in. I virtually looped around her entire body like a snake.

I had nothing else to offer this pulped witch except the "truth" as I said I had witnessed it through a bedroom window on Carp's quiet street. No solace in that; no solace in any climax I could concoct, real or otherwise. I squeezed around Janine, trying to force her to quit moving, lie still, catch her stinking breath.

"Oh Christ, Michael," she sobbed. "How could he do it? How could he hate us so much to be that perverted?"

"I don't know. I really don't. I don't know anything, baby."

She quieted down; our breathing grew more regular. Panting, panting, and then a kind of calm almost intruded. Until Janine heaved her shoulders helplessly against me and bit into my left forearm so hard her teeth actually punctured the skin and sank into my muscle.

"It cannot happen like this!" she wailed. "I forbid it! I told you *it isn't fair!*"

"Nothing is fair," I answered pathetically.

"Dead," she said bewilderedly. "Dead, you say? How could a man like that do such a thing, Michael? You're a liar. You want to rob me of my just desserts."

But it lacked a fire, suddenly, her voice. She was pooped, drained, almost servile. "I don't understand," she whimpered. "It's all a joke. A big fat fucking joke."

Some joke. Some funny bag of bones, *qué no?*

"I don't believe it," she sighed. "That man is a demon. He'll reincarnate himself tomorrow." Then she added a postscript: "God have mercy on his soul."

And she released the deepest sigh I'd ever heard, letting free all her rancid air in a long, drawn-out pitiful moan, as if hoping to rid her lungs of life itself—the godforsaken finishing wail of a rotten time.

310

And stopped.

In alarm I waited for her to suck in another breath, but it seemed she lacked that capacity, had finally given up.

Until abruptly she turned on me with a jerk, eyes blazing. "*You* killed him, Michael."

"What?"

"You killed him, didn't you?" No screams, no hysterics this time as she pushed off the bed and pointed a shaking finger at me. "You despicable son of a bitch. You did that, didn't you?"

"I don't know what you're talking about. Stop it, Janine. I told you the truth."

"'Truth'?" She stamped over to a window, kicking aside the mangled curtain on the floor. "Nobody tells me the truth anymore. Nobody ever told me the 'truth.' You're all a pack of liars. Jack and Cathie, you, you're *all* a bunch of liars."

She strode over to the chifforobe and with her arm swept off the trinkets still left there onto the floor; they crashed and tinkled in the litter. Then we faced each other, dumbfounded by the endless nightmare. I raised my hand to ward off her eyes boring into me, shook my head, and remained guilty as accused. More passions connect across the silences than ever we dare surmise.

"You're dumb, Michael," she said. Against the glass she tapped her painted fingernails; Petal Pink the shade, I believe. Or maybe Rose of Sharon. Her fingernails and her toes that matched, standing in bits of broken glass, oblivious to the sting.

"You never gave me credit for an ounce of brains," she said. "I'm just a cute repository for your jism. Like a Stepford Wife, or a Japanese fuck doll. Or that Viet Cong skull your pal rigged up with a—what was it called? A Pocket Pussy, didn't you tell me? What a charming name. I've never been anything more than your Pocket Pussy."

"You're standing in glass. You'll cut your feet."

"I hope so." She kicked among the crystal pieces, scattering sharp chips across the floor.

"Janine, I'm sorry, I—"

"Ditch your 'I'm sorry's,' Michael. I ain't interested. I'm not interested in any of your bullshit anymore." Back to the chifforobe she went, yanking out a drawer so hard it pulled free and clunked onto the floor, spilling rumpled sweaters around her feet. Stooping, she selected a pale-green number and drew it over her head.

"We've got a problem here, however." She tugged the hem down over her breasts. "You see, now we'll never know if he killed Cathie or not. We've lost the chance to force a confession. We'll never know . . ."

"That's a lie. You know it was Carp."

"Oh? And how do I know that? Where's the evidence? He left you a note? Show it to me."

"I don't have a note. I—"

"I'll just bet you don't have a note." She fumbled around the floor, hunting up a cigarette. When she found a pack she located her purse, dug out a Bic lighter, set fire to the weed.

"I'll bet you don't have a thing that connects him to her murder."

"Janine—"

"I said don't you 'Janine' me, Michael. I'm not your patsy anymore."

"You told me it was him," I said. "*You* told me that you knew beyond the shadow of a doubt."

"I lied." She almost smirked, plopping into a nearby chair. "Everybody lies, why not me? I always wanted to be part of the crowd, nobody ever let me. So I just took the bull by the horns and joined up."

"I don't think I understand what you're saying."

"I lie, you lie, we all lie, Michael." Up again, she circled the bed, eyeing me and exhaling smoke on her trip back to the chifforobe. From another drawer she selected prefaded jeans, tugging them on up under her skirt. She unbuttoned the skirt, letting it fall. Then runkled about in the closet for her Swiss-cheese sneakers. And sat down in the mess, putting them on, carefully tying the laces.

"Why are you getting dressed?"

"Because you're lying through your teeth, sweet baby. I just realized he isn't dead, is he? It's just your way of copping out. What was your plan, to move us away from here tomorrow so I'd never bump into him by accident? Well, you know something, my dear friend—?"

She approached and casually, almost affectionately tousled my hair.

"I never fell for it. Not even for a minute." She headed out the door, through the living room into the kitchen, and splashed cold water on her face, calling back at me:

"You wanna know why I threw that fit? I'll tell you."

She reappeared in the doorway, drying her face on a dish towel.

"I wanted you to think I believed you. Then, when you weren't looking, I'd take your guns and do the job myself. But if you realized I knew you were lying, you might hide the guns and try and stop me. But then I realized I need you to do the job correctly. I don't even know where he lives."

"To do what job correctly? I'm not following this at all."

Stooping, she retrieved the Magnum. Her palm held a half dozen bullets that she must have filched from the carton in the living room. She fitted them into the chamber and clicked it shut.

"Poor Michael." Again, she departed the bedroom. "He's not dead. Your story doesn't make any sense at all. You're jerking me off, baby, because you're afraid. You don't want to do it. You lie like a hound, but that's all right, I won't take it personal, I'm used to it. You found out where he lives and got cold feet. So you made up that story."

Nervously pacing, she returned and stopped, hands almost coquettishly on her hips. I realized she was crazy. Both of us were nuts.

"But that's okay, sweetie. I think I understand. Maybe you even did it for me, trying to protect me. Come on, get up, gimme a Yankee dime."

She held her arms out to me. And I obeyed her, going over nearly in a trance. Maybe like this the black widow hypnotizes her victims prior to a fatal bite. Between her hands she framed my face, planting the coldest kiss in heaven on my lips. Then, taking my hand, she led me toward the door.

"So let's let bygones be bygones, okay, my love?" Her voice had a sharp, sickly sweetness to it, almost like cajoling baby talk. "I forgive you. Poor baby, you've had a hell of a day, haven't you? I don't blame you for being shaky. But I'm strong, I really am. Don't let that little blowup of mine throw you for a loop. I'm really one tough cookie. Let's go."

She grabbed up her purse, heavy with the Magnum.

"Where are we going?"

"We're going to see Tom Carp."

"He's dead."

"I know, dumbbell. But I have to see for myself, is all." She halted, one hand on the doorknob. "Would you deny me that?"

Openly, her eyes met mine: ingenuous, partially atwinkle, cold as arctic sunshine, pupils fully dilated, absolutely off her rocker.

"No," I said at last. "I can't deny you that."

"Then that's settled, thank Christ."

And we proceeded out the door. Primly, she threaded an arm through mine; I escorted her to the truck. Janine hesitated at the door, glancing skyward.

"Such a pretty night," she murmured. "So many stars."

And wasn't that another journey to make your eyes light up and your stomach say howdy?

Janine sat way over against the passenger door, tightly clutching the purse on her lap, staring straight ahead. She never said a word. Nor did I. The night had a soft autumn luster; the main drag north, of motels, banks, fast-foods, and gas stations, was by and large deserted. When I checked my watch it surprised me to read the hour as 2:00 A.M. How time flies, so they say, when you're having fun.

Past two shopping centers and the new courthouse I drove. Past the brightly lit Kentucky Fried Chicken, resplendent in red-and-white-checkered tablecloths. A shoe store, a health-food em-

314

porium, a restaurant, a doughnut shop, and other prosaic business places. I stole a glance at Janine, but she concentrated forward, eyes fixed on Thomas Carp, willing him into view. Streetlamps cast amber shadows across her face; waves of otherworldly light swept her cheeks and eyelashes—pale baby, pale bones, all geared up to meet the man. A police car went by aimed in the opposite direction—Janine didn't notice.

When we reached his street, I punched off the headlights, and we continued on the leafy route guided only by the parking lights. I pulled over a couple of dwellings from his digs, extinguished even the parking lights, and twisted the wheel into the lock position. I had nothing to say, no suggestions, no clear idea of how to proceed, approach the house, make an entrance. The living-room lamp still burned as I had left it. More leaves had gathered on the lawn, that's all.

Janine said, "What are we waiting for? Which house is it?"

"That one, over there."

She assessed it. Then said, "It looks normal."

"It is normal."

"Apple pie," she murmured. "Come on, let's get this over with."

Quickly, she swung out and waited for me to circle the truck. But as I reached her and began to grip one elbow, suddenly something snapped and she sank onto her knees. "Oh dear, Michael," she coughed. "I don't think I can do it." I squatted down beside Janine, fumbling to grip her shoulders. "I feel faint." Her face was wet from tears.

"Now that we're here," she rasped, "it all seems like a crazy dream." She was white, white as snow, white as death itself. "I don't know how to kill him," she wept, staring at the house. "I don't know how to kill anybody. Why did you let us come?"

"You don't have to," I said, ears ringing, close to tears myself. "I already told you that."

"But then what's the point?" she sobbed, stiffening against my enfolding arms. "What's the point of anything, Michael, if I can't have my revenge?"

Her words were muffled against my shoulder; I held on tightly to my kneeling love. I felt her struggle to steel herself, quit crying, avoid collapse, keep going to the end.

"Help me up," she whispered finally. "We have to go in there."

And so I took both hands and helped raise her to her feet. She teetered there uncertainly, knuckling at her eyes. "Jesus Christ almighty," she gasped. "What's the matter with the world? Why am I such a basket case? Who does God think he is?"

And then she said, "All right. I'm okay. Please let's go."

I took her right hand; the purse was draped over her left shoulder. Up the sidewalk we went, cutting left at the coyote fence, and I led her back to the bedroom window. We halted there for her to take a peek. Nothing had changed, during the bizarre evening, except the programs on his flickering tube.

No exclamation, declaration, broken gasp or other response came from Janine. After a spell she said, "Come on, let's go inside." And she ranged ahead of me to the kitchen door.

"Don't touch the handle," I warned. "You'll leave fingerprints."

Janine fumbled around the gun in her purse for a Kleenex, and employed it like a handkerchief on the knob—the door wasn't locked. She eased it open and entered the fluorescent-bright kitchen. I followed, convinced that this last irresponsible act would condemn us. By chance, a cop car idling past would smell a rat, gear down, and they'd head for the house, catching us with our pants around our ankles. I accepted the Kleenex from Janine and lightly shut the door. When I turned around again to emphasize how careful she must be, my lollipop had disappeared.

I hurried to the living-room archway. Janine was lowering into a plastic armchair facing the sleazy Naugahyde couch on which Tom Carp reclined at a tilting angle. I could tell that she simply did not comprehend it. I never saw her mouth that agape. Nothing could have prepared her for the moment. It occurred to me then that she had never seen a dead person, but that was wrong: what about her dad? Well, certainly they never let her catch a glimpse of Cathie, that would have been too cruel.

Myself, I only dwelled an instant on Carp, making sure he was

dead, I suppose. The man seemed normal enough, except for the
back of his head, which had taken an abrupt ride into the after-
world. When he pulled the trigger, the gun barrel had leaped backward from his mouth, chipping some teeth in the process. But the
weapon still lay clutched in the stiff grip of his shooting hand. Tom
had done a thorough job; the only question was why? Newspapers
would talk about getting jilted, bad real estate deals, lingering depression over Nam.

Another nigger bites the dust.

"I wonder if he left a note," I said, moron words, zombie
sounds.

"No, he wouldn't do that."

"How do you know?"

Janine shook her head. She wanted to cry again, but struggled
to contain herself. "It makes perfect sense. Because it makes no
sense at all."

Well, what now? Not with a bang but a whimper. Here we
were; there he was. Cars screeched on the TV; guns started popping. I went over to turn it off, but Janine said, "No, don't do that.
That would be suspicious."

So I stayed my hand; she was right, I guess. Thinking better
than me at this point: how does the brain keep functioning? I felt
now that mine was turned off; numb; bye-bye, Miss American Pie.
The future had finally come to a dead halt, I couldn't think of
anywhere to go from here, or anything to say. Too pooped to pop,
kids; isn't that how we used to put it? Allee allee in come free. "The
party's all over," is what Dandy Don used to sing at the end of
Monday-night football games. Yes indeed, the party was all over.

Janine said, "I apologize, Michael. You were telling the truth."

I nodded. Well, thank God for small favors.

"You didn't do it," she said. "I understand that now."

"No, you're right, I didn't do it."

"We never could have killed him. It was a stupid game."

She pursed her lips and leaned forward a tad, unable to tear her eyes off the man on the couch. My dear buddy, Tom Carp. Oh, we sure had some times together, didn't we, old pal? Funny, how time passes by, things happen, little adventures on the face of the earth reach their petty conclusions. The mind fumbles around, seeking a handhold, a toehold, some way to belay itself across the chasms. And I wondered briefly, how come—earlier in the evening—I hadn't heard the shot? Saw him drive into the garage, yes I did, and the lights went on, the TV started to flicker—but I never heard the shot. Kids did wheelies on their BMXs, dogs sashayed along the sidewalks, cars came and parked and families trotted out. Maybe it had occurred when some other garage door was rattling up, or that bouncy teenage girl and her sister were debarking from their peppy Bug. Who knows? I just never heard the shot.

And after it, finally, all the guns lie silent. Then all us mangled survivors can trundle upon the battlefield and gather up the corpses, fitting them into Glad bags, tying ID tags around their toes. Blow that lonely trumpet, boys; play heartbreaking taps for these honored dead. No ceremony too grand, no tear too salty to commemorate their holy sacrifice; no flag too pure to wrap around their remains. Fire those twenty-one-gun salutes, and let the homilies curdle those chunks of meat headed for the worms. Brave boys, all of 'em, don't you think?—a credit to their country. From the Halls of Montezuma to the shores of Tripoli.

Janine said, "What do you suppose he was thinking?"

"What?" I woke up a little. "Who?"

"This man." She couldn't say his name.

"Maybe he was tired. I don't know. Guilt—?"

"He was a fucked-up person," she said. Her voice sounded almost reverent. "Like all of us."

"Yeah, I'll grant you that."

She kept looking at him. How still the corpse lay. How wide open the eyes. Hands just *being* there, blue and severed forever. Lumps. Big hairy quiet lumps. After awhile they stink.

Janine's face twisted, trying to hold composure. "Maybe he did it because of Cathie. Maybe he knew we were coming and took pity on us."

"Maybe." And then I summed it up stupidly, explaining everything: "Vietnam."

She couldn't take her eyes off him. And soon I couldn't take my eyes off her. Such a small, bedraggled ragamuffin. Hair frowsy and unkempt, poking out all over. Face pale, smudged around the eyes from old mascara. A small, pointy, getting-wrinkled face; not much chin to speak of; pale cheeks sagging—awfully tired, almost wizened. Pale-green sweater, kind of pretty; hands clutching the purse in her lap. Dirty jeans hiding her skinny legs. Threadbare sneakers, one lace only half tied. Not much Darlin' Sexpot visible now. Just a diminutive human being sitting there, contemplating the end of the road.

Willie Pacheco.

Two million Vietnamese.

Barbara Cicarelli.

Thomas Carp—

Janine's dry sticky tongue licked her parched lips. She said, "We need some proof." And stirred.

"Proof about what—that he's dead? You want me to check his pulse?"

"Proof about Cathie."

"I don't understand."

She stood up and could hardly maintain her balance, cut to the quick at last by a monumental weariness. Yet things remained to be done.

"Proof that he murdered Cathie."

I glanced around the room; almost bare. Beige rug, Naugahyde couch, couple of ratty armchairs, a tasteless landscape print on the wall, old brown curtains—not much pudding here to go on if proof was what she wanted.

"We have to look around the house," she said, voice quavering from fatigue. "Maybe there's some letters, or a diary, or photographs, or something." She cast about, dismayed, sliding toward a kind of torpor, it seemed—like that sleepiness generated by hypothermia.

"At least we have to look. We have to do something."

She toddled off toward the bedroom, stilted, limping, almost as if old age had suddenly withered her body, as if arthritis had abruptly jumped her bones. I followed behind her, feeling dull and witless. In the back of my head a glimmer said, Don't be stupid, leave, blow this joint before somebody happens along. But I had no will to deter her from the ritual. Let it happen, whatever must happen. Let it all happen in its appointed rhythm until at last it was done . . . on earth as it is in heaven.

She flipped on the light, then said "Oops," and dug for a Kleenex in her bag, wiping the switch clean. "I feel dizzy," she said weakly. "I'm not thinking clearly. Don't want to leave any fingerprints."

A bed, rumpled bedclothes, couple of nudie magazines—*Playboy, Penthouse*—on the floor. A man needs a bit of sex life at night, to calm his needs. Much to be said in the annals of sexual gratification for a good right hand. How did Woody Allen put it? He trusted jerking off because it was having sex with somebody that he loved. Many laughs we had shared over that.

No pictures on the wall. Not much atop the bureau either— wallet, dollar in change, a Chap Stick, half-empty pack of gum. On the surface, at least, Tom Carp had led a downright Spartan existence.

Carefully covering her tracks with the Kleenex, Janine slid open the closet door. A few clothes hung on the bar—shirts, sport jackets, slacks sheathed in plastic from the dry cleaner's. Shoes and boots on the floor; couple of guns stacked in a corner . . . the AR-15, a .22 rifle, a shotgun—not much of an arsenal, given this day and wild age.

Kneeling, Janine probed among the dirty clothes, pitching them listlessly aside. She pushed shoes, boots, sneakers around, then straightened with a sigh.

"Not much here, is there?"

She craned her neck to see on the ledge overhead. "Is there anything up there, Michael?"

I checked along the shelf: an empty shoe box, two old *Penthouse* and *Hustler* magazines, an unopened carton of Marlboros. Temporary; a temporary life. Everything seemed so temporary.

Janine heaped stuff back on the closet floor with her foot, making sure it all looked pretty much as she had found it. Then she tackled the bureau, opening drawers. Two small ones on top held socks, underwear, a watch with a broken expansion band, more packs of cigarettes, a buck knife in a sheath, and odds and ends like cuff links, a cigarette lighter from Nam, and a dime-store cedar box from Carmel, California. Inside it, jumbled, lay his medals. One, two, three, four, five—count 'em—six in all.

After that, two drawers of clothing odds and ends. T-shirts, jerseys, dungarees, socks, handkerchiefs, and so forth. Finally, Janine pulled out the bottom drawer, and at least we hit a load in a different genre. More magazines: *Playboy*, *Hustler*, *Penthouse*, and some hard-core rags and comic books of a more pornographic ilk. Plus hundreds of amateurish photographs featuring nude women, nude girls—posing for his camera. Among them were dozens of harsher Instamatic images from his boisterous days in Nam.

We kneeled together and silently poked through every one, placing them on the floor beside us. Quite a catalog of beaver shots and leeringly proffered tits. I recognized Shirley a few times, and other faces that I'd seen around town. Some of them trussed, hogtied, all trundled up—in corsets, garter belts, spike high heels.

And, of course, a number of dismembered elfin bodies from our boyhood days in Nam. It all seemed tawdry and dusty, without much passion to speak of. An odd and ugly collection of sophomoric pouts and bug-eyed nipples, and tiny dead black-pajamaed shapes sprawled across the bloody ground.

It required ten minutes to sift through this detritus of his life. We discovered nothing that resembled Cathie's roasted body. Wordlessly, we dumped it all back in and closed the drawer. Janine rose abruptly and started to put her hand against the bureau for balance; but, remembering about fingerprints, she placed it instead on my shoulder and steadied herself. Tears were beginning again to creep from her eyes. So I circled my arms tiredly around her and held her for a spell while she caught her breath.

"Nothing," she mumbled into my chest. "Nothing at all."

"Well," my distant voice said, "I guess that was to be expected."

"All right. Let's see if there's anywhere else."

Bedroom, living room—a "Barney Miller" rerun now on the TV—and little kitchen. Not much house for a big man to roam in. Janine opened the refrigerator, inspecting the meager contents, closed the door and wiped the handle clean. We opened cupboard doors, exposing his unimaginative larder. Cans of ravioli, Spaghettios, powdered chocolate, twelve-packs of M&M's—pretty seditious stuff. Pots, pans, a few utensils, toilet paper, Comet cleanser, other sundry odds and ends. She even opened the oven door—looking for a scorched head, perhaps? A baking tin full of entrails?—and closed it carefully, wiped it clean.

And that was that.

I followed her into the bathroom. Not even a ring blemished the tub. No bloodstains on the shower curtains. Nothing scrawled across the medicine cabinet mirror, and just the usual pharmaceuticals inside: toothpaste, aspirin, Pepto-Bismol, Rolaids, package of Ex-Lax, razor blades, et al. And in the linen closet?—an extra pair of sheets, couple of towels, shoe-shine kit, another can of Comet.

The man had departed without a trace.

We assembled back in the living room, bewildered, out of options. Except for, "Oh, the garage," she suggested. So yonder to that last resort we traipsed. Discovered a few paint cans on shelves, garden hose and a rake, and other implements of landscaping. But mostly it was bare. Still, we poked into every nook and cranny, just to be certain.

At last there remained the car. Absently, I held open the door while Janine crawled in and contorted herself, searching under the front seats, checking out the glove compartment. Found an empty beer can, a couple of maps, an ashtray full of cigarette butts (but no human teeth, I'm afraid), and little else.

She backed out. I closed the door and smudged it clean.

"Let's look in the trunk."

I tried, but it was locked. "Are the keys in the ignition?"

"No, they must be in the house."

"I think I saw them on the bureau."

She retraced our steps, returning a moment later with the keys. "They weren't on the bureau," she said. "They were in his pocket."

Janine sorted through them, found one that had VOLVO stamped on it, poked it into the lock, and opened the trunk, raising high the lid. Not much of note in here either, no shriveled bodies, no severed hands or feet, no collection of female heads. Just a spare, a jack, tire tools, a can of compressed air, some chains, a cloth rumpled in a corner. Janine reached for the cloth, held it up, and unraveled it—a dirty sweatshirt: she turned it around. And there was Snoopy, absurd ears flopping, and the logo: *J'aime New York.*

I love New York.

We confronted this item for a moment. The trail ends at a pot of gold at the foot of the rainbow, a lottery ticket comes through— but nobody shrieks in exaltation. Some smudges of dirt could have been dried blood. No burn marks anywhere, no rips, no tears. It must have been yanked off during the opening struggle and cast aside, then grabbed afterward in case any splotches of attackers' blood stained it. Nobody would ever know exactly why. Perhaps Carp had wanted a souvenir, and later forgot to file it in the bottom bureau drawer with all his other mementos. Janine held it up a trifle longer than Hollywood might have deemed appropriate, then rumpled it up and tucked it under her arm.

"Maybe you should leave it here," I said. "It's evidence the cops can use to solve her murder."

"No, I don't care if they ever solve the murder. That's not important." Her voice was scarcely audible as she closed the trunk and removed the keys, wiping off the lock in case an errant print remained.

"I don't want them coming around anymore," she added. "I don't want to read about it in the papers. It's over now and I want it to stay over."

I followed her back to the kitchen, to the rear door, eager to be gone—but she veered into the living room.

"Where are you going?"

"I better replace the keys where I found them."

She returned shortly, halting in the middle of the kitchen. Never had I seen her face so wan, the eyes so heavy lidded, almost asleep. Not much to say to each other, was there? The quest had ended.

"Let's go home, Michael. I'm real tired."

We left Carp at rest in his still, small dwelling, ushering ourselves outside into the early hours preceding dawn. Did a final door handle cleanup, and tiptoed around the house, up the sidewalk, down to the truck. Not a creature stirred on the slumbering street. I opened the passenger door for my lady, patting her elbow ineffectually as she climbed inside and settled with the purse and Cathie's sweatshirt in her lap.

I had to literally pull myself up behind the wheel. It required a great effort of will to turn the ignition key, bracing against the engine's explosion. No two more brittle people ever faced the uncertain future as I pulled away from the curb, heading back to the barn. Worn out, drained out, played out, sucked out—time for a little shut-eye to knit our raveled sleeves.

12

ABSOLUTION

$\mathbf{B}$ut no, it never ends: Janine still wished to perform a final act before we repaired to our lair and called it quits.

"I don't want this thing in our house." She fluffed the sweatshirt. "I don't want any evidence around. Let's drive by the house and get all your guns, then go to the mesa, to that place. You know, where we . . . you know, buried Cathie."

"Don't you want to sleep a little first?"

"No, I want to finish it all, baby. I want it *over*."

You could almost love such a quiet town. Streetlamps fizzed, casting their unreal glow on empty stores, motels, macadam. Big O tires, the drive-in theater, Kentucky Fried pullets. An aura of impending dawn cast the mountains in shadowy backdrop as we puttered along. Neon café signs and cantina logos glowed softly in this last hour of slumber. MILLER BEER . . . THINGS GO BETTER WITH COKE . . . FLOYD'S CAFÉ—BOWLING EVERY THURSDAY NITE. SLIM & JIM at the Holiday Inn; LEE'S CHINESE RESTAURANT . . . CAR WASH & OIL CHANGE, $14.95. The town had a single street cleaner, and it cranked along, smudging the gutters with water, revolving up bits and pieces of yesterday's leavings. A bus bound north for Denver idled at the Trailways station, full of snoozing people, while the driver pushed cardboard boxes into the holds beneath the windows. And a flock of magpies, up early, scavenged the remains of a dead cat: I gave them a wide berth and they didn't even scatter.

Heading home at last; heading home for all time, it seemed. End of the journey, end of my pilgrim's progress, end of my unholy little war. With that sad, battered waif beside me, clutching the sweatshirt to her breast and staring solemnly out the windshield, tears streaming down her cheeks. Maybe in another life it would have been different, I don't know. Are there any people anywhere who maintain their innocence, growing up and growing old in some kind of compassionate wholeness?—I sure don't know. We all handle the cards that are dealt us and place our bets, hoping for the best.

And what is it, out there or up there or under there, that decides who survives, who goes under, who lives beyond the rainy days and has the courage to go forward? It's all a mystery, isn't it? A mystery that travels the ages, looking for a few good men, a few good women, kids whose reaches exceed their grasp, else what's a heaven for? Heaven? I don't know anything about heaven. The morning newspaper lands on a carefully trimmed lawn, on a dilapidated front porch, or among sunflowers preening at a front gate—and coffee percolates, fried eggs blister beside bacon in the pan, concerned housewives pick out the sleepy stickums from their children's eyes. Divorced daddies shovel important papers into their briefcases; anxious mothers fold arms across their bosoms, making sure the children clamber aboard the school buses without mishap. Days begin, fruit hangs pretty from orchard limbs, cats meow for the morning meal. It all goes on apace, and has forever. Poets fly off midnight bridges, and even generals, even the president himself (according to Bob Dylan), must sometimes stand before the mirror, naked.

So we proceeded south, heading home.

Janine remained in the truck while I rounded up the arsenal and dumped it in the bed. Good-bye to war; farewell to arms.

328

Time for the tides to carry them out to sea, out of sight, out of mind. Gone, but not forgotten. Well, forgetting was another process that might weigh heavily on our shoulders. But you have to begin again, after the flames have died.

North, then, back through the snoozing burg. I stopped at all the traffic lights, and neither of us spoke. A cattle truck went by, full of stoic animals headed for slaughter, headed for auction. Woodcutters up early plodded through town, their pickups loaded above the gunwales with pungent piñon. And a great big Colorado semi toting hay bales slowed hissingly at Safeway. Society on the move, carting around the bacon that makes it function, blivets of the normal life that had escaped us for a while.

Outside town, at the blinking yellow light, I aimed west toward the mesa. Three red bulbs, warning of electric lines at the airport runway, were still illuminated. Dawn came up like pussycats: the sage radiated a sweet luminosity in any yokel's lexicon.

Janine leaned against the far door hugging the sweatshirt to her stomach. A few development homes, a gravel pit, an old sheep corral receded behind us. Light, like a fairy frost, colored the world. It was very beautiful, I thought. Ravens scavenged at the town dump, black shapes busy on the premorning air seeking vital tidbits. All activity seemed slow and casual in a landscape stretching softly for miles, gray and undisturbed.

The truck jounced along a rocky dirt road; we reached our destination. The sun remained hidden behind mountains, but its light unfurled a cloak of gleaming lavender across the windblown vegetation. I helped Janine to earth. When she staggered, I grabbed her elbow. We walked to that wild outcropping which hung over the river like a spell.

Morning . . . mourning.

At the place where Cathie's ashes were scattered, Janine kneeled, arranging the sweatshirt in a bundle on a rock. Then she held that position, hands cupping the offering. What next? No breeze yet, no swallows either—the day had not begun. All earth awaited the poky sun, which was taking its own sweet time.

Janine fumbled in her purse, found a disposable lighter, and touched fire to the cloth. It burned slowly at first, then warmed to the task. Within minutes flames had consumed the sweatshirt, and only embers darkened the stone. What little smoke there was dispersed against the blueing sky. Soon all evidence had evaporated, last remnants of the tragedy engulfed by the land of smithereens. Janine poked among the ashes, scattering them across the rock; she flicked them into crevices. The lichens were pretty and intricate; dew glistened on the spines of nearby prickly pears.

"Are you okay?" I asked.

"I think so. I'm not sure."

And the beautiful expectant morning was absolutely quiet until a small plane buzzed over the mountains, tilted its wings to catch a glare of sun, and droned sleepily toward the airport.

Then she said: "I don't see how I can carry it around with me for the rest of my life. Right now it seems an impossible burden. Cathie's death is going to torment me forever. And what happened this morning—"

She gestured futilely with one hand.

"How does a person learn to live with it and not go crazy?"

"I don't know."

After a long pause, she said, "On the way here I was just thinking about things."

"What things?"

"Oh, about you, I guess. And everything that happened in Vietnam. All your terrible stories about the Pig Boy, and that old man taking a crap in the middle of the path. And your friend the nurse in Montana, Cicarelli. All that death and devastation it seems nobody can ever halt. Or come out of alive on the other side. Or even want to be alive on the other side. Like, I sat in the truck wondering how do people even *breathe*, let alone function positively, with all that damage clogging their memories? All of it, obviously, is too much for anybody normal to bear."

Carefully shaking her head, Janine reached for another cigarette.

"But then there's you, Michael. Your attitude toward me through all this. I mean, after all the things you did and witnessed

330

in Vietnam, all the traumas you went through back home, all the terrible times we experienced together—after all that you're still alive. You survived. And you've been hustling your poor little ass off, trying to save me. What for? What's the point? What can you possibly see in the future that will make it worthwhile again?"

Turning her head, she looked at me and repeated her last sentence:

"What can you possibly *see*?"

Did she want an answer? I reached over and brushed her cheek; she kissed my fingertips.

"I don't know," she added after awhile. "I'm so confused. Because, you know, the strangest part of it all is that driving over here I started to remember our fucking. Our crazy and wonderful times together. All the hurt you splashed around me and into me, all the bruises you gave my body, and how wild and exciting it was for us both."

She rubbed her nose, poked with her toe at a rock.

"Shit, Michael. Then all this other crap came flooding in. Those basketball games with Cathie. And I even had a flash of how I made you and Cathie shake *hands*, for crissakes, after she tried to blow you away for messing with her momma."

"And then?"

She pursed her lips, wondering how to express such things.

"And then I recalled how you treated me when I doused myself in gasoline. Every detail. How you carried me to the bathroom and washed my body and shampooed my hair, and laid me down gently in the bed. I didn't care, back when that happened. Mostly I was pissed at you for interfering. But this morning I started to wonder: What made you *do* it? What was the *signal* you received that made you escape the hospital in all your pain, and come searching for me? ESP?"

I couldn't think of a response. She looked about to cry, but I let her be.

"So in the truck awhile ago it hit me like a bomb, this revelation. That you really *are* a saint, Michael. Some kind of bumbling, awkward angel who's been placed on earth to save me. And like, my God, all this time I have ignored that. Tried my damnedest to make you run away, give up on me, call it quits. But you just keep holding me in your arms, even though I never respond. Keep telling me that you love me. And so in the end I guess your power is greater than my power. What do you think of that?"

"I'm not a saint," I said. "Never was, never will be."

"Well," she said quietly. "I think I have decided to trust you. If you can see something that's worth it, then I'll tag along for a while. I'm placing myself in your hands like a little child. I don't have much belief in myself, right now, not by a long shot. But I will believe in you. In your strength, wherever the hell you got it from. I don't know where. I can't even begin to guess at it. But so long as it's there, I think I'll have faith that you've tipped to something I'm almost blind about. I don't know how else to explain it."

And she glanced up, smiling timidly, quiet and forlorn. "So there, Michael. I reckon that's the gist of my story. Doesn't make a whole lot of sense, does it?"

"I love you, Janine. Pure and simple."

"'Pure and simple.' Isn't it funny about language?"

"It's all we got."

She gestured at the oncoming day.

"Your vision, Michael. Of the future. You and me. Together, apart, whatever. How come you won't give up?"

"We made it this far. There must be a reason. We are our gift to each other."

She looked up at me. "The world is full of killers. They're still out there, running around, hacking people apart with knives and sharpened axes."

"I know."

"Well," she said, leaning back slightly, tilting her face toward the mountains. "I want to tell you one more thing."

"It is?"

"Cathie loved you. We had talks. She came to respect you, because you're really the only guy who ever cared for us. Forget how we began, that's the truth. She told me once why she loved you. You want to know why?"

Yes, of course I wanted to know why.

332

"She told me she didn't think that underneath you really had a mean bone in your body. Those were her words, 'mean bone in his body.' When she said it, I was flabbergasted. I wanted to protest, but in the end I kept my mouth shut. And I'm really glad I did. Maybe Cathie had a way of seeing things that I would never comprehend. So I'm glad I kept my mouth shut, and let her have the final say. She died feeling that way about you. And I think she was right about all that, and I was wrong."

Then she runkled for another cigarette. "And believe me, Michael Smith, it isn't all that easy, in this day and age, to come across a fellow as screwed up as you are, who still doesn't have a mean bone in his body."

And when she glanced up again she was crying. "All right," she said. "Go fetch the guns."

I climbed to the truck, amassed all my emblems of male supremacy, and returned with my gadgets held crosswise in my arms like sticks of wood.

"Throw them over." To be a part of the ritual, she selected the .45 and approached the edge. "Get rid of them, Michael. I never want to touch a gun again."

It was an easy labor: a little thrust outward and they cascaded into thin air, tumbling tinily for hundreds of feet before they banged and bounced among the boulders and slid out of sight, gone for eternity. She flipped the .45 as a postscript, and we were unarmed at last, naked in a world dependent on hardware, our statement to the gods. When the .45 hit, a bullet exploded out the barrel, and a minuscule lead projectile zipped impotently into the dawn sky.

We teetered on the precipice, awaiting the sun. Her hand found mine—so be it: this couple had made a choice.

Awakening swallows now began their prancing on the quiet air.

Janine said, "Okay, I am done with it all. Please take me home."

She squeezed my hand tightly. And on our way back to the

truck, she said, "Thank you for making me scatter her ashes out here. It was the right thing to do. I'm sorry I didn't understand. Sometimes it takes so long to understand."

What were our plans now?—return home, set the alarm, catch a few Z's, then paddle groggily awake three hours hence, and put on our respective faces to meet the working day?

"I love you, Michael," she said, hugging me at the truck. "I love you for standing fast."

Sunshine burst over the mountains, instantly cutting an all-encompassing swath of brilliance across the mesa. A canyon wren released its haunting yodel that dived down the cliffs toward the Rio Grande.

Janine opened her door and climbed inside. Wearily, she said, "Home again, home again, jiggity jog."

Couldn't argue with that. I fired it up, popped the clutch, and wrestled the steering wheel over the rocky ground. Sunshine reflecting through the windows made us warm. And the autumn day opened in beauty, like a flower.

We arrived home to a house in shambles, and helped each other inside, each step like testing thin ice before us. I went directly to the bedroom and collapsed among rumpled sheets and blankets, ready to sleep forever. Janine sat on the bed, lit a cigarette, and cast her eyes morosely around the dismantled room. Drawers were tipped over on the floor, lamps broken, clothes scattered among the litter from bureau tops and shards of broken glass.

Reflecting on who knows what, she took it all in. Barely awake, I tried enticing her down for a cuddle, but she wasn't ready yet. She remained stiffly perched, thoughtfully drawing on her cigarette, while my hand puttered sleepily on her bruised thighs. Despite my weariness I wanted to make love, curl up together in a small passion of reassurance, ending the night with tokens of gentleness and hope.

Feebly, Janine squeezed my hand. Her fingers brushed my cheek. Unable to keep my eyes open, I swam toward the darkness, lusting after oblivion. But Janine began to reconnoiter the room. Annoyed by her rustling, I fought to pry open one eye; she was stooped over, achingly picking up the mess. On hands and knees she fiddled with trinkets and small treasures, photographs of Cathie in shattered frames, pretty perfume bottles.

"Come to bed, Janine."

I extended a hand, but she paid no attention. My eye clamped shut again and weariness surrounded me. However, I could not quite succumb to sleep, not while Janine hauled herself around the room and I could faintly discern the rustle as she arranged things on the chifforobe and bedside table. Faraway magazine pages riffled; coat hangers jangled in the closet; ashtray residue tinkled into the wastebasket. Broom straws scratched against floorboards, glass bits clinked as she swept them into a pile, then into a dustpan.

Stubbornly, she attacked the shambles. Setting things in order, cleaning up the mess, her final act of defiance before repose, her gesture of starting over. Slowly, dreamily, she performed the chores. To me in my exhausted state, the mystery of it was overwhelming. Her shuffling was the last potent sound on earth. After the earthquake, after the volcano blows, after the savage strafing run that lays waste the entire village, out of their caves and tunnels and air-raid shelters they come on the following day, picking up sticks, rooting in rubble, searching for survivors, a precious cooking pot, hunting charcoal lumps to start a fire, locating food—gearing up again to repair, patch, make neat, carry on, eat.

Finally, her frail weight dented the mattress; she fired a last cigarette. "There, that makes me feel better." Though I was drugged and fading, fading, those words came through clearly to me, lodging in the center of it all. One hand ruffled in my tangled hair; she laid her palm flat against my chest. My heart thumped against her fingers. Then the hand sank into my body, saying, There there, everything's okay, now. I've engaged the mess and it is conquered. Go to sleep now, Michael, trust in me. I'm here beside you, and there's no more wolves at the door.

Janine extinguished the cigarette and snuggled under the sheets beside me. Her small body nudged into mine, her head came to rest against my shoulder: she tucked one knee between my thighs. We clung to each other, breathing deeply. And nestled close like two furry things in a deep burrow, hibernating far below the tempests.

Vietnam returned, the old dream again, the bewildering fragments, the body field and countless dismembered corpses. Alarm bells sounded when I realized the golem was stirring in my sleep, but I could not escape the unhappy scene.

Again, on that desolate terrain, I pushed my wheelbarrow, stooping to lift the mangled torsos, peering into the clay-cold features of severed heads, seeking a person, a friend, a soul I might remember. With an oh so heavy heart, I loaded up that old barrow with the pieces, driven by an urgency to somehow right all these terrible wrongs.

Yet a different mood than ever before characterized my labor. A hush among the bodies seemed almost peaceful and unregretting. As if all the pain endured by these twisted relics from the slaughterhouse had somehow been put to rest at last. I heard my own quiet breathing, and the slow squeak of the barrow's wheel as it accumulated a heavy load. I cradled fragments of the sorrowful dead in my arms, brushing back wisps of tangled hair. And soon I began to recognize the features and contours of children and old men alike, Vietnamese peasants and wounded buddies, . . . Willie Pacheco and burnt-crisp Cathie Tarr. I lifted them all up gently, adding them reverently to my cargo. Then carted them over to the edge of the field, and, as I had so often in the past, I pieced them slowly together.

Kneeling over each corpse after the reconstruction work was completed, I placed my lips against their mouths and breathed the air of life inside. Touched my lips to the skinny Pig Boy and exhaled deeply; placed my mouth over Cicarelli's sunken skull and blew warmth down her constricted throat; moved my tongue across the brown teeth of that old man we had surprised in the act of defecation; and cleaned and saturated the burnt features of Cathie Tarr with tears that never ceased streaming from my eyes.

I cradled them all in my arms, whispering words of encouragement, until at last they began to gasp and stir again. And one by one they came alive as they never had before. Faint sparkles animated their eyes; hearts began to pump again inside scarred chest cavities.

I continued about my task, resurrecting human beings, the angel Michael, if you will, striving to make amends. Slowly they twisted, fingers moving stiffly; a glow fused their dead cold skin. I touched them with my healing hands and kissed them apprehensively. The woman Carp had raped and killed in the chopper was the first to actually sit up, rubbing her bony knees as sensation returned to her feet and toes. And even Thomas Carp rolled over at last and pushed onto his hands and knees with the most searing moan I'd ever heard.

Everybody came alive at last, not as grotesque monsters from a netherworld, but as simple people once again. And as I hurried on to do them all correctly while the spell endured and my wish fulfillments were being granted, a lightness entered my own body, joyful and rare. By gum, I really *was* an angel sent earthward to mend all my friends and enemies alike!

And what a longing permeated that dream!

In the end, I had patched together without one false step each dismembered body on that dismal field. Until all that ground where once the aftermath of battle had been displayed was empty. And all across the plain beyond people returned to life. Soldiers and housewives and little kids who had been boiled in napalm, and innocent bystanders snuffed by auto accidents or brutal murders. All alive, creakily stumbling around a bit, puzzled by their good fortune. Until at last I ceased my activity, the job completed.

Haltingly, they found their sea legs again, gingerly parting the blue air almost as if swimming. Some coughed, acclimating to an oxygen which must have seared their rebirthed lungs. And as a conductor must sometimes feel about the rousing music at the tip of his creative wand, so I loved my creations.

What a triumph of persistence! But I had very little time to gloat in jubilation. Because after all was said and done, of course, they began to leave. A small group of Vietnamese hugged each other, then melted into the starry gloom. Tom Carp tucked his shirt into his pants, tightened his belt, and disappeared. Barbara Cicarelli patted a few tufts of hair remaining on her head, then placed her arms around my neck and gave me a little kiss. "I thank you, Michael Smith." And Cathie Tarr, in her insolent, sulky way—no words of gratitude—glided toward another undefined point in the horizon, and eventually dissolved.

Soon I stood alone, bereft and startled . . . also released and properly arrogant. All gone; all returned to the connective tissues and molecules of memory; absolved by history. Yet I tarried awhile longer on that deserted killing ground, excited by great feelings of love. More marvels than we can possibly imagine exist on earth, if only we could take the time to acknowledge them.

Then I laid down on the barren earth, tugged up over me the sky's comforting blanket of twinkling souls, and drifted slowly toward my wakefulness, and a fresh start with Janine.